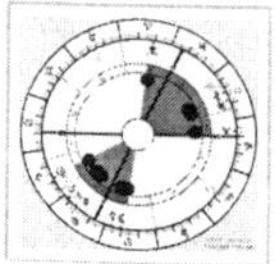

Helena Blavatsky - Birth Chart

(Helena Petrovna von Hahn)
(Yelena Petrovna Blavatskaya)

Gender: Female
Date of Birth: 12 August 1831 - 02:17h
Birth place: Ekaterinoslav, Dnipro
Country: UA, Ukraine
Age: † 59 years
Death: 8 May 1891 (Cause: Influenza)
Occupation: psychic, philosopher, journalist, founder of the Theosophical Society

Sun: ♌ Leo
Moon: ♎ Lib
ASC: ♋ Can
Life Path: 6
Compatibility

Helena Blavatsky - Astrology Birth Chart, Horoscope

Date of Birth (local time):	*12 August 1831 - 02:17* (LMT)
Universal Time (UT/GMT):	*11 August 1831 - 23:57* (-2:20h)
UA, Ekaterinoslav, Dnipro:	*48°28'N, 35°3'E*
House system:	*Placidus*

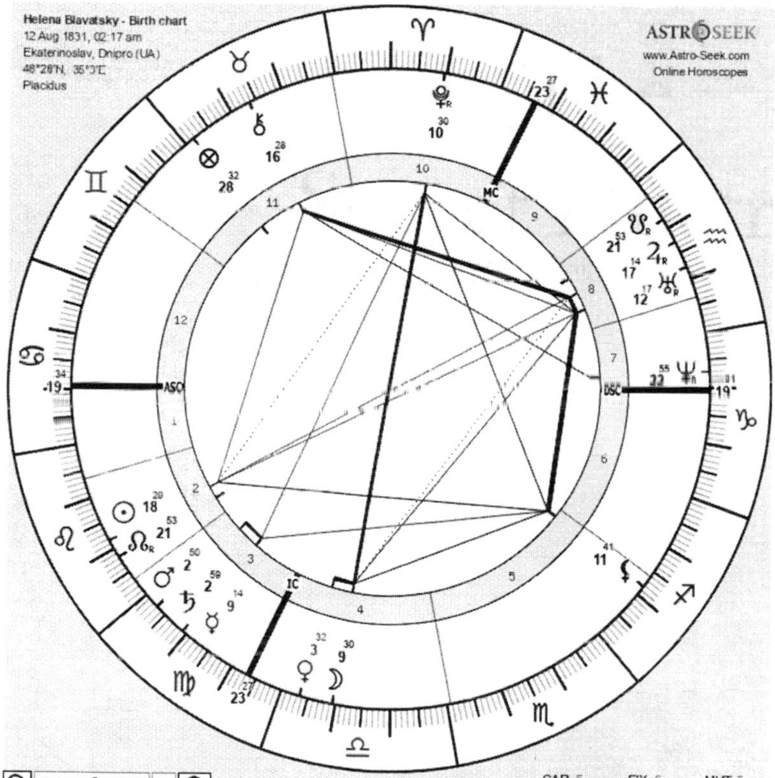

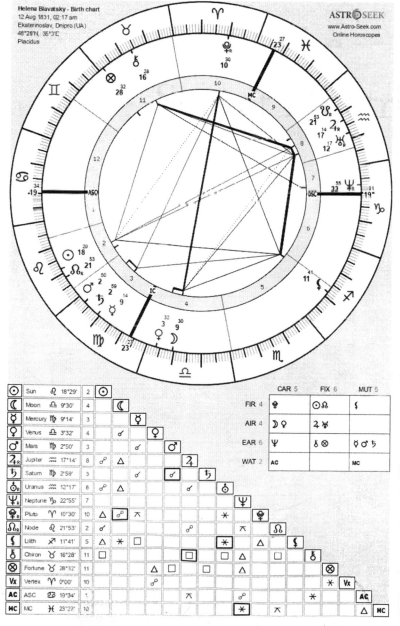

☉ Sun	♌ 18°29′	2	
☽ Moon	♎ 9°30′	4	
☿ Mercury	♍ 9°14′	3	
♀ Venus	♎ 3°32′	4	
♂ Mars	♍ 2°50′	3	
♃ Jupiter	♒ 17°14′	8	R
♄ Saturn	♍ 2°59′	3	
♅ Uranus	♒ 12°17′	8	R
♆ Neptune	♑ 22°55′	7	R
♇ Pluto	♈ 10°30′	10	R
☊ Node (M)	♌ 21°53′	2	R
⚸ Lilith (M)	♐ 11°41′	5	
⚷ Chiron	♉ 16°28′	11	
⊗ Fortune	♉ 28°32′	11	
Spirit	♍ 10°35′	3	

Houses: (Placidus system)

AC:	♋ 19°34′	**DC:**	♑ 19°34′
2:	♌ 6°32′	8:	♒ 6°32′
3:	♌ 26°39′	9:	♒ 26°39′
IC:	♍ 23°27′	**MC**	♓ 23°27′
5:	♏ 0°37′	11:	♉ 0°37′
6:	♐ 13°56′	12:	♊ 13°56′

Elements:

4x Fire 4x Earth
5x Air 4x Water

Midpoints:

ASC/MC: ♉ 21°30′ 11
Sun/Moon: ♍ 14°00′ 3

	CAR 5	FIX 6	MUT 5
FIR 4	♇	☉☊	⚸
AIR 4	☽♀	♃♅	
EAR 6	♆	⚷⊗	☿♂♄
WAT 2	AC		MC

				☉	☽	☿	♀	♂	♃	♄	♅	♆	♇	☊	⚸	⚷	⊗	Vx	AC	MC
☉ Sun	♌	18°29'	2	☉																
☽ Moon	♎	9°30'	4		☽															
☿ Mercury	♍	9°14'	3			☿														
♀ Venus	♎	3°32'	4		☌		♀													
♂ Mars	♍	2°50'	3			☌		♂												
♃R Jupiter	♒	17°14'	8	☍	△				♃											
♄ Saturn	♍	2°59'	3			☌		☌		♄										
♅R Uranus	♒	12°17'	8	☍	△				☌		♅									
♆R Neptune	♑	22°55'	7									♆								
♇R Pluto	♈	10°30'	10	△	☍	⚻					✶		♇							
☊R Node	♌	21°53'	2	☌					☍			⚻		☊						
⚸ Lilith	♐	11°41'	5	△	✶	□					✶		△		⚸					
⚷ Chiron	♉	16°28'	11	□					□		□	△		□		⚷				
⊗ Fortune	♉	28°32'	11				△	□		□		△					⊗			
Vx Vertex	♈	0°00'	10				☍										✶	Vx		
AC ASC	♋	19°34'	1						⚻			☍				✶			AC	
MC MC	♓	23°27'	10									✶		⚻					△	MC

The Secret Doctrine

THE SYNTHESIS OF SCIENCE, RELIGION, AND PHILOSOPHY

By H. P. Blavatsky

pac ps
Pacific Publishing Studio

Published in the United States by Pacific Publishing Studio.

www.PacPS.com

ISBN-13: 978-1461006282

ISBN-10: 1461006287

CONTENTS

COSMIC EVOLUTION

SEVEN STANZAS TRANSLATED WITH COMMENTARIES
FROM THE
SECRET BOOK OF DZYAN.

Nor Aught nor Nought existed; yon bright sky
Was not, nor heaven's broad roof outstretched above.
What covered all? what sheltered? what concealed?
Was it the water's fathomless abyss?
There was not death -- yet there was nought immortal,
There was no confine betwixt day and night;
The only One breathed breathless by itself,
Other than It there nothing since has been.
Darkness there was, and all at first was veiled
In gloom profound — an ocean without light --
The germ that still lay covered in the husk
Burst forth, one nature, from the fervent heat.

. . . .

Who knows the secret? who proclaimed it here?
Whence, whence this manifold creation sprang?
The Gods themselves came later into being --
Who knows from whence this great creation sprang?
That, whence all this great creation came,
Whether Its will created or was mute,
The Most High Seer that is in highest heaven,
He knows it -- or perchance even He knows not."
"Gazing into eternity . . .
Ere the foundations of the earth were laid,

. . . . .

Thou wert. And when the subterranean flame
Shall burst its prison and devour the frame . . .
Thou shalt be still as Thou wert before
And knew no change, when time shall be no more.
Oh! endless thought, divine ETERNITY."

STANZA I.

1. THE ETERNAL PARENT WRAPPED IN HER EVER INVISIBLE ROBES HAD SLUMBERED ONCE AGAIN FOR SEVEN ETERNITIES.

2. TIME WAS NOT, FOR IT LAY ASLEEP IN THE INFINITE BOSOM OF DURATION.

3. UNIVERSAL MIND WAS NOT, FOR THERE WERE NO AH-HI TO CONTAIN IT.

4. THE SEVEN WAYS TO BLISS WERE NOT. THE GREAT CAUSES OF MISERY WERE NOT, FOR THERE WAS NO ONE TO PRODUCE AND GET ENSNARED BY THEM.

5. DARKNESS ALONE FILLED THE BOUNDLESS ALL, FOR FATHER, MOTHER AND SON WERE ONCE MORE ONE, AND THE SON HAD NOT AWAKENED YET FOR THE NEW WHEEL, AND HIS PILGRIMAGE THEREON.

6. THE SEVEN SUBLIME LORDS AND THE SEVEN TRUTHS HAD CEASED TO BE, AND THE UNIVERSE, THE SON OF NECESSITY, WAS IMMERSED IN PARANISHPANNA, TO BE OUTBREATHED BY THAT WHICH IS AND YET IS NOT. NAUGHT WAS.

7. THE CAUSES OF EXISTENCE HAD BEEN DONE AWAY WITH; THE VISIBLE THAT WAS, AND THE INVISIBLE THAT IS, RESTED IN ETERNAL NON-BEING -- THE ONE BEING.

8. ALONE THE ONE FORM OF EXISTENCE STRETCHED BOUNDLESS, INFINITE, CAUSELESS, IN DREAMLESS SLEEP; AND LIFE PULSATED UNCONSCIOUS IN UNIVERSAL SPACE, THROUGHOUT THAT ALL-PRESENCE WHICH IS SENSED BY THE OPENED EYE OF THE DANGMA.

9. BUT WHERE WAS THE DANGMA WHEN THE ALAYA OF THE UNIVERSE WAS IN PARAMARTHA AND THE GREAT WHEEL WAS ANUPADAKA?

STANZA II.

1. . . . WHERE WERE THE BUILDERS, THE LUMINOUS SONS OF MANVANTARIC DAWN? . . . IN THE UNKNOWN DARKNESS IN THEIR AH-HI PARANISHPANNA. THE PRODUCERS OF FORM FROM NO-FORM -- THE ROOT OF THE WORLD -- THE DEVAMATRI AND SVABHAVAT, RESTED IN THE BLISS OF NON-BEING.

2. . . . WHERE WAS SILENCE? WHERE THE EARS TO SENSE IT? NO, THERE WAS NEITHER SILENCE NOR SOUND; NAUGHT SAVE CEASELESS ETERNAL BREATH, WHICH KNOWS ITSELF NOT.

3. THE HOUR HAD NOT YET STRUCK; THE RAY HAD NOT YET FLASHED INTO THE GERM; THE MATRIPADMA HAD NOT YET SWOLLEN.

4. HER HEART HAD NOT YET OPENED FOR THE ONE RAY TO ENTER, THENCE TO FALL, AS THREE INTO FOUR, INTO THE LAP OF MAYA.

5. THE SEVEN SONS WERE NOT YET BORN FROM THE WEB OF LIGHT. DARKNESS ALONE WAS FATHER-MOTHER, SVABHAVAT; AND SVABHAVAT WAS IN DARKNESS.

6. THESE TWO ARE THE GERM, AND THE GERM IS ONE. THE UNIVERSE WAS STILL CONCEALED IN THE DIVINE THOUGHT AND THE DIVINE BOSOM. . . .

STANZA III.

1. . . . THE LAST VIBRATION OF THE SEVENTH ETERNITY THRILLS THROUGH INFINITUDE. THE MOTHER SWELLS, EXPANDING FROM WITHIN WITHOUT, LIKE THE BUD OF THE LOTUS.

2. THE VIBRATION SWEEPS ALONG, TOUCHING WITH ITS SWIFT WING THE WHOLE UNIVERSE AND THE GERM THAT DWELLETH IN DARKNESS: THE DARKNESS THAT BREATHES OVER THE SLUMBERING WATERS OF LIFE. . .

3. DARKNESS RADIATES LIGHT, AND LIGHT DROPS ONE SOLITARY RAY INTO THE MOTHER-DEEP. THE RAY SHOOTS THROUGH THE VIRGIN EGG, THE RAY CAUSES THE ETERNAL EGG TO THRILL, AND DROP THE NON-ETERNAL GERM, WHICH CONDENSES INTO THE WORLD-EGG.

4. THEN THE THREE FALL INTO THE FOUR. THE RADIANT ESSENCE BECOMES SEVEN INSIDE, SEVEN OUTSIDE. THE LUMINOUS EGG, WHICH IN ITSELF IS THREE, CURDLES AND SPREADS IN MILK-WHITE CURDS THROUGHOUT THE DEPTHS OF MOTHER, THE ROOT THAT GROWS IN THE DEPTHS OF THE OCEAN OF LIFE.

5. THE ROOT REMAINS, THE LIGHT REMAINS, THE CURDS REMAIN, AND STILL OEAOHOO IS ONE.

6. THE ROOT OF LIFE WAS IN EVERY DROP OF THE OCEAN OF IMMORTALITY, AND THE OCEAN WAS RADIANT LIGHT, WHICH WAS FIRE, AND HEAT, AND MOTION. DARKNESS VANISHED AND WAS NO MORE; IT DISAPPEARED IN ITS OWN ESSENCE, THE BODY OF FIRE AND WATER, OR FATHER AND MOTHER.

7. BEHOLD, OH LANOO! THE RADIANT CHILD OF THE TWO, THE UNPARALLELED REFULGENT GLORY: BRIGHT SPACE SON OF DARK SPACE, WHICH EMERGES FROM THE DEPTHS OF THE GREAT DARK WATERS. IT IS OEAOHOO THE YOUNGER, THE   HE SHINES FORTH AS THE SON; HE IS THE BLAZING DIVINE DRAGON OF WISDOM; THE ONE IS FOUR, AND FOUR TAKES TO ITSELF THREE,   AND THE UNION PRODUCES THE SAPTA, IN WHOM ARE THE SEVEN WHICH BECOME THE TRIDASA (OR THE HOSTS AND THE

MULTITUDES). BEHOLD HIM LIFTING THE VEIL AND UNFURLING IT FROM EAST TO WEST. HE SHUTS OUT THE ABOVE, AND LEAVES THE BELOW TO BE SEEN AS THE GREAT ILLUSION. HE MARKS THE PLACES FOR THE SHINING ONES, AND TURNS THE UPPER INTO A SHORELESS SEA OF FIRE, AND THE ONE MANIFESTED INTO THE GREAT WATERS.

8. WHERE WAS THE GERM AND WHERE WAS NOW DARKNESS? WHERE IS THE SPIRIT OF THE FLAME THAT BURNS IN THY LAMP, OH LANOO? THE GERM IS THAT, AND THAT IS LIGHT, THE WHITE BRILLIANT SON OF THE DARK HIDDEN FATHER.

9. LIGHT IS COLD FLAME, AND FLAME IS FIRE, AND FIRE PRODUCES HEAT, WHICH YIELDS WATER: THE WATER OF LIFE IN THE GREAT MOTHER.

10. FATHER-MOTHER SPIN A WEB WHOSE UPPER END IS FASTENED TO SPIRIT -- THE LIGHT OF THE ONE DARKNESS -- AND THE LOWER ONE TO ITS SHADOWY END, MATTER; AND THIS WEB IS THE UNIVERSE SPUN OUT OF THE TWO SUBSTANCES MADE IN ONE, WHICH IS SVABHAVAT.

11. IT EXPANDS WHEN THE BREATH OF FIRE IS UPON IT; IT CONTRACTS WHEN THE BREATH OF THE MOTHER TOUCHES IT. THEN THE SONS DISSOCIATE AND SCATTER, TO RETURN INTO THEIR MOTHER'S BOSOM AT THE END OF THE GREAT DAY, AND RE-BECOME ONE WITH HER; WHEN IT IS COOLING IT BECOMES RADIANT, AND THE SONS EXPAND AND CONTRACT THROUGH THEIR OWN SELVES AND HEARTS; THEY EMBRACE INFINITUDE.

12. THEN SVABHAVAT SENDS FOHAT TO HARDEN THE ATOMS. EACH IS A PART OF THE WEB. REFLECTING THE "SELF-EXISTENT LORD" LIKE A MIRROR, EACH BECOMES IN TURN A WORLD.

STANZA IV.

1. . . . LISTEN, YE SONS OF THE EARTH, TO YOUR INSTRUCTORS -- THE SONS OF THE FIRE. LEARN, THERE IS NEITHER FIRST NOR LAST, FOR ALL IS ONE: NUMBER ISSUED FROM NO NUMBER.

2. LEARN WHAT WE WHO DESCEND FROM THE PRIMORDIAL SEVEN, WE WHO ARE BORN FROM THE PRIMORDIAL FLAME, HAVE LEARNT FROM OUR FATHERS. . . .

3. FROM THE EFFULGENCY OF LIGHT -- THE RAY OF THE EVER-DARKNESS -- SPRUNG IN SPACE THE RE-AWAKENED ENERGIES; THE ONE FROM THE EGG, THE SIX, AND THE FIVE. THEN THE THREE, THE ONE, THE FOUR, THE ONE, THE FIVE -- THE TWICE SEVEN THE SUM TOTAL. AND THESE ARE THE ESSENCES, THE FLAMES, THE ELEMENTS, THE BUILDERS, THE NUMBERS, THE ARUPA, THE RUPA, AND THE FORCE OF DIVINE MAN -- THE SUM TOTAL. AND FROM THE DIVINE MAN EMANATED THE FORMS, THE SPARKS, THE SACRED ANIMALS, AND THE MESSENGERS OF THE SACRED FATHERS WITHIN THE HOLY FOUR.

4. THIS WAS THE ARMY OF THE VOICE -- THE DIVINE MOTHER OF THE SEVEN. THE SPARKS OF THE SEVEN ARE SUBJECT TO, AND THE SERVANTS OF, THE FIRST, THE SECOND, THE THIRD, THE FOURTH, THE FIFTH, THE SIXTH, AND THE SEVENTH OF THE SEVEN. THESE "SPARKS" ARE CALLED SPHERES, TRIANGLES, CUBES, LINES, AND MODELLERS; FOR THUS STANDS THE ETERNAL NIDANA -- THE OEAOHOO, WHICH IS:

5. "DARKNESS" THE BOUNDLESS, OR THE NO-NUMBER, ADI-NIDANA SVABHAVAT: --

I. THE ADI-SANAT, THE NUMBER, FOR HE IS ONE.

II. THE VOICE OF THE LORD SVABHAVAT, THE NUMBERS, FOR HE IS ONE AND NINE.

III. THE "FORMLESS SQUARE."

AND THESE THREE ENCLOSED WITHIN THE ◯ ARE THE SACRED FOUR; AND THE TEN ARE THE ARUPA UNIVERSE. THEN COME THE "SONS," THE SEVEN FIGHTERS, THE ONE, THE EIGHTH LEFT OUT, AND HIS BREATH WHICH IS THE LIGHT-MAKER.

6. THEN THE SECOND SEVEN, WHO ARE THE LIPIKA, PRODUCED BY THE THREE. THE REJECTED SON IS ONE. THE "SON-SUNS" ARE COUNTLESS.

STANZA V.

1. THE PRIMORDIAL SEVEN, THE FIRST SEVEN BREATHS OF THE DRAGON OF WISDOM, PRODUCE IN THEIR TURN FROM THEIR HOLY CIRCUMGYRATING BREATHS THE FIERY WHIRLWIND.

2. THEY MAKE OF HIM THE MESSENGER OF THEIR WILL. THE DZYU BECOMES FOHAT, THE SWIFT SON OF THE DIVINE SONS WHOSE SONS ARE THE LIPIKA, RUNS CIRCULAR ERRANDS. FOHAT IS THE STEED AND THE THOUGHT IS THE RIDER. HE PASSES LIKE LIGHTNING THROUGH THE FIERY CLOUDS; TAKES THREE, AND FIVE, AND SEVEN STRIDES THROUGH THE SEVEN REGIONS ABOVE, AND THE SEVEN BELOW. HE LIFTS HIS VOICE, AND CALLS THE INNUMERABLE SPARKS, AND JOINS THEM.

3. HE IS THEIR GUIDING SPIRIT AND LEADER. WHEN HE COMMENCES WORK, HE SEPARATES THE SPARKS OF THE LOWER KINGDOM THAT FLOAT AND THRILL WITH JOY IN THEIR RADIANT DWELLINGS, AND FORMS THEREWITH THE GERMS OF WHEELS. HE PLACES THEM IN THE SIX DIRECTIONS OF SPACE, AND ONE IN THE MIDDLE -- THE CENTRAL WHEEL.

4. FOHAT TRACES SPIRAL LINES TO UNITE THE SIXTH TO THE SEVENTH -- THE CROWN; AN ARMY OF THE SONS OF LIGHT STANDS AT EACH ANGLE, AND THE LIPIKA IN THE MIDDLE WHEEL, THEY SAY: THIS IS GOOD, THE

FIRST DIVINE WORLD IS READY, THE FIRST IS NOW THE SECOND. THEN THE "DIVINE ARUPA" REFLECTS ITSELF IN CHHAYA LOKA, THE FIRST GARMENT OF THE ANUPADAKA.

5. FOHAT TAKES FIVE STRIDES AND BUILDS A WINGED WHEEL AT EACH CORNER OF THE SQUARE, FOR THE FOUR HOLY ONES AND THEIR ARMIES.

6. THE LIPIKA CIRCUMSCRIBE THE TRIANGLE, THE FIRST ONE, THE CUBE, THE SECOND ONE, AND THE PENTACLE WITHIN THE EGG. IT IS THE RING CALLED "PASS NOT" FOR THOSE WHO DESCEND AND ASCEND. ALSO FOR THOSE WHO DURING THE KALPA ARE PROGRESSING TOWARDS THE GREAT DAY "BE WITH US." THUS WERE FORMED THE RUPA AND THE ARUPA: FROM ONE LIGHT SEVEN LIGHTS; FROM EACH OF THE SEVEN, SEVEN TIMES SEVEN LIGHTS. THE WHEELS WATCH THE RING. . . . .

STANZA VI.

1. BY THE POWER OF THE MOTHER OF MERCY AND KNOWLEDGE -- KWAN-YIN -- THE "TRIPLE" OF KWAN-SHAI-YIN, RESIDING IN KWAN-YIN-TIEN, FOHAT, THE BREATH OF THEIR PROGENY, THE SON OF THE SONS, HAVING CALLED FORTH, FROM THE LOWER ABYSS, THE ILLUSIVE FORM OF SIEN-TCHANG AND THE SEVEN ELEMENTS:

2. THE SWIFT AND RADIANT ONE PRODUCES THE SEVEN LAYA CENTRES, AGAINST WHICH NONE WILL PREVAIL TO THE GREAT DAY "BE-WITH-US," AND SEATS THE UNIVERSE ON THESE ETERNAL FOUNDATIONS SURROUNDING TSIEN-TCHAN WITH THE ELEMENTARY GERMS.

3. OF THE SEVEN -- FIRST ONE MANIFESTED, SIX CONCEALED, TWO MANIFESTED, FIVE CONCEALED; THREE MANIFESTED, FOUR CONCEALED; FOUR PRODUCED, THREE HIDDEN; FOUR AND ONE TSAN REVEALED, TWO AND ONE HALF CONCEALED; SIX TO BE MANIFESTED, ONE LAID ASIDE. LASTLY, SEVEN SMALL WHEELS REVOLVING; ONE GIVING BIRTH TO THE OTHER.

4. HE BUILDS THEM IN THE LIKENESS OF OLDER WHEELS, PLACING THEM ON THE IMPERISHABLE CENTRES.

HOW DOES FOHAT BUILD THEM? HE COLLECTS THE FIERY DUST. HE MAKES BALLS OF FIRE, RUNS THROUGH THEM, AND ROUND THEM, INFUSING LIFE THEREINTO THEN' SETS THEM INTO MOTION; SOME ONE WAY, SOME THE OTHER WAY. THEY ARE COLD, HE MAKES THEM HOT. THEY ARE DRY, HE MAKES THEM MOIST. THEY SHINE, HE FANS AND COOLS THEM. THUS ACTS FOHAT FROM ONE TWILIGHT TO THE OTHER, DURING SEVEN ETERNITIES.

5. AT THE FOURTH, THE SONS ARE TOLD TO CREATE THEIR IMAGES. ONE THIRD REFUSES -- TWO OBEY.

THE CURSE IS PRONOUNCED; THEY WILL BE BORN ON THE FOURTH, SUFFER AND CAUSE SUFFERING; THIS IS THE FIRST WAR.

6. THE OLDER WHEELS ROTATED DOWNWARDS AND UPWARDS. . . . THE MOTHER'S SPAWN FILLED THE WHOLE. THERE WERE BATTLES FOUGHT BETWEEN THE CREATORS AND THE DESTROYERS, AND BATTLES FOUGHT FOR SPACE; THE SEED APPEARING AND RE-APPEARING CONTINUOUSLY.

7. MAKE THY CALCULATIONS, LANOO, IF THOU WOULDEST LEARN THE CORRECT AGE OF THY SMALL WHEEL. ITS FOURTH SPOKE IS OUR MOTHER. REACH THE FOURTH "FRUIT" OF THE FOURTH PATH OF KNOWLEDGE THAT LEADS TO NIRVANA, AND THOU SHALT COMPREHEND, FOR THOU SHALT SEE . . . . .

STANZA VII.

1. BEHOLD THE BEGINNING OF SENTIENT FORMLESS LIFE.

FIRST THE DIVINE, THE ONE FROM THE MOTHER-SPIRIT; THEN THE SPIRITUAL; THE THREE FROM THE ONE, THE FOUR FROM THE ONE, AND THE FIVE FROM WHICH THE THREE, THE FIVE, AND THE SEVEN. THESE ARE THE THREE-FOLD, THE FOUR-FOLD DOWNWARD; THE "MIND-BORN" SONS OF THE FIRST LORD; THE SHINING SEVEN.

IT IS THEY WHO ARE THOU, ME, HIM, OH LANOO. THEY, WHO WATCH OVER THEE, AND THY MOTHER EARTH.

2. THE ONE RAY MULTIPLIES THE SMALLER RAYS. LIFE PRECEDES FORM, AND LIFE SURVIVES THE LAST ATOM OF FORM. THROUGH THE COUNTLESS RAYS PROCEEDS THE LIFE-RAY, THE ONE, LIKE A THREAD THROUGH MANY JEWELS.

3. WHEN THE ONE BECOMES TWO, THE THREEFOLD APPEARS, AND THE THREE ARE ONE; AND IT IS OUR THREAD, OH LANOO, THE HEART OF THE MAN-PLANT CALLED SAPTASARMA.

4. IT IS THE ROOT THAT NEVER DIES; THE THREE-TONGUED FLAME OF THE FOUR WICKS. THE WICKS ARE THE SPARKS, THAT DRAW FROM THE THREE TONGUED FLAME SHOT OUT BY THE SEVEN -- THEIR FLAME -- THE BEAMS AND SPARKS OF ONE MOON REFLECTED IN THE RUNNING WAVES OF ALL THE RIVERS OF EARTH.

5. THE SPARK HANGS FROM THE FLAME BY THE FINEST THREAD OF FOHAT. IT JOURNEYS THROUGH THE SEVEN WORLDS OF MAYA. IT STOPS IN THE FIRST, AND IS A METAL AND A STONE; IT PASSES INTO THE SECOND AND BEHOLD -- A PLANT; THE PLANT WHIRLS THROUGH SEVEN CHANGES AND BECOMES A SACRED ANIMAL. FROM THE COMBINED ATTRIBUTES OF THESE, MANU, THE THINKER IS FORMED. WHO FORMS HIM? THE SEVEN LIVES, AND THE ONE LIFE. WHO COMPLETES HIM? THE FIVE-FOLD LHA. AND WHO PERFECTS THE LAST BODY? FISH, SIN, AND SOMA. . . . .

6. FROM THE FIRST-BORN THE THREAD BETWEEN THE SILENT WATCHER AND HIS SHADOW BECOMES MORE STRONG AND RADIANT WITH EVERY CHANGE. THE MORNING SUN-LIGHT HAS CHANGED INTO NOON-DAY GLORY. . . . .

7. THIS IS THY PRESENT WHEEL, SAID THE FLAME TO THE SPARK. THOU ART MYSELF, MY IMAGE, AND MY SHADOW. I HAVE CLOTHED MYSELF IN THEE, AND THOU ART MY VAHAN TO THE DAY, "BE WITH US," WHEN THOU SHALT RE-BECOME MYSELF AND OTHERS, THYSELF AND ME. THEN THE BUILDERS, HAVING DONNED THEIR FIRST CLOTHING, DESCEND ON RADIANT EARTH AND REIGN OVER MEN -- WHO ARE THEMSELVES. . . .

Thus ends this portion of the archaic narrative, dark, confused, almost incomprehensible. An attempt will now be made to throw light into this darkness, to make sense out of this apparent NON-SENSE.

COMMENTARIES

ON THE SEVEN STANZAS AND THEIR TERMS, ACCORDING TO THEIR
NUMERATION, IN STANZAS AND SLOKAS.

STANZA I.

1. "THE ETERNAL PARENT (Space), WRAPPED IN HER EVER INVISIBLE ROBES, HAD
SLUMBERED ONCE AGAIN FOR SEVEN ETERNITIES (*a*)."

The "Parent Space" is the eternal, ever present cause of all -- the incomprehensible
DEITY, whose "invisible robes" are the mystic root of all matter, and of the Universe.
Space is the *one eternal thing* that we can most easily imagine, immovable in its
abstraction and uninfluenced by either the presence or absence in it of an objective
Universe. It is without dimension, in every sense, and self-existent. Spirit is the first
differentiation from THAT, the causeless cause of both Spirit and Matter. It is, as taught
in the esoteric catechism, neither limitless void, nor conditioned fulness, but both. It was
and ever will be. (See Proem pp. 2 *et seq.*)

Thus, the "Robes" stand for the noumenon of undifferentiated Cosmic Matter. It is not
matter as we know it, but the spiritual essence of matter, and is co-eternal and even one
with Space in its abstract sense. Root-nature is also the source of the subtile invisible
properties in visible matter. It is the Soul, so to say, of the ONE infinite Spirit. The Hindus
call it Mulaprakriti, and say that it is the primordial substance, which is the basis of the
Upadhi or vehicle of every phenomenon, whether physical, mental or psychic. It is the
source from which Akasa radiates.

(*a*) By the Seven "Eternities," aeons or periods are meant. The word "Eternity," as
understood in Christian theology, has no meaning to the Asiatic ear, except in its
application to the ONE existence; nor is the term sempiternity, the eternal only in futurity,
anything better than a misnomer. Such words do not and cannot exist in philosophical
metaphysics, and were unknown till the advent of ecclesiastical Christianity. The Seven
Eternities meant are the seven periods, or a period answering in its duration to the seven
periods, of a Manvantara, and extending throughout a Maha-Kalpa or the "Great Age" --
100 years of Brahma -- making a total of 311,040,000,000,000 of years; each year of
Brahma being composed of 360 "days," and of the same number of "nights" of Brahma
(reckoning by the Chandrayana or lunar year); and a "Day of Brahma" consisting of
4,320,000,000 of mortal years. These "Eternities" belong to the most secret calculations, in
which, in order to arrive at the true total, every figure must be $7x$ (7 to the power of x); x
varying according to the nature of the cycle in the subjective or real world; and every
figure or number relating to, or representing all the different cycles from the greatest to
the smallest -- in the objective or unreal world -- must necessarily be multiples of seven.
The key to this cannot be given, for herein lies the mystery of esoteric calculations, and
for the purposes of ordinary calculation it has no sense. "The number seven," says the
Kabala, "is the great number of the Divine Mysteries;" number ten is that of all human
knowledge (Pythagorean decade); 1,000 is the number ten to the third power, and
therefore the number 7,000 is also symbolical. In the Secret Doctrine the figure and
number 4 are the male symbol only on the highest plane of abstraction; on the plane of
matter the 3 is the masculine and the 4 the female: the upright and the horizontal in the
fourth stage of symbolism, when the symbols became the glyphs of the generative powers
on the physical plane.

2. TIME WAS NOT, FOR IT LAY ASLEEP IN THE INFINITE BOSOM OF DURATION (*a*).

(*a*) Time is only an illusion produced by the succession of our states of consciousness as we travel through eternal duration, and it does not exist where no consciousness exists in which the illusion can be produced; but "lies asleep." The present is only a mathematical line which divides that part of eternal duration which we call the future, from that part which we call the past. Nothing on earth has real duration, for nothing remains without change -- or the same -- for the billionth part of a second; and the sensation we have of the actuality of the division of "time" known as the present, comes from the blurring of that momentary glimpse, or succession of glimpses, of things that our senses give us, as those things pass from the region of ideals which we call the future, to the region of memories that we name the past. In the same way we experience a sensation of duration in the case of the instantaneous electric spark, by reason of the blurred and continuing impression on the retina. The real person or thing does not consist solely of what is seen at any particular moment, but is composed of the sum of all its various and changing conditions from its appearance in the material form to its disappearance from the earth. It is these "sum-totals" that exist from eternity in the "future," and pass by degrees through matter, to exist for eternity in the "past." No one could say that a bar of metal dropped into the sea came into existence as it left the air, and ceased to exist as it entered the water, and that the bar itself consisted only of that cross-section thereof which at any given moment coincided with the mathematical plane that separates, and, at the same time, joins, the atmosphere and the ocean. Even so of persons and things, which, dropping out of the to-be into the has-been, out of the future into the past -- present momentarily to our senses a cross-section, as it were, of their total selves, as they pass through time and space (as matter) on their way from one eternity to another: and these two constitute that "duration" in which alone anything has true existence, were our senses but able to cognize it there.

3. . . . UNIVERSAL MIND WAS NOT, FOR THERE WERE NO AH-HI (celestial beings) TO CONTAIN (hence to manifest) IT (*a*).

(*a*) Mind is a name given to the sum of the states of Consciousness grouped under Thought, Will, and Feeling. During deep sleep, ideation ceases on the physical plane, and memory is in abeyance; thus for the time-being "Mind is not," because the organ, through which the Ego manifests ideation and memory on the material plane, has temporarily ceased to function. A noumenon can become a phenomenon on any plane of existence only by manifesting on that plane through an appropriate basis or vehicle; and during the long night of rest called Pralaya, when all the existences are dissolved, the "UNIVERSAL MIND" remains as a permanent possibility of mental action, or as that abstract absolute thought, of which mind is the concrete relative manifestation. The AH-HI (Dhyan-Chohans) are the collective hosts of spiritual beings -- the Angelic Hosts of Christianity, the Elohim and "Messengers" of the Jews -- who are the vehicle for the manifestation of the divine or universal thought and will. They are the Intelligent Forces that give to and enact in Nature her "laws," while themselves acting according to laws imposed upon them in a similar manner by still higher Powers; but they are not "the personifications" of the powers of Nature, as erroneously thought. This hierarchy of spiritual Beings, through which the Universal Mind comes into action, is like an army -- a "Host," truly -- by means of which the fighting power of a nation manifests itself, and which is composed of army corps, divisions, brigades, regiments, and so forth, each with its separate individuality or life, and its limited freedom of action and limited responsibilities; each contained in a larger individuality, to which its own interests are subservient, and each containing lesser individualities in itself.

4. THE SEVEN WAYS TO BLISS (Moksha or Nirvana) WERE NOT (*a*). THE GREAT CAUSES OF MISERY (Nidana and Maya) WERE NOT, FOR THERE WAS NO ONE TO PRODUCE AND GET ENSNARED BY THEM (*b*).

(*a*) There are seven "Paths" or "Ways" to the bliss of Non-Exist- ence, which is absolute Being, Existence, and Consciousness. They were not, because the Universe was, so far, empty, and existed only in the Divine Thought. For it is . . .

(*b*) The twelve Nidanas or causes of being. Each is the effect of its antecedent cause, and a cause, in its turn, to its successor; the sum total of the Nidanas being based on the four truths, a doctrine especially characteristic of the Hinayana System. They belong to the theory of the stream of catenated law which produces merit and demerit, and finally brings Karma into full sway. It is based upon the great truth that re-incarnation is to be dreaded, as existence in this world only entails upon man suffering, misery and pain; Death itself being unable to deliver man from it, since death is merely the door through which he passes to another life on earth after a little rest on its threshold -- Devachan. The Hinayana System, or School of the "Little Vehicle," is of very ancient growth; while the Mahayana is of a later period, having originated after the death of Buddha. Yet the tenets of the latter are as old as the hills that have contained such schools from time immemorial, and the Hinayana and Mahayana Schools (the latter, that of the "Great Vehicle") both teach the same doctrine in reality. *Yana,* or Vehicle (in Sanskrit, Vahan) is a mystic expression, both "vehicles" inculcating that man may escape the sufferings of rebirths and even the false bliss of Devachan, by obtaining Wisdom and Knowledge, which alone can dispel the Fruits of Illusion and Ignorance.

Maya or illusion is an element which enters into all finite things, for everything that exists has only a relative, not an absolute, reality, since the appearance which the hidden noumenon assumes for any observer depends upon his power of cognition. To the untrained eye of the savage, a painting is at first an unmeaning confusion of streaks and daubs of color, while an educated eye sees instantly a face or a landscape. Nothing is permanent except the one hidden absolute existence which contains in itself the noumena of all realities. The existences belonging to every plane of being, up to the highest Dhyan-Chohans, are, in degree, of the nature of shadows cast by a magic lantern on a colourless screen; but all things are relatively real, for the cogniser is also a reflection, and the things cognised are therefore as real to him as himself. Whatever reality things possess must be looked for in them before or after they have passed like a flash through the material world; but we cannot cognise any such existence directly, so long as we have sense-instruments which bring only material existence into the field of our consciousness. Whatever plane our consciousness may be acting in, both we and the things belonging to that plane are, for the time being, our only realities. As we rise in the scale of development we perceive that during the stages through which we have passed we mistook shadows for realities, and the upward progress of the Ego is a series of progressive awakenings, each advance bringing with it the idea that now, at last, we have reached "reality;" but only when we shall have reached the absolute Consciousness, and blended our own with it, shall we be free from the delusions produced by Maya.

5. **D**ARKNESS ALONE FILLED THE BOUNDLESS ALL (*a*), FOR FATHER, MOTHER AND SON WERE ONCE MORE ONE, AND THE SON HAD NOT AWAKENED YET FOR THE NEW WHEEL AND HIS PILGRIMAGE THEREON (*b*).

(*a*) "Darkness is Father-Mother: light their son," says an old Eastern proverb. Light is inconceivable except as coming from some source which is the cause of it; and as, in the instance of primordial light, that source is unknown, though as strongly demanded by reason and logic, therefore it is called "Darkness" by us, from an intellectual point of view. As to borrowed or secondary light, whatever its source, it can be but of a temporary mayavic character. Darkness, then, is the eternal is added to darkness to make of it light, or to light to make it darkness, on this our plane. They are interchangeable, and scientifically light is but a mode of darkness and *vice versa*. Yet both are phenomena of the same noumenon -- which is absolute darkness to the scientific mind, and but a gray twilight to the perception of the average mystic, though to that of the spiritual eye of the Initiate it is absolute light. How far we discern the light that shines in darkness depends upon our powers of vision. What is light to us is darkness to certain insects, and the eye of the clairvoyant sees illumination where the normal eye perceives only blackness. When the whole universe was plunged in sleep -- had returned to its one primordial element -- there was neither centre of luminosity, nor eye to perceive light, and darkness necessarily filled the boundless all.

(*b*) The Father-Mother are the male and female principles in root-nature, the opposite poles that manifest in all things on every plane of Kosmos, or Spirit and Substance, in a less allegorical aspect, the resultant of which is the Universe, or the Son. They are "once more One" when in "The Night of Brahma," during Pralaya, all in the objective Universe has returned to its one primal and eternal cause, to reappear at the following Dawn -- as it does periodically. "Karana" -- eternal cause -- was alone. To put it more plainly: Karana is alone during the "Nights of Brahma." The previous objective Universe has dissolved into its one primal and eternal cause, and is, so to say, held in solution in space, to differentiate again and crystallize out anew at the following Manvantaric dawn, which is the commencement of a new "Day" or new activity of Brahma -- the symbol of the Universe. In esoteric parlance, Brahma is Father-Mother-Son, or Spirit, Soul and Body at once; each personage being symbolical of an attribute, and each attribute or quality being a graduated efflux of Divine Breath in its cyclic differentiation, involutionary and evolutionary. In the cosmicophysical sense, it is the Universe, the planetary chain and the earth; in the purely spiritual, the Unknown Deity, Planetary Spirit, and Man -- the Son of the two, the creature of Spirit and Matter, and a manifestation of them in his periodical appearances on Earth during the "wheels," or the Manvantaras. -- (*See* Part II. §: "*Days and Nights of Brahma.*")

6. THE SEVEN SUBLIME LORDS AND THE SEVEN TRUTHS HAD CEASED TO BE (*a*), AND THE UNIVERSE, THE SON OF NECESSITY, WAS IMMERSED IN PARANISHPANNA (*b*) (absolute perfection, Paranirvana, which is Yong-Grub) TO BE OUT-BREATHED BY THAT WHICH IS AND YET IS NOT. NAUGHT WAS (*c*).

(*a*) The seven sublime lords are the Seven Creative Spirits, the Dhyan-Chohans, who correspond to the Hebrew Elohim. It is the same hierarchy of Archangels to which St. Michael, St. Gabriel, and others belong, in the Christian theogony. Only while St. Michael, for instance, is allowed in dogmatic Latin theology to watch over all the promontories and gulfs, in the Esoteric System, the Dhyanis watch successively over one of the Rounds and the great Root-races of our planetary chain. They are, moreover, said to send their Bhodisatvas, the human correspondents of the Dhyani-Buddhas (of whom *vide infra*) during every Round and Race. Out of the Seven Truths and Revelations, or rather revealed secrets, four only have been handed to us, as we are still in the Fourth Round, and the world also has only had four Buddhas, so far. This is a very complicated question, and will receive more ample treatment later on.

So far "There are only Four Truths, and Four Vedas" -- say the Hindus and Buddhists. For a similar reason Irenaeus insisted on the necessity of Four Gospels. But as every new Root-race at the head of a Round must have its revelation and revealers, the next Round will bring the Fifth, the following the Sixth, and so on.

(*b*) "*Paranishpanna*" is the absolute perfection to which all existences attain at the close of a great period of activity, or Maha-Manvantara, and in which they rest during the succeeding period of repose. In Tibetan it is called Yong-Grub. Up to the day of the Yogacharya school the true nature of Paranirvana was taught publicly, but since then it has become entirely esoteric; hence so many contradictory interpretations of it. It is only a true Idealist who can understand it. Everything has to be viewed as ideal, with the exception of Paranirvana, by him who would comprehend that state, and acquire a knowledge of how Non Ego, Voidness, and Darkness are Three in One and alone Self-existent and perfect. It is absolute, however, only in a relative sense, for it must give room to still further absolute perfection, according to a higher standard of excellence in the following period of activity -- just as a perfect flower must cease to be a perfect flower and die, in order to grow into a perfect fruit, -- if a somewhat Irish mode of expression may be permitted.

The Secret Doctrine teaches the progressive development of everything, worlds as well as atoms; and this stupendous development has neither conceivable beginning nor imaginable end. Our "Universe" is only one of an infinite number of Universes, all of them "Sons of Necessity," because links in the great Cosmic chain of Universes, each one standing in the relation of an effect as regards its predecessor, and being a cause as regards its successor.

The appearance and disappearance of the Universe are pictured as an outbreathing and inbreathing of "the Great Breath," which is eternal, and which, being Motion, is one of the three aspects of the Absolute -- Abstract Space and Duration being the other two. When the "Great Breath" is projected, it is called the Divine Breath, and is regarded as the breathing of the Unknowable Deity -- the One Existence -- which breathes out a thought, as it were, which becomes the Kosmos. (See "Isis Unveiled.") So also is it when the Divine Breath is inspired again the Universe disappears into the bosom of "the Great Mother," who then sleeps "wrapped in her invisible robes."

(c) By "that which is and yet is not" is meant the Great Breath itself, which we can only speak of as absolute existence, but cannot picture to our imagination as any form of existence that we can distinguish from Non-existence. The three periods -- the Present, the Past, and the Future -- are in the esoteric philosophy a compound time; for the three are a composite number only in relation to the phenomenal plane, but in the realm of noumena have no abstract validity. As said in the Scriptures: "The Past time is the Present time, as also the Future, which, though it has not come into existence, still is"; according to a precept in the Prasanga Madhyamika teaching, whose dogmas have been known ever since it broke away from the purely esoteric schools. Our ideas, in short, on duration and time are all derived from our ensations according to the laws of Association. Inextricably bound up with the relativity of human knowledge, they nevertheless can have no existence except in the experience of the individual ego, and perish when its evolutionary march dispels the Maya of phenomenal existence. What is Time, for instance, but the panoramic succession of our states of consciousness? In the words of a Master, "I feel irritated at having to use these three clumsy words -- Past, Present, and Future -- miserable concepts of the objective phases of the subjective whole, they are about as ill-adapted for the purpose as an axe for fine carving." One has to acquire *Paramartha* lest one should become too easy a prey to *Samvriti* -- is a philosophical axiom.

7. **T**HE CAUSES OF EXISTENCE HAD BEEN DONE AWAY WITH (a); THE VISIBLE THAT WAS, AND THE INVISIBLE THAT IS, RESTED IN ETERNAL NON-BEING, THE ONE BEING (b).

(a) "The Causes of Existence" mean not only the physical causes known to science, but the metaphysical causes, the chief of which is the desire to exist, an outcome of Nidana and Maya. This desire for a sentient life shows itself in everything, from an atom to a sun, and is a reflection of the Divine Thought propelled into objective existence, into a law that the Universe should exist. According to esoteric teaching, the real cause of that supposed desire, and of all existence, remains for ever hidden, and its first emanations are the most complete abstractions mind can conceive. These abstractions must of necessity be postulated as the cause of the material Universe which presents itself to the senses and intellect; and they underlie the secondary and subordinate powers of Nature, which, anthropomorphized, have been worshipped as God and gods by the common herd of every age. It is impossible to conceive anything without a cause; the attempt to do so makes the mind a blank.

This is virtually the condition to which the mind must come at last when we try to trace back the chain of causes and effects, but both science and religion jump to this condition of blankness much more quickly than is necessary; for they ignore the metaphysical abstractions which are the only conceivable cause of physical concretions. These abstractions become more and more concrete as they approach our plane of existence, until finally they phenomenalise in the form of the material Universe, by a process of conversion of metaphysics into physics, analogous to that by which steam can be condensed into water, and the water frozen into ice.

(b) The idea of Eternal Non-Being, which is the One Being, will appear a paradox to anyone who does not remember that we limit our ideas of being to our present consciousness of existence; making it a specific, instead of a generic term. An unborn infant, could it think in our acceptation of that term, would necessarily limit its conception of being, in a similar manner, to the intrauterine life which alone it knows; and were it to endeavour to express to its consciousness the idea of life after birth (death to it), it would, in the absence of data to go upon, and of faculties to comprehend such data, probably express that life as "Non-Being which is Real Being." In our case the One Being is the noumenon of all the noumena which we know must underlie phenomena, and give them whatever shadow of reality they possess, but which we have not the senses or the intellect to cognize at present. The impalpable atoms of gold scattered through the substance of a ton of auriferous quartz may be imperceptible to the naked eye of the miner, yet he knows that they are not only present there but that they alone give his quartz any appreciable value; and this relation of the gold to the quartz may faintly shadow forth that of the noumenon to the phenomenon. But the miner knows what the gold will look like when extracted from the quartz, whereas the common mortal can form no conception of the reality of things separated from the Maya which veils them, and in which they are hidden. Alone the Initiate, rich with the lore acquired by numberless generations of his predecessors, directs the "Eye of Dangma" toward the essence of things in which no Maya can have any influence. It is here that the teachings of esoteric philosophy in relation to the Nidanas and the Four Truths become of the greatest importance; but they are secret.

8. ALONE, THE ONE FORM OF EXISTENCE STRETCHED BOUNDLESS, INFINITE, CAUSELESS, IN DREAMLESS SLEEP (a); AND LIFE PULSATED UNCONSCIOUS IN UNIVERSAL SPACE, THROUGHOUT THAT ALL-PRESENCE WHICH IS SENSED BY THE "OPENED EYE" OF THE DANGMA (b).

(a) The tendency of modern thought is to recur to the archaic idea of a homogeneous basis for apparently widely different things -- heterogeneity developed from homogeneity. Biologists are now searching for their homogeneous protoplasm and chemists for their protyle, while science is looking for the force of which electricity, magnetism, heat, and so forth, are the differentiations. The Secret Doctrine carries this idea into the region of metaphysics and postulates a "One Form of Existence" as the basis and source of all things. But perhaps the phrase, the "One Form of Existence," is not altogether correct. The Sanskrit word is Prabhavapyaya, "the place, or rather plane, whence emerges the origination, and into which is the resolution of all things," says a commentator. It is not the "Mother of the World," as translated by Wilson (see Book I., Vishnu Purana); for Jagad Yoni (as shown by FitzEdward Hall) is scarcely so much "the Mother of the World" or "the Womb of the World" as the "Material Cause of the Universe." The Puranic Commentators explain it by Karana -- "Cause" -- but the Esoteric philosophy, by the *ideal spirit of that cause*. It is, in its secondary stage, the Svabhavat of the Buddhist philosopher, the eternal cause and effect, omnipresent yet abstract, the self-existent plastic Essence and the root of all things, viewed in the same dual light as the Vedantin views his Parabrahm and Mulaprakriti, the one under two aspects. It seems indeed extraordinary to find great scholars speculating on the possibility of the Vedanta, and the Uttara-Mimansa especially, having been "evoked by the teachings of the Buddhists," whereas, it is on the contrary Buddhism (of Gautama, the Buddha) that was "evoked" and entirely upreared on the tenets of the Secret Doctrine, of which a partial sketch is here attempted, and on which, also, the Upanishads are made to rest. The above, according to the teachings of Sri Sankaracharya, is undeniable.

(b) Dreamless sleep is one of the seven states of consciousness known in Oriental esotericism. In each of these states a different portion of the mind comes into action; or as a Vedantin would express it, the individual is conscious in a different plane of his being. The term "dreamless sleep," in this case is applied allegorically to the Universe to express a condition somewhat analogous to that state of consciousness in man, which, not being remembered in a waking state, seems a blank, just as the sleep of the mesmerised subject seems to him an unconscious blank when he returns to his normal condition, although he has been talking and acting as a conscious individual would.

9. BUT WHERE WAS THE DANGMA WHEN THE ALAYA OF THE UNIVERSE (*Soul as the basis of all, Anima Mundi*) WAS IN PARAMARTHA (a) (*Absolute Being and Consciousness which are Absolute Non-Being and Unconsciousness*) AND THE GREAT WHEEL WAS ANUPADAKA (b)?

(a) Here we have before us the subject of centuries of scholastic disputations. The two terms "Alaya" and "Paramartha" have been the causes of dividing schools and splitting the truth into more different aspects than any other mystic terms. Alaya is literally the "Soul of the World" or Anima Mundi, the "Over-Soul" of Emerson, and according to esoteric teaching it changes periodically its nature. Alaya, though eternal and changeless in its inner essence on the planes which are unreachable by either men or Cosmic Gods (Dhyani Buddhas), alters during the active life-period with respect to the lower planes, ours included. During that time not only the Dhyani-Buddhas are one with Alaya in Soul and Essence, but even the man strong in the Yoga (mystic meditation) "is able to merge his soul with it" (Aryasanga, the *Bumapa* school). This is not Nirvana, but a condition next to it. Hence the disagreement. Thus, while the Yogacharyas (of the Mahayana school) say that Alaya is the personification of the Voidness, and yet Alaya (*Nyingpo* and *Tsang* in Tibetan) is the basis of every visible and invisible thing, and that, though it is eternal and immutable in its essence, it reflects itself in every object of the Universe "like the moon in clear tranquil water"; other schools dispute the statement. The same for Paramartha: the Yogacharyas interpret the term as that which is also dependent upon other things (*paratantra*); and the Madhyamikas say that Paramartha is limited to Paranishpanna or absolute perfection; *i.e.*, in the exposition of these "two truths" (out of four), the former believe and maintain that (on this plane, at any rate) there exists only Samvritisatya or relative truth; and the latter teach the existence of Paramarthasatya, the "absolute truth." "No Arhat, oh mendicants, can reach absolute knowledge before he becomes one with Paranirvana. *Parikalpita* and *Paratantra* are his two great enemies" (Aphorisms of the Bodhisattvas). *Parikalpita* (in Tibetan *Kun-ttag*) is error, made by those unable to realize the emptiness and illusionary nature of all; who believe something to exist which does not -- *e.g.*, the Non-Ego. And

"Paramartha" is self-consciousness in Sanskrit, Svasamvedana, or the "self-analysing reflection" -- from two words, parama (above everything) and artha (comprehension), Satya meaning absolute true being, or Esse. In Tibetan Paramarthasatya is Dondampaidenpa. The opposite of this absolute reality, or actuality, is Samvritisatya -- the relative truth only -- "Samvriti" meaning "false conception" and being the origin of illusion, Maya; in Tibetan Kundzabchi-denpa, "illusion-creating appearance."

Paratantra is that, whatever it is, which exists only through a dependent or causal connexion, and which has to disappear as soon as the cause from which it proceeds is removed -- *e.g.*, the light of a wick. Destroy or extinguish it, and light disappears.

Esoteric philosophy teaches that everything lives and is conscious, but not that all life and consciousness are similar to those of human or even animal beings. Life we look upon as "the one form of existence," manifesting in what is called matter; or, as in man, what, incorrectly separating them, we name Spirit, Soul and Matter. Matter is the vehicle for the manifestation of soul on this plane of existence, and soul is the vehicle on a higher plane for the manifestation of spirit, and these three are a trinity synthesized by Life, which pervades them all. The idea of universal life is one of those ancient conceptions which are returning to the human mind in this century, as a consequence of its liberation from anthropomorphic theology. Science, it is true, contents itself with tracing or postulating the signs of universal life, and has not yet been bold enough even to whisper "Anima Mundi!" The idea of "crystalline life," now familiar to science, would have been scouted half a century ago. Botanists are now searching for the nerves of plants; not that they suppose that plants can feel or think as animals do, but because they believe that some structure, bearing the same relation functionally to plant life that nerves bear to animal life, is necessary to explain vegetable growth and nutrition. It hardly seems possible that science can disguise from itself much longer, by the mere use of terms such as "force" and "energy," the fact that things that have life are living things, whether they be atoms or planets.

But what is the belief of the inner esoteric Schools? the reader may ask. What are the doctrines taught on this subject by the Esoteric "Buddhists"? With them "Alaya" has a double and even a triple meaning. In the Yogacharya system of the contemplative Mahayana school, Alaya is both the Universal Soul (Anima Mundi) and the Self of a progressed adept. "He who is strong in the Yoga can introduce at will his Alaya by means of meditation into the true Nature of Existence." The "Alaya has an absolute eternal existence," says Aryasanga -- the rival of Nagarjuna. In one sense it is *Pradhana;* which cause, is emphatically called by the most eminent sages Pradhana, original base, which is subtile Prakriti, viz., that which is eternal, and which at once is (or comprehends) what is and what is not, or is mere process." "Prakriti," however, is an incorrect word, and Alaya would explain it better; for Prakriti is not the "uncognizable Brahma." It is a mistake of those who know nothing of the Universality of the Occult doctrines from the very cradle of the human races, and especially so of those scholars who reject the very idea of a "primordial revelation," to teach that the Anima Mundi, the One Life or "Universal Soul," was made known only by Anaxagoras, or during his age. This philosopher brought the teaching forward simply to oppose the too materialistic conceptions on Cosmogony of Democritus, based on his exoteric theory of *blindly* driven atoms. Anaxagoras of Clazomene was not its inventor but only its propagator, as also was Plato. That which he called Mundane Intelligence, the nous ([[*nous*]]), the principle that according to his views is absolutely separated and free from matter and acts on design, was called Motion, the ONE LIFE, or *Jivatma*, ages before the year 500 B.C. in India. Only the Aryan philosophers never endowed the principle, which with them is infinite, with the finite "attribute" of "thinking."

This leads the reader naturally to the "Supreme Spirit" of Hegel and the German Transcendentalists as a contrast that it may be useful to point out. The schools of Schelling and Fichte have diverged widely from the primitive archaic conception of an ABSOLUTE principle, and have mirrored only an aspect of the basic idea of the Vedanta. Even the "Absoluter Geist" shadowed forth by von Hartman in his pessimistic philosophy of the Unconscious, while it is, perhaps, the closest approximation made by European speculation to the Hindu Adwaitee Doctrines, similarly falls far short of the reality.

According to Hegel, the "Unconscious" would never have undertaken the vast and laborious task of evolving the Universe, except in the hope of attaining clear Self-consciousness. In this connection it is to be borne in mind that in designating Spirit, which the European Pantheists use as equivalent to Parabrahm, as unconscious, they do not attach to that expression of "Spirit" -- one employed in the absence of a better to symbolise a profound mystery -- the connotation it usually bears.

The "Absolute Consciousness," they tell us, "behind" phenomena, which is only termed unconsciousness in the absence of any element of personality, transcends human conception. Man, unable to form one concept except in terms of empirical phenomena, is powerless from the very constitution of his being to raise the veil that shrouds the majesty of the Absolute. Only the liberated Spirit is able to faintly realise the nature of the source whence it sprung and whither it must eventually return. . . . As the highest Dhyan Chohan, however, can but bow in ignorance before the awful mystery of Absolute Being; and since, even in that culmination of conscious existence -- "the merging of the individual in the universal consciousness" -- to use a phrase of Fichte's -- the Finite cannot conceive the Infinite, nor can it apply to it its own standard of mental experiences, how can it be said that the "Unconscious" and the Absolute can have even an instinctive impulse or hope of attaining clear self-consciousness? A Vedantin would never admit this Hegelian idea; and the Occultist would say that it applies perfectly to the awakened MAHAT, the Universal Mind already projected into the phenomenal world as the first aspect of the changeless ABSOLUTE, but never to the latter. "Spirit and Matter, or Purusha and Prakriti are but the two primeval aspects of the One and Secondless," we are taught.

The matter-moving Nous, the animating Soul, immanent in every atom, manifested in man, latent in the stone, has different degrees of power; and this pantheistic idea of a general Spirit-Soul pervading all Nature is the oldest of all the philosophical notions. Nor was the Archaeus a discovery of Paracelsus nor of his pupil Van Helmont; for it is again the same Archaeus or "Father-Ether," -- the manifested basis of life -- localised. The whole series of the numberless speculations of this kind are but variations on this theme, the key-note of which was struck in this primeval Revelation. (See Part II., "Primordial Substance.")

(*b*) The term Anupadaka, "parentless," or without progenitors, is a mystical designation having several meanings in the philosophy. By this name celestial beings, the Dhyan-Chohans or Dhyani-Buddhas, are generally meant. But as these correspond mystically to the human Buddhas and Bodhisattwas, known as the "Manushi (or human) Buddhas," the latter are also designated "Anupadaka," once that their whole personality is merged in their compound sixth and seventh principles -- or Atma-Buddhi, and that they have become the "diamond-souled" (Vajra-sattvas), the full Mahatmas. The "Concealed Lord" (Sangbai Dag-po), "the one merged with the absolute," can have no parents since he is Self-existent, and one with the Universal Spirit (Svayambhu), the Svabhavat in the highest aspect. The mystery in the hierarchy of the Anupadaka is great, its apex being the universal Spirit-Soul, and the lower rung the Manushi-Buddha; and even every Soul-endowed man is an Anupadaka in a latent state. Hence, when speaking of the Universe in its formless, eternal, or absolute condition, before it was fashioned by the "Builders" -- the expression, "the Universe was Anupadaka." (See Part II., "Primordial Substance.")

STANZA II.

COMMENTARY

1. . . . . WHERE WERE THE BUILDERS, THE LUMINOUS SONS OF MANVANTARIC DAWN (*a*)? .
. . . IN THE UNKNOWN DARKNESS IN THEIR AH-HI (*Chohanic, Dhyani-Buddhic*)
PARANISHPANNA, THE PRODUCERS OF FORM (*rupa*) FROM NO-FORM (*arupa*), THE ROOT
OF THE WORLD -- THE DEVAMATRI AND SVABHAVAT, RESTED IN THE BLISS OF NON-
BEING (*b*).

(*a*) The "Builders," the "Sons of Manvantaric Dawn," are the real creators of the Universe;
and in this doctrine, which deals only with our Planetary System, they, as the architects of
the latter, are also called the "Watchers" of the Seven Spheres, which exoterically are the
Seven planets, and esoterically the seven earths or spheres (planets) of our chain also. The
opening sentence of Stanza I., when mentioning "Seven Eternities," is made to apply both
to the *Maha-Kalpa* or "the (great) Age of Brahma," as well as to the Solar *pralaya* and
subsequent resurrection of our Planetary System on a higher plane. There are many kinds
of *pralaya* (dissolution of a thing visible), as will be shown elsewhere.

(*b*) Paranishpanna, remember, is the *summum bonum*, the Absolute, hence the same as
Paranirvana. Besides being the final state it is that condition of subjectivity which has no
relation to anything but the one absolute truth (Para-marthasatya) on its plane. It is that
state which leads one to appreciate correctly the full meaning of Non-Being, which, as
explained, is *absolute* Being. Sooner or later, all that now *seemingly* exists, will be in
reality and actually in the state of Paranishpanna. But there is a great difference between
conscious and *unconscious* "being." The condition of Paranishpanna, without Paramartha,
the Self-analysing consciousness (Svasamvedana), is no bliss, but simply extinction (for
Seven Eternities). Thus, an iron ball placed under the scorching rays of the sun will get
heated through, but will not feel or appreciate the warmth, while a man will. It is only
"with a mind clear and undarkened by personality, and an assimilation of the merit of
manifold existences devoted to being in its collectivity (the whole living and sentient
Universe)," that one gets rid of personal existence, merging into, becoming one with, the
Absolute, and continuing in full possession of Paramartha.

2. . . . . WHERE WAS SILENCE? WHERE WERE THE EARS TO SENSE IT? NO! THERE WAS
NEITHER SILENCE, NOR SOUND (*a*). NAUGHT SAVE CEASELESS, ETERNAL BREATH (*Motion*)
WHICH KNOWS ITSELF NOT (*b*).

(*a*) The idea that things can cease to exist and still BE, is a fundamental one in Eastern
psychology. Under this apparent contradiction in terms, there rests a fact of Nature to
realise which in the mind, rather than to argue about words, is the important thing. A
familiar instance of a similar paradox is afforded by chemical combination. The question
whether Hydrogen and Oxygen cease to exist, when they combine to form water, is still a
moot one, some arguing that since they are found again when the water is decomposed
they must be there all the while; others contending that as they actually turn into
something totally different they must cease to exist as themselves for the time being; but
neither side is able to form the faintest conception of the real condition of a thing, which
has become something else and yet has not ceased to be itself. Existence as water may be
said to be, for Oxygen and Hydrogen, a state of Non-being which is "more real being" than
their existence as gases; and it may faintly symbolise the condition of the Universe when
it goes to sleep, or ceases to be, during the "Nights of Brahma" -- to awaken or reappear
again, when the dawn of the new Manvantara recalls it to what we call existence.

(*b*) The "Breath" of the One Existence is used in its application only to the spiritual aspect of Cosmogony by Archaic esotericism; otherwise, it is replaced by its equivalent in the material plane -- Motion. The One Eternal Element, or element-containing Vehicle, is *Space*, dimensionless in every sense; co-existent with which are -- endless *duration*, primordial (hence indestructible) *matter*, and *motion* -- absolute "perpetual motion" which is the "breath" of the "One" Element. This breath, as seen, can never cease, not even during the Pralayic eternities. (*See* "*Chaos, Theos, Kosmos,*" in Part II.)

But the "Breath of the One Existence" does not, all the same, apply to the *One Causeless Cause* or the "All Be-ness" (in contradistinction to All-Being, which is Brahma, or the Universe). Brahma (or Hari) the four-faced god who, after lifting the Earth out of the waters, "accomplished the Creation," is held to be only the instrumental, and not, as clearly implied, the ideal Cause. No Orientalist, so far, seems to have thoroughly comprehended the real sense of the verses in the Purana, that treat of "creation."

Therein Brahma is the cause of the potencies that are to be generated subsequently for the work of "creation." When a translator says, "And from him proceed the potencies to be created, after they had become the real cause": "and from IT proceed the potencies that *will create* as they *become* the real cause" (on the material plane) would perhaps be more correct? Save that one (causeless) ideal cause there is no other to which the universe can be referred. "Worthiest of ascetics! through its potency -- *i.e.*, through the potency of that cause -- every created thing comes by its inherent or proper nature." If, in the Vedanta and Nyaya, *nimitta* is the efficient cause, as contrasted with *upadana,* the material cause, (and in the Sankhya, *pradhana* implies the functions of both); in the Esoteric philosophy, which reconciles all these systems, and the nearest exponent of which is the Vedanta as expounded by the Advaita Vedantists, none but the *upadana* can be speculated upon; that which is in the minds of the Vaishnavas (the Vasishta-dvaita) as the ideal in contradistinction to the real -- or Parabrahm and Isvara -- can find no room in published speculations, since that ideal even is a misnomer, when applied to that of which no human reason, even that of an adept, can conceive.

To know itself or oneself, necessitates consciousness and perception (both limited faculties in relation to any subject except Parabrahm), to be cognized. Hence the "Eternal Breath which knows itself not." Infinity cannot comprehend Finiteness. The Boundless can have no relation to the bounded and the conditioned. In the occult teachings, the Unknown and the Unknowable MOVER, or the Self-Existing, is the absolute divine Essence. And thus being *Absolute* Consciousness, and *Absolute* Motion -- to the limited senses of those who describe this indescribable -- it is unconsciousness and immoveableness. Concrete consciousness cannot be predicated of abstract Consciousness, any more than the quality wet can be predicated of water -- wetness being its own attribute and the cause of the wet quality in other things. Consciousness implies limitations and qualifications; something to be conscious of, and someone to be conscious of it. But Absolute Consciousness contains the cognizer, the thing cognized and the cognition, all three in itself and all three *one.* No man is conscious of more than that portion of his knowledge that happens to have been recalled to his mind at any particular time, yet such is the poverty of language that we have no term to distinguish the knowledge not actively thought of, from knowledge we are unable to recall to memory. To forget is synonymous with not to remember. How much greater must be the difficulty of finding terms to describe, and to distinguish between, abstract metaphysical facts or differences. It must not be forgotten, also, that we give names to things according to the appearances they assume for ourselves. We call absolute consciousness "unconsciousness," because it seems to us that it must necessarily be so, just as we call the Absolute, "Darkness," because to our finite understanding it appears quite impenetrable, yet we recognize fully that our perception of such things does not do them justice. We involuntarily distinguish in our minds, for instance, between unconscious absolute consciousness, and unconsciousness, by secretly endowing the former with some indefinite quality that corresponds, on a higher plane than our thoughts can reach, with what we know as consciousness in ourselves. But this is not any kind of consciousness that we can manage to distinguish from what appears to us as unconsciousness.

3. **THE HOUR HAD NOT YET STRUCK; THE RAY HAD NOT YET FLASHED INTO THE GERM** (*a*); **THE MATRI-PADMA** (*mother lotus*) **HAD NOT YET SWOLLEN** (*b*).

(*a*) The ray of the "Ever Darkness" becomes, as it is emitted, a ray of effulgent light or life, and flashes into the "Germ" -- the point in the Mundane Egg, represented by matter in its abstract sense. But the term "Point" must not be understood as applying to any particular point in Space, for a germ exists in the centre of every atom, and these collectively form "the Germ;" or rather, as no atom can be made visible to our physical eye, the collectivity of these (if the term can be applied to something which is boundless and infinite) forms the noumenon of eternal and indestructible matter.

(*b*) One of the symbolical figures for the Dual creative power in Nature (matter and force on the material plane) is *Padma*, the water-lily of India. The Lotus is the product of heat (fire) and water (vapour or Ether); fire standing in every philosophical and religious system as a representation of the Spirit of Deity,   the active, male, generative principle; and Ether, or the Soul of matter, the light of the fire, for the passive female principle from which everything in this Universe emanated. Hence, Ether or Water is the Mother, and Fire is the Father. Sir W. Jones (and before him archaic botany) showed that the seeds of the Lotus contain -- even before they germinate -- perfectly formed leaves, the miniature shape of what one day, as perfect plants, they will become: nature thus giving us a specimen of the preformation of its production . . . the seed of all phanerogamous plants bearing proper flowers containing an embryo plantlet ready formed.   (See Part II., "The Lotus Flower as an Universal Symbol.") This explains the sentence "The Mother had not yet swollen" -- the form being usually sacrificed to the inner or root idea in Archaic symbology.

The Lotus, or Padma, is, moreover, a very ancient and favourite simile for the Kosmos itself, and also for man. The popular reasons given are, firstly, the fact just mentioned, that the Lotus-seed contains within itself a perfect miniature of the future plant, which typifies the fact that the spiritual prototypes of all things exist in the immaterial world before those things become materialised on Earth. Secondly, the fact that the Lotus plant grows up through the water, having its root in the Ilus, or mud, and spreading its flower in the air above. The Lotus thus typifies the life of man and also that of the Kosmos; for the Secret Doctrine teaches that the elements of both are the same, and that both are developing in the same direction. The root of the Lotus sunk in the mud represents material life, the stalk passing up through the water typifies existence in the astral world, and the flower floating on the water and opening to the sky is emblematical of spiritual being.

4. **HER HEART HAD NOT YET OPENED FOR THE ONE RAY TO ENTER, THENCE TO FALL AS THREE INTO FOUR IN THE LAP OF MAYA** (*a*).

(*a*) The Primordial Substance had not yet passed out of its precosmic latency into differentiated objectivity, or even become the (to man, so far,) invisible Protyle of Science. But, as the hour strikes and it becomes receptive of the Fohatic impress of the Divine Thought (the Logos, or the male aspect of the Anima Mundi, Alaya) -- its heart opens. It differentiates, and the THREE (Father, Mother, Son) are transformed into four. Herein lies the origin of the double mystery of the Trinity and the immaculate Conception. The first and Fundamental dogma of Occultism is Universal Unity (or Homogeneity) under three aspects. This led to a possible conception of Deity, which as an absolute unity must remain forever incomprehensible to finite intellects. "If thou wouldest believe in the Power which acts within the root of a plant, or imagine the root concealed under the soil, thou hast to think of its stalk or trunk and of its leaves and flowers. Thou canst not imagine that Power independently of these objects. Life can be known only by the Tree of Life. . . ." (Precepts for Yoga). The idea of *Absolute* Unity would be broken entirely in our conception, had we not something concrete before our eyes to contain that Unity. And the deity being absolute, must be omnipresent, hence not an atom but contains IT within itself. The roots, the trunk and its many branches are three distinct objects, yet they are one tree. Say the Kabalists: "The Deity is one, because It is infinite. It is triple, because it is ever manifesting." This manifestation is triple in its aspects, for it requires, as Aristotle has it, three principles for every natural body to become objective: privation, form, and matter. Privation meant in the mind of the great philosopher that which the Occultists call the prototypes impressed in the Astral Light -- the lowest plane and world of Anima Mundi. The union of these three principles depends upon a fourth -- the LIFE which radiates from the summits of the Unreachable, to become an universally diffused Essence on the manifested planes of Existence. And this QUATERNARY (Father, Mother, Son, as a UNITY, and a quaternary, as a living manifestation) has been the means of leading to the very archaic Idea of Immaculate Conception, now finally crystallized into a dogma of the Christian Church, which carnalized this metaphysical idea beyond any common sense. For one has but to read the Kabala and study its numerical methods of interpretation to find the origin of that dogma. It is purely astronomical, mathematical, and pre-eminently metaphysical: the Male element in Nature (personified by the male deities and Logoi -- Viraj, or Brahma; Horus, or Osiris, etc., etc.) is born through, not from, an immaculate source, personified by the "Mother"; because that Male having a Mother cannot have a "Father" -- the abstract Deity being sexless, and not even a Being but Be-ness, or Life itself. Let us render this in the mathematical language of the author of "The Source of Measures." Speaking of the "Measure of a Man" and his numerical (Kabalistic) value, he writes that in Genesis, ch. iv., v. 1, "It is called the 'Man even Jehovah' Measure, and this is obtained in this way, viz.: $113 \times 5 = 565$, and the value 565 can be placed under the form of expression $56.5 \times 10 = 565$. Here the Man-number 113 becomes a factor of 56.5×10, and the (Kabalistic) reading of this last numbered expression is Jod, He, Vau, He, or Jehovah. . . . The expansion of 565 into 56.5×10 is purposed to show the emanation of the male (Jod) from the female (Eva) principle; or, so to speak, the birth of a male element from an immaculate source, in other words, an immaculate conception."

Thus is repeated on Earth the mystery enacted, according to the Seers, on the divine plane. The "Son" of the immaculate Celestial Virgin (or the undifferentiated cosmic protyle, Matter in its infinitude) is born again on Earth as the Son of the terrestrial Eve -- our mother Earth, and becomes Humanity as a total -- past, present, and future -- for Jehovah or Jod-he-vau-he is androgyne, or both male and female. Above, the Son is the whole KOSMOS; below, he is MANKIND. The triad or triangle becomes Tetraktis, the Sacred Pythagorean number, the perfect Square, and a 6-faced cube on Earth. The Macroprosopus (the Great Face) is now Microprosopus (the lesser face); or, as the Kabalists have it, the "Ancient of Days," descending on Adam Kadmon whom he uses as his vehicle to manifest through, gets transformed into Tetragrammaton. It is now in the "Lap of Maya," the Great Illusion, and between itself and the Reality has the Astral Light, the great Deceiver of man's limited senses, unless Knowledge through Paramarthasatya comes to the rescue.

5. THE SEVEN (*Sons*) *WERE* NOT YET BORN FROM THE WEB OF LIGHT. DARKNESS ALONE WAS FATHER-MOTHER, SVABHAVAT, AND SVABHAVAT WAS IN DARKNESS (*a*).

(*a*) The Secret Doctrine, in the Stanzas given here, occupies itself chiefly, if not entirely, with our Solar System, and especially with our planetary chain. The "Seven Sons," therefore, are the creators of the latter. This teaching will be explained more fully hereafter. (See Part II., "Theogony of the Creative Gods.")

Svabhavat, the "Plastic Essence" that fills the Universe, is the root of all things. Svabhavat is, so to say, the Buddhistic concrete aspect of the abstraction called in Hindu philosophy *Mulaprakriti*. It is the body of the Soul, and that which Ether would be to Akasa, the latter being the informing principle of the former. Chinese mystics have made of it the synonym of "being." In the *Ekasloka-Shastra* of *Nagarjuna* (the *Lung-shu* of China) called by the Chinese the *Yih-shu-lu-kia-lun*, it is said that the original word of Yeu is "Being" or "Subhava," "the Substance giving substance to itself," also explained by him as meaning " without action and with action," "the nature which has no nature of its own." *Subhava*, from which *Svabhavat*, is composed of two words: Su "fair," "handsome," "good"; Sva, "self"; and bhava, "being" or "states of being."

6. THESE TWO ARE THE GERM, AND THE GERM IS -- ONE. THE UNIVERSE WAS STILL CONCEALED IN THE DIVINE THOUGHT AND THE DIVINE BOSOM.

The "*Divine Thought*" does not imply the idea of a Divine thinker. The Universe, not only past, present, and future -- which is a human and finite idea expressed by finite thought -- but in its totality, the *Sat* (an untranslateable term), the absolute being, with the Past and Future crystallized in an eternal Present, is that Thought itself reflected in a secondary or manifest cause. Brahma (neuter) as the Mysterium Magnum of Paracelsus is an absolute mystery to the human mind. Brahma, the male-female, its aspect and anthropomorphic reflection, is conceivable to the perceptions of blind faith, though rejected by human intellect when it attains its majority. (See Part II., "Primordial Substance and Divine Thought.")

Hence the statement that during the prologue, so to say, of the drama of Creation, or the beginning of cosmic evolution, the Universe or the "Son" lies still concealed "in the Divine Thought," which had not yet penetrated "into the Divine Bosom." This idea, note well, is at the root, and forms the origin of all the allegories about the "Sons of God" born of immaculate virgins.

STANZA III.

COMMENTARY

1. THE LAST VIBRATION OF THE SEVENTH ETERNITY THRILLS THROUGH INFINITUDE (*a*). THE MOTHER SWELLS, EXPANDING FROM WITHIN WITHOUT LIKE THE BUD OF THE LOTUS (*b*).

(*a*) The seemingly paradoxical use of the sentence "Seventh Eternity," thus dividing the indivisible, is sanctified in esoteric philosophy. The latter divides boundless duration into unconditionally eternal and universal Time and a conditioned one (*Khandakala*). One is the abstraction or noumenon of infinite time (Kala); the other its phenomenon appearing periodically, as the effect of *Mahat* (the Universal Intelligence limited by Manvantaric duration). With some schools, Mahat is "the first-born" of Pradhana (undifferentiated substance, or the periodical aspect of Mulaprakriti, the root of Nature), which (Pradhana) is called Maya, the Illusion. In this respect, I believe, esoteric teaching differs from the Vedantin doctrines of both the Adwaita and the Visishtadwaita schools. For it says that, while Mulaprakriti, the noumenon, is self-existing and without any origin -- is, in short, parentless, Anupadaka (as one with Brahmam) -- Prakriti, its phenomenon, is periodical and no better than a phantasm of the former, so Mahat, with the Occultists, the first-born of Gnana (or *gnosis*) knowledge, wisdom or the Logos -- is a phantasm reflected from the Absolute NIRGUNA (Parabrahm, the one reality, "devoid of attributes and qualities"; see Upanishads); while with some Vedantins Mahat is a manifestation of Prakriti, or Matter.

(*b*) Therefore, the "last vibration of the Seventh Eternity" was "fore-ordained" -- by no God in particular, but occurred in virtue of the eternal and changeless LAW which causes the great periods of Activity and Rest, called so graphically, and at the same time so poetically, the "Days and Nights of Brahma." The expansion "from within without" of the Mother, called elsewhere the "Waters of Space," "Universal Matrix," etc., does not allude to an expansion from a small centre or focus, but, without reference to size or limitation or area, means the development of limitless subjectivity into as limitless objectivity. "The ever (to us) invisible and immaterial Substance present in eternity, threw its periodical shadow from its own plane into the lap of Maya." It implies that this expansion, not being an increase in size -- for infinite extension admits of no enlargement -- was a change of condition. It "expanded like the bud of the Lotus"; for the Lotus plant exists not only as a miniature embryo in its seed (a physical characteristic), but its prototype is present in an ideal form in the Astral Light from "Dawn" to "Night" during the Manvantaric period, like everything else, as a matter of fact, in this objective Universe; from man down to mite, from giant trees down to the tiniest blades of grass.

All this, teaches the hidden Science, is but the temporary reflection, the shadow of the eternal ideal prototype in Divine Thought -- the word "Eternal," note well again, standing here only in the sense of "AEon," as lasting throughout the seemingly interminable, but still limited cycle of activity, called by us Manvantara. For what is the real esoteric meaning of Manvantara, or rather a Manu-Antara? It means, esoterically, "between two Manus," of whom there are fourteen in every "Day of Brahma," such a "Day" consisting of 1,000 aggregates of four ages, or 1,000 "Great Ages," Mahayugas. Let us now analyse the word or name Manu. Orientalists and their Dictionaries tell us that the term "Manu" is from the root *Man,* "to think"; hence "the thinking man." But, esoterically, every Manu, as an anthropomorphized patron of his special cycle (or Round), is but the personified idea of the "Thought Divine" (as the Hermetic "Pymander"); each of the Manus, therefore, being the special god, the creator and fashioner of all that appears during his own respective cycle of being or Manvantara. Fohat runs the Manus' (or Dhyan-Chohans') errands, and causes the ideal prototypes to expand from within without -- viz., to cross gradually, on a descending scale, all the planes from the noumenon to the lowest phenomenon, to bloom finally on the last into full objectivity -- the acme of illusion, or the grossest matter.

2. THE VIBRATION SWEEPS ALONG, TOUCHING WITH ITS SWIFT WING (*simultaneously*) THE WHOLE UNIVERSE, AND THE GERM THAT DWELLETH IN DARKNESS: THE DARKNESS THAT BREATHES (*moves*) OVER THE SLUMBERING WATERS OF LIFE (*a*).

(*a*) The Pythagorean Monad is also said to dwell in solitude and darkness like the "germ." The idea of the "breath" of Darkness moving over "the slumbering Waters of life," which is primordial matter with the latent Spirit in it, recalls the first chapter of Genesis. Its original is the Brahminical Narayana (the mover on the Waters), who is the personification of the eternal Breath of the unconscious All (or Parabrahm) of the Eastern Occultists. The Waters of Life, or Chaos -- the female principle in symbolism -- are the vacuum (to our mental sight) in which lie the latent Spirit and Matter. This it was that made Democritus assert, after his instructor Leucippus, that the primordial principles of all were atoms and a vacuum, in the sense of space, but not of empty space, as "Nature abhors a vacuum" according to the Peripatetics, and every ancient philosopher.

In all Cosmogonies "Water" plays the same important part. It is the base and source of material existence. Scientists, mistaking the word for the thing, understood by water the definite chemical combination of oxygen and hydrogen, thus giving a specific meaning to a term used by Occultists in a generic sense, and which is used in Cosmogony with a metaphysical and mystical meaning. Ice is not water, neither is steam, although all three have precisely the same chemical composition.

3. "DARKNESS" RADIATES LIGHT, AND LIGHT DROPS ONE SOLITARY RAY INTO THE WATERS, INTO THE MOTHER DEEP. THE RAY SHOOTS THROUGH THE VIRGIN-EGG; THE RAY CAUSES THE ETERNAL EGG TO THRILL, AND DROP THE NON ETERNAL (*periodical*) GERM, WHICH CONDENSES INTO THE WORLD EGG (*a*).

(*a*) The solitary ray dropping into the mother deep may be taken as meaning Divine Thought or Intelligence, impregnating chaos. This, however, occurs on the plane of metaphysical abstraction, or rather the plane whereon that which we call a metaphysical abstraction is a reality. The Virgin-egg being in one sense abstract Egg-ness, or the power of becoming developed through fecundation, is eternal and for ever the same. And just as the fecundation of an egg takes place before it is dropped; so the non-eternal periodical germ which becomes later in symbolism the mundane egg, contains in itself, when it emerges from the said symbol, "the promise and potency" of all the Universe. Though the idea *per se* is, of course, an abstraction, a symbolical mode of expression, it is a symbol truly, as it suggests the idea of infinity as an endless circle. It brings before the mind's eye the picture of Kosmos emerging from and in boundless space, a Universe as shoreless in magnitude if not as endless in its objective manifestation. The simile of an egg also expresses the fact taught in Occultism that the primordial form of everything manifested, from atom to globe, from man to angel, is spheroidal, the sphere having been with all nations the emblem of eternity and infinity -- a serpent swallowing its tail. To realize the meaning, however, the sphere must be thought of as seen from its centre. The field of vision or of thought is like a sphere whose radii proceed from one's self in every direction, and extend out into space, opening up boundless vistas all around. It is the symbolical circle of Pascal and the Kabalists, "whose centre is everywhere and circumference nowhere," a conception which enters into the compound idea of this emblem.

The "Mundane Egg" is, perhaps, one of the most universally adopted symbols, highly suggestive as it is, equally in the spiritual, physiological, and cosmological sense. Therefore, it is found in every world-theogony, where it is largely associated with the serpent symbol; the latter being everywhere, in philosophy as in religious symbolism, an emblem of eternity, infinitude, regeneration, and rejuvenation, as well as of wisdom. (See Part II. "Tree and Serpent and Crocodile Worship.") The mystery of apparent self-generation and evolution through its own creative power repeating in miniature the process of Cosmic evolution in the egg, both being due to heat and moisture under the efflux of the unseen creative spirit, justified fully the selection of this graphic symbol.

The "Virgin Egg" is the microcosmic symbol of the macrocosmic prototype -- the "Virgin Mother" -- Chaos or the Primeval Deep. The male Creator (under whatever name) springs forth from the Virgin female, the immaculate root fructified by the Ray. Who, if versed in astronomy and natural sciences, can fail to see its suggestiveness? Cosmos as receptive Nature is an Egg fructified -- yet left immaculate; once regarded as boundless, it could have no other representation than a spheroid. The Golden Egg was surrounded by seven natural elements (ether, fire, air, water), "four ready, three secret." It may be found stated in Vishnu Purana, where elements are translated "Envelopes" and a *secret* one is added: "Aham-kara" (see Wilson's Vishnu Purana, Book I., p. 40). The original text has no "Aham-kara;" it mentions seven Elements without specifying the last three (see Part II. on "The Mundane Egg").

4. (*Then*) THE THREE (*triangle*) FALL INTO THE FOUR (*quaternary*). THE RADIANT ESSENCE BECOMES SEVEN INSIDE, SEVEN OUTSIDE (*a*). THE LUMINOUS EGG (*Hiranyagarbha*), WHICH IN ITSELF IS THREE (*the triple hypostases of Brahma, or Vishnu, the three "Avasthas"*), CURDLES AND SPREADS IN MILK-WHITE CURDS THROUGHOUT THE DEPTHS OF MOTHER, THE ROOT THAT GROWS IN THE OCEAN OF LIFE (*b*).

The use of geometrical figures and the frequent allusions to figures in all ancient scriptures (see Puranas, Egyptian papyri, the "Book of the Dead" and even the Bible) must be explained. In the "Book of Dzyan," as in the Kabala, there are two kinds of numerals to be studied -- the figures, often simple blinds, and the Sacred Numbers, the values of which are all known to the Occultists through Initiation. The former is but a conventional glyph, the latter is the basic symbol of all. That is to say, that one is purely physical, the other purely metaphysical, the two standing in relation to each other as matter stands to spirit -- the extreme poles of the ONE Substance.

As Balzac, the unconscious Occultist of French literature, says somewhere, the Number is to Mind the same as it is to matter: "an incomprehensible agent;" (perhaps so to the profane, never to the Initiated mind). Number is, as the great writer thought, an Entity, and, at the same time, a Breath emanating from what he called God and what we call the ALL; the breath which alone could organize the physical Kosmos, "where naught obtains its form but through the Deity, which is an effect of Number." It is instructive to quote Balzac's words upon this subject: --

"The smallest as the most immense creations, are they not to be distinguished from each other by their quantities, their qualities, their dimensions, their forces and attributes, all begotten by the NUMBER? The infinitude of the Numbers is a fact proven to our mind, but of which no proof can be physically given. The mathematician will tell us that the infinitude of the numbers exists but is not to be demonstrated. God is a Number endowed with motion, which is felt but not demonstrated. As Unity, it begins the Numbers, with which it has nothing in common. . . . . *The existence of the Number depends on Unity, which, without a single Number, begets them all. . . . . What! unable either to measure the first abstraction yielded to you by the Deity, or to get hold of it, you still hope to subject to your measurements the mystery of the Secret Sciences which emanate from that Deity? . . . . And what would you feel, were I to plunge you into the abysses of MOTION, the Force which organizes the Number? What would you think, were I to add that* Motion *and* Number *are begotten by the WORD, the Supreme Reason of the Seers and Prophets, who, in days of old, sensed the mighty Breath of God, a witness to which is the Apocalypse?"*

(*b*) "The radiant essence curdled and spread throughout the depths" of Space. From an astronomical point of view this is easy of explanation: it is the "milky way," the world-stuff, or primordial matter in its first form. It is more difficult, however, to explain it in a few words or even lines, from the standpoint of Occult Science and Symbolism, as it is the most complicated of glyphs. Herein are enshrined more than a dozen symbols. To begin with, the whole pantheon of mysterious objects, every one of them having some definite Occult meaning, extracted from the allegorical "churning of the ocean" by the Hindu gods.

Besides *Amrita*, the water of life or immortality, "*Surabhi*" the "cow of plenty," called "the fountain of milk and curds," was extracted from this "Sea of Milk." Hence the universal adoration of the cow and bull, one the productive, the other the generative power in Nature: symbols connected with both the Solar and the Cosmic deities. The specific properties, for occult purposes, of the "fourteen precious things," being explained only at the fourth Initiation, cannot be given here; but the following may be remarked. In the "Satapatha Brahmana" it is stated that the churning of the "Ocean of Milk" took place in the Satya Yug, the first age which immediately followed the "Deluge." As, however, neither the Rig-Veda nor Manu -- both preceding Vaivasvata's "deluge," that of the bulk of the Fourth Race -- mention this deluge, it is evident that it is not the "great" deluge, nor that which carried away Atlantis, nor even the deluge of Noah, which is meant here. This "churning" relates to a period before the earth's formation, and is in direct connection with that other universal legend, the various and contradictory versions of which culminated in the Christian dogma of the "War in Heaven," and the fall of the Angels (see Book II., also Revelations chap. xii.). The Brahmanas, reproached by the Orientalists with their versions on the same subjects, often clashing with each other, *are pre-eminently occult works*, hence used purposely as blinds. They were allowed to survive for public use and property only because they were and are absolutely unintelligible to the masses. Otherwise they would have disappeared from circulation as long ago as the days of Akbar.

5. THE ROOT REMAINS, THE LIGHT REMAINS, THE CURDS REMAIN, AND STILL OEAOHOO (*a*) IS ONE (*b*).

(*a*) OEAOHOO is rendered "*Father-Mother of the Gods*" in the Commentaries, or the SIX IN ONE, *or the septenary root from which all proceeds*. All depends upon the accent given to these seven vowels, which may be pronounced as *one*, three, or even seven syllables by adding an *e* after the letter "o." This mystic name is given out, because without a thorough mastery of the triple pronunciation it remains for ever ineffectual.

(*b*) This refers to the Non-Separateness of all that lives and has its being, whether in active or passive state. In one sense, Oeaohoo is the "Rootless Root of All"; hence, one with Parabrahmam; in another sense it is a name for the manifested ONE LIFE, the Eternal living Unity. The "Root" means, as already explained, pure knowledge (Sattva), eternal (*Nitya*) unconditioned reality or SAT (*Satya*), whether we call it Parabrahmam or Mulaprakriti, for these are the two aspects of the ONE. The "Light" is the same Omnipresent Spiritual Ray, which has entered and now fecundated the Divine Egg, and calls cosmic matter to begin its long series of differentiations. The curds are the first differentiation, and probably refer also to that cosmic matter which is supposed to be the origin of the "Milky Way" -- the matter we know. This "matter," which, according to the revelation received from the primeval Dhyani-Buddhas, is, during the periodical sleep of the Universe, of the ultimate tenuity conceivable to the eye of the perfect Bodhisatva -- this matter, radical and cool, becomes, at the first reawakening of cosmic motion, scattered through Space; appearing, when seen from the Earth, in clusters and lumps, like curds in thin milk. These are the seeds of the future worlds, the "Star-stuff."

6. THE ROOT OF LIFE WAS IN EVERY DROP OF THE OCEAN OF IMMORTALITY (*Amrita*) AND THE OCEAN WAS RADIANT LIGHT, WHICH WAS FIRE AND HEAT AND MOTION. DARKNESS VANISHED AND WAS NO MORE. IT DISAPPEARED IN ITS OWN ESSENCE, THE BODY OF FIRE AND WATER, OF FATHER AND MOTHER (*a*).

(*a*) The essence of darkness being absolute light, Darkness is taken as the appropriate allegorical representation of the condition of the Universe during Pralaya, or the term of absolute rest, or non-being, as it appears to our finite minds. The "fire," "heat," and "motion" here spoken of, are, of course, not the fire, heat, and motion of physical science, but the underlying abstractions, the noumena, or the soul, of the essence of these material manifestations -- the "things in themselves," which, as modern science confesses, entirely elude the instruments of the laboratory, and which even the mind cannot grasp, although it can equally little avoid the conclusion that these underlying essences of things must exist. Fire and Water, or Father and Mother, may be taken here to mean the divine Ray and Chaos. "Chaos, from this union with Spirit obtaining sense, shone with pleasure, and thus was produced the Protogonos (the first-born light)," says a fragment of Hermas. Damascius calls it Dis in "Theogony" -- "The disposer of all things." (See Cory's "*Ancient Fragments*," p. 314.)

According to the Rosicrucian tenets, as handled and explained by the profane for once correctly, if only partially, so "Light and Darkness are identical in themselves, being only divisible in the human mind"; and according to Robert Fludd, "Darkness adopted illumination in order to make itself visible" (*On Rosenkranz*). According to the tenets of Eastern Occultism, DARKNESS is the one true actuality, the basis and the root of light, without which the latter could never manifest itself, nor even exist. Light is matter, and DARKNESS pure Spirit. Darkness, in its radical, metaphysical basis, is subjective and absolute light; while the latter in all its seeming effulgence and glory, is merely a mass of shadows, as it can never be eternal, and is simply an illusion, or Maya.

Even in the mind-baffling and science-harassing Genesis, light is created out of darkness "and darkness was upon the face of the deep" (ch. i. v. 2.) -- and not *vice versa.* "In him (in darkness) was life; and the life *was the light of men*" (John i. 4). A day may come when the eyes of men will be opened; and then they may comprehend better than they do now, that verse in the Gospel of John that says "And the light shineth in darkness; and the darkness comprehendeth it not." They will see then that the word "darkness" does not apply to man's spiritual eyesight, but indeed to "Darkness," the absolute, that comprehendeth not (cannot cognize) transient light, however transcendent to human eyes. *Demon est Deus inversus.* The devil is now called Darkness by the Church, whereas, in the Bible he is called the "Son of God" (see Job), the bright star of the early morning, Lucifer (see Isaiah). There is a whole philosophy of dogmatic craft in the reason why the first Archangel, who sprang from the depths of Chaos, was called Lux (Lucifer), the "Luminous Son of the Morning," or manvantaric Dawn. He was transformed by the Church into Lucifer or Satan, because he is higher and older than Jehovah, and had to be sacrificed to the new dogma. (See Book II.)

7. BEHOLD, OH LANOO! THE RADIANT CHILD OF THE TWO, THE UNPARALLELED REFULGENT GLORY, BRIGHT SPACE, SON OF DARK SPACE, WHO EMERGES FROM THE DEPTHS OF THE GREAT DARK WATERS. IT IS OEAOHOO, THE YOUNGER, THE   (*whom thou knowest now as Kwan-Shai-Yin. -- Comment*) (*a*). HE SHINES FORTH AS THE SUN. HE IS THE BLAZING DIVINE DRAGON OF WISDOM. THE EKA IS CHATUR (*four*), AND CHATUR TAKES TO ITSELF THREE, AND THE UNION PRODUCES THE SAPTA (*seven*) IN WHOM ARE THE SEVEN WHICH BECOME THE TRIDASA   (*the thrice ten*) THE HOSTS AND THE MULTITUDES (*b*). BEHOLD HIM LIFTING THE VEIL, AND UNFURLING IT FROM EAST TO WEST. HE SHUTS OUT THE ABOVE AND LEAVES THE BELOW TO BE SEEN AS THE GREAT ILLUSION. HE MARKS THE PLACES FOR THE SHINING ONES (*stars*) AND TURNS THE UPPER (*space*) INTO A SHORELESS SEA OF FIRE, AND THE ONE MANIFESTED (*element*) INTO THE GREAT WATERS (*c*).

"Bright Space, son of dark Space," corresponds to the Ray dropped at the first thrill of the new "Dawn" into the great Cosmic depths, from which it re-emerges differentiated as Oeaohoo the younger, (the "new LIFE"), to become, to the end of the life-cycle, the germ of all things. He is "the Incorporeal man who contains in himself the divine Idea," -- the generator of Light and Life, to use an expression of Philo Judaeus. He is called the "Blazing Dragon of Wisdom," because, firstly, he is that which the Greek philosophers called the Logos, the Verbum of the Thought Divine; and secondly, because in Esoteric philosophy this first manifestation, being the synthesis or the aggregate of Universal Wisdom, Oeaohoo, "the Son of the Son," contains in himself the Seven Creative Hosts (The Sephiroth), and is thus the essence of manifested Wisdom. "He who bathes in the light of Oeaohoo will never be deceived by the veil of Maya."

Kwan-Shai-Yin is identical with, and an equivalent of the Sanskrit *Avalokiteshwara*, and as such he is an androgynous deity, like the Tetragrammaton and all the Logoi of antiquity. It is only by some sects in China that he is anthropomorphized and represented with female attributes,   when, under his female aspect, he becomes Kwan-Yin, the goddess of mercy, called the "Divine Voice."   The latter is the patron deity of Thibet and of the island of Puto in China, where both deities have a number of monasteries.   (See Part II. Kwan-Shai-Yin and Kwan-yin.)

(b) "The "Dragon of Wisdom" is the One, the "Eka" (Sanskrit) or Saka. It is curious that Jehovah's name in Hebrew should also be One, Echod. "His name is Echod": say the Rabbins. The philologists ought to decide which of the two is derived from the other -- linguistically and symbolically: surely, not the Sanskrit? The "One" and the Dragon are expressions used by the ancients in connection with their respective Logoi. Jehovah -- esoterically (as Elohim) -- is also the Serpent or Dragon that tempted Eve, and the "Dragon" is an old glyph for "Astral Light" (Primordial Principle), "which is the Wisdom of Chaos." Archaic philosophy, recognizing neither Good nor Evil as a fundamental or independent power, but starting from the Absolute ALL (Universal Perfection eternally), traced both through the course of natural evolution to pure Light condensing gradually into form, hence becoming Matter or Evil. It was left with the early and ignorant Christian fathers to degrade the philosophical and highly scientific idea of this emblem (the Dragon) into the absurd superstition called the "Devil." They took it from the later Zoroastrians, who saw devils or the Evil in the Hindu Devas, and the word Evil thus became by a double transmutation D'Evil in every tongue (Diabolos, Diable, Diavolo, Teufel). But the Pagans have always shown a philosophical discrimination in their symbols. The primitive symbol of the serpent symbolised divine Wisdom and Perfection, and had always stood for psychical Regeneration and Immortality. Hence -- Hermes, calling the serpent the most spiritual of all beings; Moses, initiated in the wisdom of Hermes, following suit in Genesis; the Gnostic's Serpent with the seven vowels over its head, being the emblem of the seven hierarchies of the Septenary or Planetary Creators. Hence, also, the Hindu serpent Sesha or Ananta, "the Infinite," a name of Vishnu, whose first Vahan or vehicle on the primordial waters is this serpent. Yet they all made a difference between the good and the bad Serpent (the Astral Light of the Kabalists) -- between the former, the embodiment of divine Wisdom in the region of the Spiritual, and the latter, Evil, on the plane of matter. Jesus accepted the serpent as a synonym of Wisdom, and this formed part of his teaching: "Be ye wise as serpents," he says. "In the beginning, before Mother became Father-Mother, the fiery Dragon moved in the infinitudes alone" (*Book of Sarparajni*.) The Aitareya Brahmana calls the Earth Sarparajni, "the Serpent Queen," and "the Mother of all that moves." Before our globe became egg-shaped (and the Universe also) "a long trail of Cosmic dust (or fire mist) moved and writhed like a serpent in Space." The "Spirit of God moving on Chaos" was symbolized by every nation in the shape of a fiery serpent breathing fire and light upon the primordial waters, until it had incubated cosmic matter and made it assume the annular shape of a serpent with its tail in its mouth -- which symbolises not only Eternity and Infinitude, but also the globular shape of all the bodies formed within the Universe from that fiery mist. The Universe, as well as the Earth and Man, cast off periodically, serpent-like, their old skins, to assume new ones after a time of rest. The serpent is, surely, a not less graceful or a more unpoetical image than the caterpillar and chrysalis from which springs the butterfly, the Greek emblem of Psyche, the human soul. The "Dragon" was also the symbol of the Logos with the Egyptians, as with the Gnostics. In the "Book of Hermes," Pymander, the oldest and the most spiritual of the Logoi of the Western Continent, appears to Hermes in the shape of a Fiery Dragon of "Light, Fire, and Flame." Pymander, the "Thought Divine" personified, says: The Light is me, I am the Nous (the mind or Manu), I am thy God, and I am far older than the human principle which escapes from the shadow ("*Darkness*," or the concealed Deity). I am the germ of thought, the resplendent *Word,* the *Son* of God. All that thus sees and hears in thee is the *Verbum* of the Master, it is the Thought (*Mahat*) which is God, the Father.

The celestial Ocean, the 'Ether . . . . is the *Breath* of the Father, the life-giving principle, the *Mother*, the Holy Spirit, for these are not separated, and their union is LIFE."

Here we find the unmistakeable echo of the Archaic Secret Doctrine, as now expounded. Only the latter does not place at the head and Evolution of Life "the Father," who comes third and is the "Son of the Mother," but the "Eternal and Ceaseless Breath of the ALL." The *Mahat* (Understanding, Universal Mind, Thought, etc.), before it manifests itself as Brahma or Siva, appears as Vishnu, says *Sankhya Sara* (p. 16); hence *Mahat* has several aspects, just as the *logos* has. *Mahat* is called the Lord, in the *Primary* Creation, and is, in this sense, Universal Cognition or *Thought Divine*; but, "That Mahat which was first produced is (afterwards) called *Ego-ism*, when it is born as "I," that is said to be the *second* Creation" (*Anugita*, ch. xxvi.). And the translator (an able and learned Brahmin, not a European Orientalist) explains in a foot-note (6), "*i.e.*, when Mahat develops into the feeling of Self-Consciousness -- I -- then it assumes the name of Egoism," which, translated into our esoteric phraseology, means when *Mahat* is transformed into the human *Manas* (or even that of the finite gods), and becomes *Aham*-ship. Why it is called the *Mahat* of the *Second* creation (or the *ninth*, that of the *Kumara* in *Vishnu Purana*) will be explained in Book II. The "Sea of Fire" is then the Super-Astral (*i.e.*, noumenal) Light, the first radiation from the *Root,* the Mulaprakriti, the undifferentiated Cosmic Substance, which becomes *Astral* Matter. It is also called the "Fiery Serpent," as above described. If the student bears in mind that there is but One Universal Element, which is infinite, unborn, and undying, and that all the rest -- as in the world of phenomena -- are but so many various differentiated aspects and transformations (correlations, they are now called) of that One, from Cosmical down to microcosmical effects, from super-human down to human and sub-human beings, the totality, in short, of objective existence -- then the first and chief difficulty will disappear and Occult Cosmology may be mastered.   All the Kabalists and Occultists, Eastern and Western, recognise (*a*) the identity of "Father-Mother" with primordial *AEther* or *Akasa*, (Astral Light) ; and (*b*) its homogeneity before the evolution of the "Son," cosmically *Fohat,* for it is Cosmic Electricity. "Fohat hardens and scatters the seven brothers" (Book III. Dzyan); which means that the primordial Electric Entity -- for the Eastern Occultists insist that Electricity is an Entity -- electrifies into life, and separates primordial stuff or pregenetic matter into atoms, themselves the source of all life and consciousness. "There exists an universal *agent unique* of all forms and of life, that is called Od,   Ob, and Aour, active and passive, positive and negative, like day and night: it is the first light in Creation" (Eliphas Levi's Kabala): --- the first Light of the primordial Elohim -- the Adam, "male and female" -- or (scientifically) ELECTRICITY AND LIFE.

(*c*) The ancients represented it by a serpent, for "Fohat hisses as he glides hither and thither" (in zigzags). The Kabala figures it with the Hebrew letter Teth ﬨ, whose symbol is the serpent which played such a prominent part in the Mysteries. Its universal value is nine, for it is the ninth letter of the alphabet and the ninth door of the fifty portals or gateways that lead to the concealed mysteries of being. It is the magical agent *par excellence*, and designates in Hermetic philosophy "Life infused into primordial matter," the essence that composes all things, and the spirit that determines their form. But there are two secret Hermetical operations, one spiritual, the other material-correlative, and for ever united. "Thou shalt separate the earth from the fire, the subtile from the solid . . . that which ascends from earth to heaven and descends again from heaven to earth. It (the subtile light), is the strong force of every force, for it conquers every subtile thing and penetrates into every solid. Thus was the world formed" (*Hermes*).

It was not Zeno alone, the founder of the Stoics, who taught that the Universe evolves, when its primary substance is transformed from the state of fire into that of air, then into water, etc. Heracleitus of Ephesus maintained that the one principle that underlies all phenomena in Nature is fire. The intelligence that moves the Universe is fire, and fires is intelligence. And while Anaximenes said the same of air, and Thales of Miletus (600 years B.C.) of water, the Esoteric Doctrine reconciles all those philosophers by showing that though each was right the system of none was complete.

8. WHERE WAS THE GERM, AND WHERE WAS NOW DARKNESS? WHERE IS THE SPIRIT OF THE FLAME THAT BURNS IN THY LAMP, OH LANOO? THE GERM IS THAT, AND THAT IS LIGHT; THE WHITE BRILLIANT SON OF THE DARK HIDDEN FATHER (*a*).

(*a*) The answer to the first question, suggested by the second, which is the reply of the teacher to the pupil, contains in a single phrase one of the most essential truths of occult philosophy. It indicates the existence of things imperceptible to our physical senses which are of far greater importance, more real and more permanent, than those that appeal to these senses themselves. Before the Lanoo can hope to understand the transcendentally metaphysical problem contained in the first question he must be able to answer the second, while the very answer he gives to the second will furnish him with the clue to the correct reply to the first.

In the Sanscrit Commentary on this Stanza, the terms used for the concealed and the unrevealed Principle are many. In the earliest MSS. of Indian literature this Unrevealed, Abstract Deity has no name. It is called generally "*That*" (*Tad* in Sanskrit), and means all that is, was, and will be, or that can be so received by the human mind.

Among such appellations, given, of course, only in esoteric philosophy, as the "Unfathomable Darkness," the "Whirlwind," etc. -- it is also called the "It of the Kalahansa, the Kala-ham-sa," and even the "Kali Hamsa," (Black swan). Here the *m* and the *n* are convertible, and both sound like the nasal French *an* or *am,* or, again, *en* or *em* (*Ennui, Embarras,* etc.) As in the Hebrew Bible, many a mysterious sacred name in Sanscrit conveys to the profane ear no more than some ordinary, and often vulgar word, because it is concealed anagrammatically or otherwise. This word of Hansa or esoterically "hamsa" is just such a case. Hamsa is equal to a-ham-sa, three words meaning "I am he" (in English), while divided in still another way it will read "So-ham," "he (is) I" -- Soham being equal to Sah, "he," and aham, "I," or "I am he." In this alone is contained the universal mystery, the doctrine of the identity of man's essence with god-essence, for him who understands the language of wisdom. Hence the glyph of, and the allegory about, Kalahansa (or hamsa), and the name given to Brahma neuter (later on, to the male Brahma) of "Hansa-Vahana," he who uses the Hansa as his vehicle." The same word may be read "Kalaham-sa" or "I am I" in the eternity of Time, answering to the Biblical, or rather Zoroastrian "I am that I am." The same doctrine is found in the Kabala, as witness the following extract from an unpublished MS. by Mr. S. Liddell McGregor Mathers, the learned Kabalist: "The three pronouns אֲנִי, אַתָּה, הִיא, Hoa, Atah, Ani; He, Thou, I; are used to symbolize the ideas of Macroprosopus and Microprosopus in the Hebrew Qabalah. Hoa, "He," is applied to the hidden and concealed Macroprosopus; Atah, "Thou," to Microprosopus; and Ani, "I," to the latter when He is represented as speaking. (See *Lesser Holy Assembly*, 204 *et seq.*) It is to be noted that each of these names consists of three letters, of which the letter Aleph א, A, forms the conclusion of the first word Hoa, and the commencement of Atah and Ani, as if it were the connecting link between them. But א is the symbol of the Unity and consequently of the unvarying Idea of the Divine operating through all these. But behind the א in the name Hoa are the letters י and ה, the symbols of the numbers Six and Five, the Male and the Female, the Hexagram and the Pentagram. And the numbers of these three words, Hoa Atah Ani, are 12, 406, and 61, which are resumed in the key numbers of 3, 10, and 7, by the Qabalah of the Nine Chambers, which is a form of the exegetical rule of Temura."

It is useless to attempt to explain the mystery in full. Materialists and the men of modern Science will never understand it, since, in order to obtain clear perception of it, one has first of all to admit the postulate of a universally diffused, omnipresent, eternal Deity in Nature; secondly, to have fathomed the mystery of electricity in its true essence; and thirdly, to credit man with being the septenary symbol, on the terrestrial plane, of the One Great UNIT (the Logos), which is Itself the Seven-vowelled sign, the Breath crystallized into the WORD. He who believes in all this, has also to believe in the multiple combination of the seven planets of Occultism and of the Kabala, with the twelve zodiacal signs; to attribute, as we do, to each planet and to each constellation an influence which, in the words of Ely Star (a French Occultist), "is proper to it, beneficent or maleficent, and this, after the planetary Spirit which rules it, who, in his turn, is capable of influencing men and things which are found in harmony with him and with which he has any affinity." For these reasons, and since few believe in the foregoing, all that can now be given is that in both cases the symbol of Hansa (whether "I," "He," Goose or Swan) is an important symbol, representing, for instance, Divine Wisdom, Wisdom in darkness beyond the reach of men. For all exoteric purposes, Hansa, as every Hindu knows, is a fabulous bird, which, when given milk mixed with water for its food (in the allegory) separated the two, drinking the milk and leaving the water; thus showing inherent wisdom -- milk standing symbolically for spirit, and water for matter.

That this allegory is very ancient and dates from the very earliest archaic period, is shown by the mention (in Bhagavata Purana) of a certain caste named "Hamsa" or "Hansa," which was the "one caste" *par excellence*; when far back in the mists of a forgotten past there was among the Hindus only "One Veda, One Deity, One Caste." There is also a range in the Himalayas, described in the old books as being situated north of Mount Meru, called "Hamsa," and connected with episodes pertaining to the history of religious mysteries and initiations. As to the name of Kala-Hansa being the supposed vehicle of Brahma-Prajapati, in the exoteric texts and translations of the

Orientalists, it is quite a mistake. Brahma, the neuter, is called by them Kala-Hansa and Brahma, the male, Hansa-Vahana, because forsooth "his vehicle or Vahan is a swan or goose" (vide "the Hindu Classical Dictionary.") This is a purely exoteric gloss. Esoterically and logically, if Brahma, the infinite, is all that is described by the Orientalists, namely, agreeably with the Vedantic texts, an abstract deity in no way characterised by the description of any human attributes, and it is still maintained that he or it is called Kala-Hansa -- then how can it ever become the Vahan of Brahma, the manifested finite god? It is quite the reverse. The "Swan or goose" (Hansa) is the symbol of that male or temporary deity, as he, the emanation of the primordial Ray, is made to serve as a Vahan or vehicle for that divine Ray, which otherwise could not manifest itself in the Universe, being, antiphrastically, itself an emanation of "Darkness" -- for our human intellect, at any rate. It is Brahma, then, who is Kala-Hansa, and the Ray, the Hansa-Vahana.

As to the strange symbol chosen, it is equally suggestive; the true mystic significance being the idea of a universal matrix, figured by the primordial waters of the "deep," or the opening for the reception, and subsequently for the issue, of that one ray (the Logos), which contains in itself the other seven procreative rays or powers (the logoi or builders). Hence the choice by the Rosecroix of the aquatic fowl -- whether swan or pelican, with seven young ones for a symbol, modified and adapted to the religion of every country. En-Soph is called the "Fiery Soul of the Pelican" in the Book of Numbers. (See Part II. "The Hidden Deity and its Symbols and Glyphs.") Appearing with every Manvantara as Narayan, or Swayambhuva (the

9. LIGHT IS COLD FLAME, AND FLAME IS FIRE, AND THE FIRE PRODUCES HEAT, WHICH YIELDS WATER, THE WATER OF LIFE IN THE GREAT MOTHER (*Chaos*) (*a*).

(*a*) It must be remembered that the words "Light," "Fire," and "Flame" used in the Stanzas have been adopted by the translators thereof from the vocabulary of the old "Fire philosophers," in order to render better the meaning of the archaic terms and symbols employed in the original. Otherwise they would have remained entirely unintelligible to a European reader. But to a student of the Occult the terms used will be sufficiently clear.

All these -- "Light," "Flame," "Hot," "Cold," "Fire," "Heat," "Water," and the "water of life" are all, on our plane, the progeny; or as a modern physicist would say, the correlations of ELECTRICITY. Mighty word, and a still mightier symbol! Sacred generator of a no less sacred progeny; of fire -- the creator, the preserver and the destroyer; of light -- the essence of our divine ancestors; of flame -- the Soul of things. Electricity, the ONE Life at the upper rung of Being, and Astral Fluid, the Athanor of the Alchemists, at its lowest; GOD and DEVIL, GOOD and EVIL. . . .

Now, why is Light called in the Stanzas "cold flame"? Because in the order of Cosmic evolution (as taught by the Occultist), the energy that actuates matter after its first formation into atoms is generated on our plane by Cosmic heat; and because Kosmos, in the sense of dissociated matter, was not, before that period. The first primordial matter, eternal and coeval with Space, "which has neither a beginning nor an end," is "neither hot nor cold, but is of its own special nature," says the Commentary (Book II). Heat and cold are relative qualities and pertain to the realms of the manifested worlds, which all proceed from the manifested *Hyle*, which, in its absolutely latent aspect, is referred to as the "cold Virgin," and when awakened to life, as the "Mother." The ancient Western Cosmogonic myths state that at first there was but cold mist which was the Father, and the prolific slime (the Mother, Ilus or Hyle), from which crept forth the Mundane snake-matter, (*Isis,* vol. i., p. 146). Primordial matter, then, before it emerges from the plane of the never-manifesting, and awakens to the thrill of action under the impulse of Fohat, is but "a cool Radiance, colourless, formless, tasteless, and devoid of every quality and aspect." Even such are her first-born, the "four sons," who "are One, and become Seven," -- the entities, by whose qualifications and names the ancient Eastern Occultists called the four of the seven primal "centres of Forces," or atoms, that develop later into the great Cosmic "Elements," now divided into the seventy or so sub-elements, known to science. The four primal natures of the first Dhyan Chohans, are the so-called (for want of better terms) "Akasic," "Ethereal," "Watery," and "Fiery," answering, in the terminology of practical occultism, to scientific definitions of gases, which, to convey a clear idea to both Occultists and laymen, must be defined as Parahydrogenic, Paraoxygenic, Oxyhydrogenic, and Ozonic, or perhaps Nitr-ozonic; the latter forces or gases (in Occultism, supersensuous, yet atomic substances) being the most effective and active when energising on the plane of more grossly differentiated matter. These are both electro-positive and electro-negative.

10. FATHER-MOTHER SPIN A WEB WHOSE UPPER END IS FASTENED TO SPIRIT (*Purusha*), THE LIGHT OF THE ONE DARKNESS, AND THE LOWER ONE TO MATTER (*Prakriti*) ITS (*the Spirit's*) SHADOWY END; AND THIS WEB IS THE UNIVERSE SPUN OUT OF THE TWO SUBSTANCES MADE IN ONE, WHICH IS SWABHAVAT (*a*).

(*a*) In the Mandukya (Mundaka) Upanishad it is written, "As a spider throws out and retracts its web, as herbs spring up in the ground . . . so is the Universe derived from the undecaying one" (I. 1. 7). Brahma, as "the germ of unknown Darkness," is the material from which all evolves and develops "as the web from the spider, as foam from the water," etc. This is only graphic and true, if Brahma the "Creator" is, as a term, derived from the root *brih,* to increase or expand. Brahma "expands" and becomes the Universe woven out of his own substance.

The same idea has been beautifully expressed by Goethe, who says:
> *"Thus at the roaring loom of Time I ply,*
> *And weave for God the garment thou see'st Him by."*

The expanding of the Universe under the breath of FIRE is very suggestive in the light of the "Fire mist" period of which modern science speaks so much, and knows in reality so little.

Great heat breaks up the compound elements and resolves the heavenly bodies into their primeval one element, explains the commentary. "Once disintegrated into its primal constituent by getting within the attraction and reach of a focus, or centre of heat (energy), of which many are carried about to and fro in space, a body, whether alive or dead, will be vapourised and held in "the bosom of the Mother" until Fohat, gathering a few of the clusters of Cosmic matter (nebulae) will, by giving it an impulse, set it in motion anew, develop the required heat, and then leave it to follow its own new growth.

The expanding and contracting of the Web -- *i.e.,* the world stuff or atoms -- expresses here the pulsatory movement; for it is the regular contraction and expansion of the infinite and shoreless Ocean of that which we may call the noumenon of matter emanated by Swabhavat, which causes the universal vibration of atoms. But it is also suggestive of something else. It shows that the ancients were acquainted with that which is now the puzzle of many scientists and especially of astronomers: the cause of the first ignition of matter or the world-stuff, the paradox of the heat produced by the refrigerative contraction and other such Cosmic riddles. For it points unmistakeably to a knowledge by the ancients of such phenomena. "There is heat internal and heat external in every atom," say the manuscript Commentaries, to which the writer has had access; "the breath of the Father (or Spirit) and the breath (or heat) of the Mother (matter);" and they give explanations which show that the modern theory of the extinction of the solar fires by loss of heat through radiation, is erroneous. The assumption is false even on the Scientists' own admission. For as Professor Newcomb points out (Popular Astronomy, pp. 506-508), "by losing heat, a gaseous body contracts, and the heat generated by the contraction exceeds that which it had to lose in order to produce the contraction." This paradox, that a body gets hotter as the shrinking produced by its getting colder is greater, led to long disputes. The surplus of heat, it was argued, was lost by radiation, and to assume that the temperature is not lowered *pari passu* with a decrease of volume under a constant pressure, is to set at nought the law of Charles (Nebular Theory, Winchell). Contraction develops heat, it is true; but contraction (from cooling) is incapable of developing the whole amount of heat at any time existing in the mass, or even of maintaining a body at a constant temperature, etc. Professor Winchell tries to reconcile the paradox -- only a seeming one in fact, as

Homer Lanes proved, -- by suggesting "something besides heat." "May it not be," he asks, "simply a repulsion among the molecules, which varies according to some law of the distance?" But even this will be found irreconcileable, unless this "something besides heat" is ticketed "Causeless Heat," the "Breath of Fire," the all-creative Force Plus ABSOLUTE INTELLIGENCE, which physical science is not likely to accept.

However it may be, the reading of this Stanza shows it, notwithstanding its archaic phraseology, to be more scientific than even modern science.

11. THEN SVABHAVAT SENDS FOHAT TO HARDEN THE ATOMS. EACH (*of these*) IS A PART OF THE WEB (*Universe*). REFLECTING THE "SELF-EXISTENT LORD" (*Primeval Light*) LIKE A MIRROR, EACH BECOMES IN TURN A WORLD. . .

"Fohat hardens the atoms"; *i.e.*, by infusing energy into them: he scatters the atoms or primordial matter. "He scatters himself while scattering matter into atoms" (**MSS**. Commentaries.)

It is through Fohat that the ideas of the Universal Mind are impressed upon matter. Some faint idea of the nature of Fohat may be gathered from the appellation "Cosmic Electricity" sometimes applied to it; but to the commonly known properties of electricity must, in this case, be added others, including intelligence. It is of interest to note that modern science has come to the conclusion, that all cerebration and brain-activity are attended by electrical phenomena. (*For further details as to* "*Fohat*" *See Stanza V. and Comments.*")

STANZA IV.

COMMENTARY

1. LISTEN, YE SONS OF THE EARTH, TO YOUR INSTRUCTORS -- THE SONS OF THE FIRE (*a*). LEARN THERE IS NEITHER FIRST NOR LAST; FOR ALL IS ONE NUMBER, ISSUED FROM NO NUMBER (*b*).

(*a*) These terms, the "Sons of the Fire," the "Sons of the Fire-Mist," and the like, require explanation. They are connected with a great primordial and universal mystery, and it is not easy to make it clear. There is a passage in the *Bhagavatgita* (ch. viii.) wherein Krishna, speaking symbolically and *esoterically*, says: "I will state the times (conditions) . . . at which devotees departing (from this life) do so never to return (be reborn), or to return (to incarnate again). The Fire, the Flame, the day, the bright (lucky) fortnight, the six months of the Northern solstice, departing (dying) in these, those who know the Brahman (Yogis) go to the Brahman. Smoke, night, the dark (unlucky) fortnight, the six months of the Southern solstice, (dying) in these, the devotee goes to the lunar light (or mansion the astral light also) and returns (is reborn). These two paths, bright and dark, are said to be eternal in this world (or great kalpa, 'Age'). By the one a man goes never to come back, by the other he returns." Now these names, "Fire," "Flame," "Day," the "bright fortnight," etc., as "Smoke," "Night," and so on, leading only to the end of the lunar path are incomprehensible without a knowledge of Esotericism. These are *all names of various deities* which preside over the Cosmo-psychic Powers. We often speak of the Hierarchy of "Flames" (see Book II.) of the "Sons of Fire," etc. Sankaracharya the greatest of the Esoteric masters of India, says that *fire* means a deity which presides over Time (kala). The able translator of Bhagavatgita, Kashinath Trimbak Telang, **M.A.**, of Bombay, confesses he has "no clear notion of the meaning of these verses". It seems quite clear, on the contrary, to him who knows the occult doctrine. With these verses the mystic sense of the solar and lunar symbols are connected: the Pitris are *lunar* deities and our ancestors, because they *created the physical man.*

The Agnishwatha, the Kumara (the seven mystic sages), are solar deities, though the former are Pitris also; and these are the "fashioners of the *Inner* Man." (See Book II.) They are: --

"The Sons of Fire" -- because they are the first Beings (in the Secret Doctrine they are called "Minds"), evolved from Primordial Fire. "The Lord is a consuming Fire" (Deuteronomy iv. 24); "The Lord (Christos) shall be revealed with his mighty angels in flaming fire" (2 Thessal. i. 7, 8). The Holy Ghost descended on the Apostles like "cloven tongues of fire," (Acts ii. v. 3); Vishnu will return on *Kalki*, the White Horse, as the last Avatar amid fire and flames; and *Sosiosh* will be brought down equally on a White Horse in a "tornado of fire." "And I saw heaven open and behold a white horse, and he that sat upon him . . . . is called the Word of God," (Rev. xix. 13) amid flaming Fire. Fire is AEther in its purest form, and hence is not regarded as matter, but it is the unity of Aether -- the second manifested deity -- in its universality. But there are two "Fires" and a distinction is made between them in the Occult teachings. The first, or the purely *Formless and invisible* Fire concealed in the *Central Spiritual Sun*, is spoken of as "triple" (metaphysically); while the Fire of the manifested Kosmos is Septenary, throughout both the Universe and our Solar System. "The fire or knowledge burns up all action on the plane of illusion," says the commentary. "Therefore, those who have acquired it and are emancipated, are called 'Fires.' " Speaking of the *seven* senses symbolised as *Hotris,* priests, the Brahmana says in *Anugita*: "Thus these *seven* (senses, smell and taste, and colour, and sound, etc., etc.) are the causes of emancipation;" and the commentator adds: "It is from these seven from which the Self is to be emancipated. 'I' (am here devoid of qualities) must mean the Self, not the Brahmana who speaks." ("*Sacred Books of the East*," ed. by Max Muller, Vol. VIII., 278.)

(*b*) The expression "All is One Number, issued from No Number" relates again to that universal and philosophical tenet just explained in Stanza III. (Comm. 4). That which is absolute is of course No Number; but in its later significance it has an application in Space as in Time. It means that not only every increment of time is part of a larger increment, up to the most indefinitely prolonged duration conceivable by the human intellect, but also that no manifested thing can be thought of except as part of a larger whole: the total aggregate being the One manifested Universe that issues from the unmanifested or Absolute -- called Non-Being or "No-Number," to distinguish it from BEING or "the One Number."

2. LEARN WHAT WE, WHO DESCEND FROM THE PRIMORDIAL SEVEN, WE, WHO ARE BORN FROM THE PRIMORDIAL FLAME, HAVE LEARNED FROM OUR FATHERS (*a*).

(*a*) This is explained in Book II., and this name, "Primordial Flame," corroborates what is said in the first paragraph of the preceding commentary on Stanza IV.

The distinction between the "Primordial" and the subsequent seven Builders is this: The former are the Ray and direct emanation of the first "Sacred Four," the *Tetraktis,* that is, the eternally Self-Existent One (Eternal *in Essence* note well, not in manifestation, and distinct from the universal ONE). Latent, during Pralaya, and active, during Manvantara, the "Primordial" proceed from "Father-Mother" (Spirit-Hyle, or *Ilus*); whereas the other manifested Quaternary and the Seven proceed from the Mother alone. It is the latter who is the immaculate Virgin-Mother, who is overshadowed, not impregnated, by the Universal MYSTERY -- when she emerges from her state of Laya or undifferentiated condition. In reality, they are, of course, all one; but their aspects on the various planes of being are different. (See Part II., "Theogony of the Creative Gods.")

The first "Primordial" are the highest Beings on the Scale of Existence. They are the Archangels of Christianity, those who refuse -- as Michael did in the latter system, and as did the eldest "Mind-born sons" of Brahma (Veddhas) -- to create or rather to multiply.

3. FROM THE EFFULGENCY OF LIGHT -- THE RAY OF THE EVER-DARKNESS -- SPRUNG IN SPACE THE RE-AWAKENED ENERGIES (*Dhyan Chohans*): THE ONE FROM THE EGG, THE SIX AND THE FIVE (*a*); THEN THE THREE, THE ONE,

THE FOUR, THE ONE, THE FIVE -- THE TWICE SEVEN, THE SUM TOTAL (*b*). AND THESE ARE: THE ESSENCES, THE FLAMES, THE ELEMENTS, THE BUILDERS, THE NUMBERS, THE ARUPA (*formless*), THE RUPA (*with bodies*), AND THE FORCE OR DIVINE MAN -- THE SUM TOTAL. AND FROM THE DIVINE MAN EMANATED THE FORMS, THE SPARKS, THE SACRED ANIMALS, AND THE MESSENGERS OF THE SACRED FATHERS (*the Pitris*) WITHIN THE HOLY FOUR.

(*a*) This relates to the sacred Science of the Numerals: so sacred, indeed, and so important in the study of Occultism that the subject can hardly be skimmed, even in such a large work as the present. It is on the Hierarchies and correct numbers of these Beings invisible (to us) except upon very rare occasions, that the mystery of the whole Universe is built. The *Kumaras*, for instance, are called the "Four" though in reality seven in number, because Sanaka, Sananda, Sanatana and Sanat-Kumara are the chief Vaidhatra (their patronymic name), as they spring from the "four-fold mystery." To make the whole clearer we have to turn for our illustrations to tenets more familiar to some of our readers, namely, the Brahminical.

According to Manu, Hiranyagarbha is Brahma *the first male* formed by the undiscernible Causeless CAUSE in a "Golden Egg resplendent as the Sun," as states the Hindu Classical Dictionary. "Hiranyagarbha" means the golden, or rather the "Effulgent Womb" or Egg. The meaning tallies awkwardly with the epithet of "male." Surely the esoteric meaning of the sentence is clear enough. In the Rig Veda it is said: -- "THAT, the one Lord of all beings . . . . the one animating principle of gods and man," arose, in the beginning, in the Golden Womb, Hiranyagarbha -- which is the Mundane Egg or sphere of our Universe. That Being is surely androgynous, and the allegory of Brahma separating into two and recreating in one of his halves (the female Vach) himself as Viraj, is a proof of it.

"The One from the Egg, the Six and the Five," give the number 1065, the value of the first-born (later on the male and female Brahma-Prajapati), who answers to the numbers 7, and 14, and 21 respectively. The Prajapati are, like the Sephiroth, only seven, including the synthetic Sephira of the triad from which they spring. Thus from Hiranyagarbha or Prajapati, the *triune* (primeval Vedic Trimurti, Agni, Vayu, and Surya), emanate the other seven, or again ten, if we separate the first three which exist in one, and one in three, all, moreover, being comprehended within that one "supreme" Parama, called Guhya or " secret," and Sarvatma, the "Super-Soul." "The seven Lords of Being lie concealed in Sarvatma like thoughts in one brain." So are the Sephiroth. It is either seven when counting from the upper Triad headed by Kether, or ten -- exoterically. In the Mahabharata the Prajapati are 21 in number, or ten, six, and five (1065), thrice seven.

(*b*) "The Three, the One, the Four, the One, the Five" (in their totality -- twice seven) represent 31415 -- the numerical hierarchy of the Dhyan-Chohans of various orders, and of the inner or circumscribed world. When placed on the boundary of the great circle of "Pass not" (see Stanza V.), called also the Dhyanipasa, the "rope of the Angels," the "rope" that hedges off the phenomenal from the noumenal Kosmos, (not falling within the range of our present objective consciousness); this number, when not enlarged by permutation and expansion, is ever 31415 anagrammatically and Kabalistically, being both the number of the circle and the mystic Svastica, the twice seven once more; for whatever way the two sets of figures are counted, when added separately, one figure after another, whether crossways, from right or from left, they will always yield fourteen. Mathematically they represent the well-known calculation, namely, that the ratio of the diameter to the circumference of a circle is as 1 to 3.1415, or the value of the (pi), as this ratio is called -- the symbol being always used in mathematical formulae to express it. This set of figures must have the same meaning, since the 1 : 314,159, and then again 1 : 3 : 1,415,927 are worked out in the secret calculations to express the various cycles and ages of the "first born," or 311,040,000,000,000 with fractions, and yield the same 13,415 by a process we are not concerned with at present. And it may be shown that Mr. Ralston Skinner, author of *The Source of Measures*, reads the Hebrew word Alhim in the same number values, by

omitting, as said, the ciphers and by permutation -- 13,514: since א (a) is 1 : ל (l) is 3 (or 30); ה (h) is 5; י (i) 1 for 10; and ם (m) is 4 (40), and anagrammatically -- 31,415 as explained by him.

Thus, while in the metaphysical world, the circle with the one central Point in it has no number, and is called Anupadaka (parentless and numberless) -- viz., it can fall under no calculation, -- in the manifested world the mundane Egg or Circle is circumscribed within the groups called the Line, the Triangle, the Pentacle, the second Line and the Cube (or 13514); and when the Point having generated a Line, thus becomes a diameter which stands for the androgynous Logos, then the figures become 31415, or a triangle, a line, a cube, the second line, and a pentacle. "When the Son separates from the Mother he becomes the Father," the diameter standing for Nature, or the feminine principle. Therefore it is said: "In the world of being, the one Point fructifies the Line -- the Virgin Matrix of Kosmos (the egg-shaped zero) -- and the immaculate Mother gives birth to the form that combines all forms." Prajapati is called the first procreating male, and "his Mother's husband." This gives the key-note to all the later divine sons from immaculate mothers. It is greatly corroborated by the significant fact that Anna (the name of the Mother of the Virgin Mary) now represented by the Roman Catholic church as having given birth to her daughter in an immaculate way ("Mary conceived without sin"), is derived from the Chaldean Ana, heaven, or Astral Light, Anima Mundi; whence Anaitia, Devi-durga, the wife of Siva, is also called Annapurna, and Kanya, the Virgin; "Uma-Kanya" being her esoteric name, and meaning the "Virgin of light," Astral Light in one of its multitudinous aspects.

(*c*) The Devas, Pitris, Rishis; the Suras and the Asuras; the Daityas and Adityas; the Danavas and Gandharvas, etc., etc., have all their synonyms in our Secret Doctrine, as well as in the Kabala and the Hebrew Angelology; but it is useless to give their ancient names, as it would only create confusion. Many of these may be also found now, even in the Christian hierarchy of divine and celestial powers. All those Thrones and Dominions,

Virtues and Principalities, Cherubs, Seraphs and demons, the various denizens of the Sidereal World, are the modern copies of archaic prototypes. The very symbolism in their names, when transliterated and arranged in Greek and Latin, are sufficient to show it, as will be proved in several cases further on.

The "Sacred Animals" are found in the Bible as well as in the Kabala, and they have their meaning (a very profound one, too) on the page of the origins of Life. In the Sepher Jezirah it is stated that "God engraved in the Holy Four the throne of his glory, the Ophanim (Wheels or the World-Spheres), the Seraphim, the Sacred Animals, and the ministering angels, and from these three (the Air, Water, and Fire or Ether) he formed his habitation." Thus was the world made "through three Seraphim -- Sepher, Saphar, and Sipur," or "through Number, Numbers, and Numbered." With the astronomical key these "Sacred Animals" become the signs of the Zodiac.

Kabala, as in India, the Deity was considered as the Universe, and was not, in his origin, the extra-cosmic God he is now.

4. THIS WAS THE ARMY OF THE VOICE -- THE DIVINE SEPTENARY. THE SPARKS OF THE SEVEN ARE SUBJECT TO, AND THE SERVANTS OF, THE FIRST, SECOND, THIRD, FOURTH, FIFTH, SIXTH, AND THE SEVENTH OF THE SEVEN (*a*). THESE ("*sparks*") ARE CALLED SPHERES, TRIANGLES, CUBES, LINES, AND MODELLERS; FOR THUS STANDS THE ETERNAL NIDANA -- THE OI-HA-HOU (*the Permutation of Oeaohoo*) (*b*).

(*a*) This Sloka gives again a brief analysis of the Hierarchies of the Dhyan Chohans, called Devas (gods) in India, or the conscious intelligent powers in Nature. To this Hierarchy correspond the actual types into which humanity may be divided; for humanity, as a whole, is in reality a materialized though as yet imperfect expression thereof. The "army of the Voice" is a term closely connected with the mystery of Sound and Speech, as an effect and corollary of the cause -- Divine Thought. As beautifully expressed by P. Christian, the learned author of "The History of Magic" and of "L'Homme Rouge des Tuileries," the word spoken by, as well as the name of, every individual largely determine his future fate. Why? Because --

"When our Soul (mind) creates or evokes a thought, the representative sign of that thought is self-engraved upon the astral fluid, which is the receptacle and, so to say, the mirror of all the manifestations of being.

"The sign expresses the thing: the thing is the (hidden or occult) virtue of the sign.

"To pronounce a word is to evoke a thought, and make it present: the magnetic potency of the human speech is the commencement of every manifestation in the Occult World. To utter a Name is not only to define a Being (an Entity), but to place it under and condemn it through the emission of the Word (Verbum), to the influence of one or more Occult potencies. Things are, for every one of us, that which it (the Word) makes them while naming them. The Word (Verbum) or the speech of every man is, quite unconsciously to himself, a BLESSING or a CURSE; this is why our present ignorance about the properties or attributes of the IDEA as well as about the attributes and properties of MATTER, is often fatal to us.

"Yes, names (and words) are either BENEFICENT or MALEFICENT; they are, in a certain sense, either venomous or health-giving, according to the hidden influences attached by Supreme Wisdom to their elements, that is to say, to the LETTERS which compose them, and the NUMBERS correlative to these letters."

This is strictly true as an esoteric teaching accepted by all the Eastern Schools of Occultism. In the Sanskrit, as also in the Hebrew and all other alphabets, every letter has its occult meaning and its rationale; it is a cause and an effect of a preceding cause and a combination of these very often produces the most magical effect. The vowels, especially, contain the most occult and formidable potencies. The Mantras (esoterically, magical rather than religious) are chanted by the Brahmins and so are the Vedas and other Scriptures.

The "Army of the Voice," is the prototype of the "Host of the Logos," or the "WORD" of the Sepher Jezirah, called in the Secret Doctrine "the One Number issued from No-

Number" -- the One Eternal Principle. The esoteric theogony begins with the One, manifested, therefore not eternal in its presence and being, if eternal in its essence; the number of the numbers and numbered -- the latter proceeding from the Voice, the feminine Vach, Satarupa "of the hundred forms," or Nature. It is from this number 10, or creative nature, the Mother (the occult cypher, or "nought," ever procreating and multiplying in union with the Unit "I," one, or the Spirit of Life), that the whole Universe proceeded.

In the *Anugita* a conversation is given (ch. vi., 15) between a Brahmana and his wife, on the origin of Speech and its occult properties. The wife asks how Speech came into existence, and which was prior to the other, Speech or Mind. The Brahmana tells her that the Apana (*inspirational breath*) becoming lord, changes that intelligence, which does not understand Speech or Words, into the state of Apana, and thus opens the mind. Thereupon he tells her a story, a dialogue between Speech and Mind. "Both went to the Self of Being (*i.e.*, to the individual Higher Self, as Nilakantha thinks, to Prajapati, according to the commentator Arjuna Misra), and asked him to destroy their doubts and decide which of them preceded and was superior to the other. To this the lord said: 'Mind is Superior.' But Speech answered the Self of Being, by saying: 'I verily yield (you) your desires,' meaning that by speech he acquired what he desired. Thereupon again, the Self told her that there are two minds, the 'movable' and the 'immovable.' 'The immovable is with me,' he said, 'the movable is in your dominion' (*i.e.* of Speech) on the plane of matter. To that you are superior. But inasmuch, O beautiful one, as you came personally to speak to me (in the way you did, *i.e.* proudly), therefore, O, Sarasvati! you shall never speak after (hard) exhalation." "The goddess Speech" (Sarasvati, a later form or aspect of Vach, the goddess also of secret learning or Esoteric Wisdom), "verily, dwelt always between the Prana and the Apana. But O noble one! going with the Apana wind (vital air), though impelled, without the Prana (expirational breath), she ran up to Prajapati (Brahma), saying, 'Be pleased, O venerable sir!' Then the Prana appeared again, nourishing Speech. And, therefore, Speech never speaks after (hard or inspirational) exhalation. It is always noisy or noiseless. Of these two, the noiseless is the superior to the noisy (Speech) . . . . The (speech) which is produced in the body by means of the Prana, and which then goes (is transformed) into Apana, and then becoming assimilated with the Udana (physical organs of Speech) . . . then finally dwells in the Samana ('at the navel in the form of sound, as the material cause of all words,' says Arjuna Misra). So Speech formerly spoke. Hence the mind is distinguished by reason of its being immovable, and the Goddess (Speech) by reason of her being movable."

This allegory is at the root of the Occult law, which prescribes silence upon the knowledge of certain secret and invisible things perceptible only to the spiritual mind (the 6th sense), and which cannot be expressed by "noisy" or uttered speech. This chapter of *Anugita* explains, says Arjuna Misra, Pranayama, or regulation of the breath in Yoga practices. This mode, however, without the previous acquisition of, or at least full understanding of the two higher senses, of which there are seven, as will be shown, pertains rather to the lower Yoga. The *Hatha* so called was and still is discountenanced by the Arhats. It is injurious to the health and alone can never develop into Raj Yoga. This story is quoted to show how inseparably connected are, in the metaphysics of old, intelligent beings, or rather "Intelligences," with every sense or function whether physical or mental. The Occult claim that there are seven senses in man, as in nature, as there are seven states of consciousness, is corroborated in the same work, chapter vii., on Pratyahara (the restraint and regulation of the senses, Pranayama being that of the "vital winds" or breath). The Brahmana speaks in it "of the institution of the seven sacrificial Priests (Hotris). He says: "The nose and the eyes, and the tongue, and the skin and the ear as the fifth (or smell, sight, taste, touch and hearing), mind and understanding are the seven sacrificial priests separately stationed"; and which "dwelling in a minute space (still) do not perceive each other" on this sensuous plane, none of them except mind. For mind says: "The nose smells not without me, the eye does not take in colour, etc., etc. I am the eternal chief among all elements (*i.e.*, senses). Without me, the senses never shine, like an empty dwelling, or like fires the flames of which are extinct. Without me, all beings, like fuel half dried and half moist, fail to apprehend qualities or objects even with the senses exerting themselves."

This, of course, with regard only to *mind on the sensuous plane.* Spiritual mind (the upper portion or aspect of the *impersonal* MANAS) takes no cognisance of the senses in physical man. How well the ancients were acquainted with the correlation of forces and all the recently discovered phenomena of mental and physical faculties and functions, with many more mysteries also -- may be found in reading chapters vii. and viii. of this (in philosophy and mystic learning) priceless work. See the quarrel of the senses about their respective superiority and their taking the Brahman, the lord of all creatures, for their arbiter. "You are all greatest and not greatest," or superior to objects, as A. Misra says, none being independent of the other. "You are all possessed of one another's qualities. All are greatest in their own spheres and all support one another. There is one unmoving (life-wind or breath, the '*Yoga inhalation,*' so called, which is the breath of the *One* or Higher SELF). That is the (or my) own Self, accumulated in numerous (forms)."

This Breath, Voice, Self or "Wind" (*pneuma?*) is the Synthesis of the Seven Senses, *noumenally* all minor deities and esoterically -- the *septenary* and the "Army of the VOICE."

(*b*) Next we see Cosmic matter scattering and forming itself into elements; grouped into the mystic four within the fifth element -- Ether, the lining of Akasa, the Anima Mundi or Mother of Kosmos. "Dots, Lines, Triangles, Cubes, Circles" and finally "Spheres" -- why or how? Because, says the Commentary, such is the first law of Nature, and because Nature geometrizes universally in all her manifestations. There is an inherent law -- not only in the primordial, but also in the manifested matter of our phenomenal plane -- by which Nature correlates her geometrical forms, and later, also, her compound elements; and in which there is no place for accident or chance. It is a fundamental law in Occultism, that there is no rest or cessation of motion in Nature. That which seems rest is only the change of one form into another; the change of substance going hand in hand with that of form -- as we are taught in Occult physics, which thus seem to have anticipated the discovery of the "Conservation of matter" by a considerable time. Says the ancient Commentary to Stanza IV.: --

"*The Mother is the fiery Fish of Life. She scatters her spawn and the Breath (Motion) heats and quickens it. The grains (of spawn) are soon attracted to each other and form the curds in the Ocean (of Space). The larger lumps coalesce and receive new spawn -- in fiery dots, triangles and cubes, which ripen, and at the appointed time some of the lumps detach themselves and assume spheroidal form, a process which they effect only when not interfered with by the others. After which, law No.   comes into operation. Motion (the Breath) becomes the whirlwind and sets them into rotation.*"

5. . . . . . . WHICH IS: ----

"DARKNESS," THE BOUNDLESS OR THE NO-NUMBER, ADI-NIDANA SVABHAVAT: THE

O *(for x, unknown quantity):*

I. THE ADI-SANAT, THE NUMBER, FOR HE IS ONE (*a*).
II. THE VOICE OF THE WORD, SVABHAVAT, THE NUMBERS, FOR HE IS ONE AND NINE.
III. THE "FORMLESS SQUARE." (*Arupa.*) (*b*).

AND THESE THREE ENCLOSED WITHIN THE **O** (*boundless circle*), ARE THE SACRED FOUR, AND THE TEN ARE THE ARUPA (*subjective, formless*) UNIVERSE (*c*); THEN COME THE "SONS," THE SEVEN FIGHTERS, THE ONE, THE EIGHTH LEFT OUT, AND HIS BREATH WHICH IS THE LIGHT-MAKER (*Bhaskara*) (*d*).

(*a*) "Adi-Sanat," translated literally is the First or "primeval" ancient, which name identifies the Kabalistic "Ancient of Days" and the "Holy Aged" (Sephira and Adam Kadmon) with Brahma the Creator, called also *Sanat* among his other names and titles.

Svabhavat is the mystic Essence, the plastic root of physical Nature -- "Numbers" when manifested; the Number, in its Unity of Substance, on the highest plane. The name is of Buddhist use and a Synonym for the four-fold Anima Mundi, the Kabalistic "Archetypal

World," from whence proceed the "Creative, Formative, and the by the descent of FLAME into primordial matter causes its particles to move, which motion becomes Whirlwind." A drop of liquid assumes a spheroidal form owing to its atoms moving around themselves in their ultimate, unresolvable, and noumenal essence; unresolvable for physical science, at any rate.

(*b*) ⭕ This means that the "Boundless Circle" (Zero) becomes a figure or number, only when one of the nine figures precedes it, and thus manifests its value and potency, the Word or Logos in union with VOICE and Spirit (the expression and source of Consciousness) standing for the nine figures and thus forming, with the Cypher, the Decade which contains in itself all the Universe. The triad forms within the circle the Tetraktis or Sacred Four, the Square within the Circle being the most potent of all the magical figures.

(*c*) The "One Rejected" is the Sun of our system. The exoteric version may be found in the oldest Sanskrit Scriptures. In the Rig Veda, Aditi, "The Boundless" or infinite Space, translated by Mr. Max Muller, "the visible infinite, visible by the naked eye (!!); the endless expanse beyond the Earth, beyond the clouds, beyond the sky," is the equivalent of "Mother-Space" coeval with "Darkness." She is very properly called "The Mother of the Gods," DEVA-MATRI, as it is from her Cosmic matrix that all the heavenly bodies of our system were born -- Sun and Planets. Thus she is described, allegorically, in this wise: "Eight Sons were born from the body of Aditi; she approached the gods with seven, but cast away the eighth, Martanda," our sun. The seven sons called the Aditya are, cosmically or astronomically, the seven planets; and the Sun being excluded from their number shows plainly that the Hindus may have known, and in fact knew of a seventh planet, without calling it Uranus.   But esoterically and theologically,

The Secret Doctrine teaches that the Sun is a central Star and not a planet. Yet the Ancients knew of and worshipped seven great gods, excluding the Sun and Earth. Which was that "Mystery God" they set apart? Of course not Uranus, discovered only by Herschel in 1781. But could it not be known by another name? Says the so to say, the Adityas are, in their primitive most ancient meanings, the eight, and the twelve great gods of the Hindu Pantheon. "The Seven allow the mortals to see their dwellings, but show themselves only to the Arhats," says an old proverb, "their dwellings" standing here for planets. The ancient Commentary gives an allegory and explains it: --

"*Eight houses were built by Mother. Eight houses for her Eight Divine sons; four large and four small ones. Eight brilliant suns, according to their age and merits. Bal-ilu (Martanda) was not satisfied, though his house was the largest. He began (to work) as the huge elephants do. He breathed (drew in) into his stomach the vital airs of his brothers. He sought to devour them. The larger four were far away; far, on the margin of their kingdom. They were not robbed (affected), and laughed. Do your worst, Sir, you cannot reach us, they said. But the smaller wept. They complained to the Mother. She exiled Bal-i-lu to the centre of her Kingdom, from whence he could not move. (Since then) he (only) watches and threatens. He pursues them, turning slowly around himself, they turning swiftly from him, and he following from afar the direction in which his brothers move on the path that encircles their houses. From that day he feeds on the sweat of the Mother's body. He fills himself with her breath and refuse. Therefore, she rejected him.*"

Thus the "rejected Son" being our Sun, evidently, as shown above, the "Sun-Sons" refer not only to our planets but to the heavenly bodies in general. Himself only a reflection of the Central Spiritual Sun, *Surya* is the prototype of all those bodies that evolved after him. In the Vedas he is called *Loka-Chakshuh,* "the Eye of the World" (our planetary world), and he is one of the three chief deities. He is called indifferently the Son of *Dyaus* and of *Aditi,* because no distinction is made with reference to, or scope allowed for, the esoteric meaning. Thus he is depicted as drawn by seven horses, and by one horse with seven heads; the former referring to his seven planets, the latter to their one common origin from the One Cosmic Element. This "One Element" is called figuratively "FIRE." The Vedas (Aitareya-Brahmana of Haug also; p. i) teach "that the fire verily is all the deities." (Narada in Anugita).

The meaning of the allegory is plain, for we have both the Dzyan Commentary and modern science to explain it, though the two differ in more than one particular. The Occult Doctrine rejects the hypothesis born out of the Nebular Theory, that the (seven) great planets have evolved from the Sun's central mass, not of this our visible Sun, at any rate. The first condensation of Cosmic matter of course took place about a central nucleus, its parent Sun; but our sun, it is taught, merely detached itself earlier than all the others, as the rotating mass contracted, and is their elder, bigger brother therefore, not their father. The eight Adityas, "the gods," are all formed from the eternal substance (Cometary matter -- the Mother) or the "World-Stuff " which is both the fifth and the sixth COSMIC Principle, the Upadhi or basis of the Universal Soul, just as in man, the Microcosm, Manas is the Upadhi of Buddhi.

(d) There is a whole poem on the pregenetic battles fought by the growing planets before the final formation of Kosmos, thus accounting for the seemingly disturbed position of the systems of several planets, the plane of the satellites of some (of Neptune and Uranus, for instance, of which the ancients knew nothing, it is said) being tilted over, thus giving them an appearance of retrograde motion. These planets are called the warriors, the Architects, and are accepted by the Roman Church as the leaders of the heavenly Hosts, thus showing the same traditions. Having evolved from Cosmic Space, and before the final formation of the primaries and the annulation of the planetary nebula, the Sun, we are taught, drew into the depths of its mass all the Cosmic vitality he could, threatening to engulf his weaker "brothers" before the law of attraction and repulsion was finally adjusted; after which he began feeding on "The Mother's refuse and sweat"; in other words, on those portions of Ether (the "breath of the Universal Soul") of the existence and constitution of which science is as yet absolutely ignorant. A theory of this kind having been propounded by Sir William Grove (see "*Correlation of the Physical Forces*," 1843, p. 81; and "*Address to the British Association*, 1866"), who theorized that the systems "are gradually changing by atmospheric additions or subtractions, or by accretions and diminutions arising from nebular substances" . . . and again that "the Sun may condense gaseous matter as it travels in Space and so heat may be produced" -- the archaic teaching seems scientific enough, even in this age. Mr. W. Mattieu Williams suggested that the diffused matter or Ether which is the recipient of the heat radiations of the Universe is thereby drawn into the depths of the solar mass. Expelling thence the previously condensed and thermally exhausted Ether, it becomes compressed and gives up its heat, to be in turn itself driven out in a rarified and cooled state, to absorb a fresh supply of heat, which he supposes to be in this way taken up by the Ether, and again concentrated and redistributed by the Suns of the Universe.

This is about as close an approximation to the Occult teachings as Science ever imagined; for Occultism explains it by "the dead breath" given back by Martanda and his feeding on the "sweat and refuse" of "Mother Space." What could affect Neptune, Saturn and Jupiter, but little, would have killed such comparatively small "Houses" as Mercury, Venus and Mars. As Uranus was not known before the end of the eighteenth century, the name of the fourth planet mentioned in the allegory must remain to us, so far, a mystery.

The "Breath" of all the "seven" is said to be Bhaskara (light-making), because they (the planets) were all comets and suns in their origin. They evolve into Manvantaric life from primaeval Chaos (now the noumenon of irresolvable nebulae) by aggregation and accumulation of the primary differentiations of the eternal matter, according to the beautiful expression in the Commentary, "Thus the Sons of Light clothed themselves in the fabric of Darkness." They are called allegorically "the Heavenly Snails," on account of their (to us) formless INTELLIGENCES inhabiting unseen their starry and planetary homes, and, so to speak, carrying them as the snails do along with themselves in their revolution. The doctrine of a common origin for all the heavenly bodies and planets, was, as we see, inculcated by the Archaic astronomers, before Kepler, Newton, Leibnitz, Kant, Herschel and Laplace. Heat (the Breath), attraction and repulsion -- the three great factors of Motion -- are the conditions under which all the members of all this primitive family are born, developed, and die, to be reborn after a "Night of Brahma," during which eternal matter relapses periodically into its primary undifferentiated state. The most attenuated gases can give no idea of its nature to the modern physicist. Centres of Forces at first, the invisible sparks of primordial atoms differentiate into molecules, and become Suns -- passing gradually into objectivity gaseous, radiant, cosmic, the one "Whirlwind" (or motion) finally giving the impulse to the form, and the initial motion, regulated and sustained by the never-resting Breaths -- the Dhyan Chohans.

6. . . . . THEN THE SECOND SEVEN, WHO ARE THE LIPIKA, PRODUCED BY THE THREE (*Word, Voice, and Spirit*). THE REJECTED SON IS ONE, THE "SON-SUNS" ARE COUNTLESS.

The *Lipi-ka*, from the word *lipi*, "writing," means literally the "Scribes." Mystically, these Divine Beings are connected with Karma, the Law of Retribution, for they are the Recorders or Annalists who impress on the (to us) invisible tablets of the Astral Light, "the great picture gallery of eternity" -- a faithful record of every act, and even thought, of man, of all that was, is, or ever will be, in the phenomenal Universe. As said in "*Isis*," this divine and unseen canvas is the BOOK OF LIFE. As it is the Lipika who project into objectivity from the passive Universal Mind the ideal plan of the universe, upon which the "Builders" reconstruct the Kosmos after every Pralaya, it is they who stand parallel to the Seven Angels of the Presence, whom the Christians recognise in the Seven "Planetary Spirits" or the "Spirits of the Stars;" for thus it is they who are the direct amanuenses of the Eternal Ideation -- or, as called by Plato, the "Divine Thought." The Eternal Record is no fantastic dream, for we meet with the same records in the world of gross matter. "A shadow never falls upon a wall without leaving thereupon a permanent trace which might be made visible by resorting to proper processes," says Dr. Draper. . . . "The portraits of our friends or landscape-views may be hidden on the sensitive surface from the eye, but they are ready to make their appearance as soon as proper developers are resorted to. A spectre is concealed on a silver or a glassy surface, until, by our necromancy, we make it come forth into the visible world. Upon the walls of our most private apartments, where we think the eye of intrusion is altogether shut out, and our retirement can never be profaned, there exist the vestiges of all our acts, silhouettes of whatever we have done." Drs. Jevons and Babbage believe that every thought, displacing the particles of the brain and setting them in motion, scatters them throughout the Universe, and they think that "each particle of the existing matter must be a register of all that has happened." (Principles of Science, Vol. II. p. 455.) Thus the ancient doctrine has begun to acquire rights of citizenship in the speculations of the scientific world.

The forty "Assessors" who stand in the region of *Amenti* as the accusers of the Soul before *Osiris*, belong to the same class of deities as the Lipika, and might stand paralleled, were not the Egyptian gods so little understood in their esoteric meaning. The Hindu *Chitra-Gupta* who reads out the account of every Soul's life from his register, called Agra-Sandhani; the "Assessors" who read theirs from the heart of the defunct, which becomes an open book before (whether) Yama, Minos, Osiris, or Karma -- are all so many copies of, and variants from the Lipika, and their Astral Records. Nevertheless, the Lipi-ka are not deities connected with Death, but with Life Eternal.

Connected as the Lipika are with the destiny of every man and the birth of every child, whose life is already traced in the Astral Light not fatalistically, but only because the future, like the PAST, is ever alive in the PRESENT -- they may also be said to exercise an influence on the Science of Horoscopy. We must admit the truth of the latter whether we will or not. For, as observed by one of the modern adepts of Astrology, "Now that photography has revealed to us the chemical influence of the Sidereal system, by fixing on the sensitized plate of the apparatus milliards of stars and planets that had hitherto baffled the efforts of the most powerful telescopes to discover them, it becomes easier to understand how our solar system can, at the birth of a child, influence his brain -- virgin of any impression -- in a definite manner and according to the presence on the zenith of such or another zodiacal constellation."

STANZA V.

COMMENTARY

1. THE PRIMORDIAL SEVEN, THE FIRST SEVEN BREATHS OF THE DRAGON OF WISDOM, PRODUCE IN THEIR TURN FROM THEIR HOLY CIRCUMGYRATING BREATHS THE FIERY WHIRLWIND (*a*). This is, perhaps, the most difficult of all the Stanzas to explain. Its language is comprehensible only to him who is thoroughly versed in Eastern allegory and its purposely obscure phraseology. The question will surely be asked, "Do the Occultists believe in all these 'Builders,' 'Lipika,' and 'Sons of Light' as Entities, or are they merely imageries?" To this the answer is given as plainly: "After due allowance for the imagery of personified Powers, we must admit the existence of these Entities, if we would not reject the existence of spiritual humanity within physical mankind. For the hosts of these Sons of Light and 'Mind-born Sons' of the first manifested Ray of the UNKNOWN ALL, are the very root of spiritual man." Unless we want to believe the unphilosophical dogma of a specially created soul for every human birth -- a fresh supply of these pouring in daily, since "Adam" -- we have to admit the occult teachings. This will be explained in its place. Let us see, now, what may be the occult meaning of this Stanza.

The Doctrine teaches that, in order to become a divine, fully conscious god, -- aye, even the highest -- the Spiritual primeval INTELLIGENCES must pass through the human stage. And when we say human, this does not apply merely to our terrestrial humanity, but to the mortals that inhabit any world, *i.e.*, to those Intelligences that have reached the appropriate equilibrium between matter and spirit, as *we* have now, since the middle point of the Fourth Root Race of the Fourth Round was passed. Each Entity must have won for itself the right of becoming divine, through self-experience. Hegel, the great German thinker, must have known or sensed intuitionally this truth when saying, as he did, that the Unconscious evolved the Universe only "in the hope of attaining clear self-consciousness," of becoming, in other words, MAN; for this is also the secret meaning of the usual Puranic phrase about Brahma being constantly "moved by the desire to create." This explains also the hidden Kabalistic meaning of the saying: "The *Breath* becomes a stone; the stone, a plant; the plant, an animal; the animal, a man; the man, a spirit; and the spirit, a god." The Mind-born Sons, the Rishis, the Builders, etc., were all men -- of whatever forms and shapes -- in other worlds and the preceding Manvantaras.

This subject, being so very mystical, is therefore the most difficult to explain in all its details and bearings; since the whole mystery of evolutionary creation is contained in it. A sentence or two in it vividly recalls to mind similar ones in the Kabala and the phraseology of the King Psalmist (civ.), as both, when speaking of God, show him making the wind his messenger and his "ministers a flaming fire." But in the Esoteric doctrine it is used figuratively. The "fiery Wind" is the incandescent Cosmic dust which only follows magnetically, as the iron filings follow the magnet, the directing thought of the "Creative Forces." Yet, this cosmic dust is something more; for every atom in the Universe has the potentiality of self-consciousness in it, and is, like the Monads of Leibnitz, a Universe in itself, and *for* itself. *It is an atom and an angel.*

In this connection it should be noted that one of the luminaries of the modern Evolutionist School, Mr. A. R. Wallace, when discussing the inadequacy of "natural selection" as the sole factor in the development of physical man, practically concedes the whole point here discussed. He holds that the evolution of man was directed and furthered by superior Intelligences, whose agency is a necessary factor in the scheme of Nature. But once the operation of these Intelligences is admitted in one place, it is only a logical deduction to extend it still further. No hard and fast line can be drawn.

2. THEY MAKE OF HIM THE MESSENGER OF THEIR WILL (*a*). THE DZYU BECOMES FOHAT; THE SWIFT SON OF THE DIVINE SONS, WHOSE SONS ARE THE LIPIKA, RUNS CIRCULAR ERRANDS. HE IS THE STEED, AND THE THOUGHT IS THE RIDER (*i.e., he is under the influence of their guiding thought*). HE PASSES LIKE LIGHTNING THROUGH THE FIERY CLOUDS (*cosmic mists*) (*b*); TAKES THREE, AND FIVE, AND SEVEN STRIDES THROUGH THE SEVEN REGIONS ABOVE AND THE SEVEN BELOW (*the world to be*). HE LIFTS HIS VOICE, AND CALLS THE INNUMERABLE SPARKS (*atoms*) AND JOINS THEM TOGETHER (*c*).

(*a*) This shows the "Primordial Seven" using for their *Vahan* (vehicle, or the manifested subject which becomes the symbol of the Power directing it), Fohat, called in consequence, the "Messenger of their will" -- the fiery whirlwind.

"Dzyu becomes Fohat" -- the expression itself shows it. Dzyu is the one real (magical) knowledge, or Occult Wisdom; which, dealing with eternal truths and primal causes, becomes almost omnipotence when applied in the right direction. Its antithesis is Dzyu-mi, that which deals with illusions and false appearances only, as in our exoteric modern sciences. In this case, Dzyu is the expression of the collective Wisdom of the Dhyani-Buddhas.

(*b*) As the reader is supposed not to be acquainted with the Dhyani-Buddhas, it is as well to say at once that, *according to the Orientalists*, there are five Dhyanis who are the "celestial" Buddhas, of whom the human Buddhas are the manifestations in the world of form and matter. Esoterically, however, the Dhyani-Buddhas are seven, of whom five only have hitherto manifested, and two are to come in the sixth and seventh Root-races. They are, so to speak, the eternal prototypes of the Buddhas who appear on this earth, each of whom has his particular divine prototype. So, for instance, Amitabha is the Dhyani-Buddha of Gautama Sakyamuni, manifesting through him whenever this great Soul incarnates on earth as He did in Tzon-kha-pa. As the synthesis of the seven Dhyani-Buddhas, Avalokiteswara was the first Buddha (the Logos), so Amitabha is the inner "God" of Gautama, who, in China, is called Amita(-Buddha). They are, as Mr. Rhys Davids correctly states, "the glorious counterparts in the mystic world, free from the debasing conditions of this material life" of every earthly mortal Buddha -- the liberated Manushi-Buddhas appointed to govern the Earth in this Round. They are the "Buddhas of Contemplation," and are all Anupadaka (parentless), *i.e.*, self-born of divine essence. The exoteric teaching which says that every Dhyani-Buddha has the faculty of creating from himself, an equally celestial son -- a Dhyani-Bodhisattva -- who, after the decease of the Manushi (human) Buddha, has to carry out the work of the latter, rests on the fact that owing to the highest initiation performed by one overshadowed by the "Spirit of Buddha" -- (who is credited by the Orientalists with having created the five Dhyani-Buddhas!), -- a candidate becomes virtually a Bodhisattva, created such by the High Initiator.

(*c*) Fohat, being one of the most, if not the most important character in esoteric Cosmogony, should be minutely described. As in the oldest Grecian Cosmogony, differing widely from the later mythology, Eros is the third person in the primeval trinity: Chaos, Gaea, Eros: answering to the Kabalistic En-Soph (for Chaos is SPACE, [[*Chaino*]], "void") the Boundless ALL, Shekinah and the Ancient of Days, or the Holy Ghost; so Fohat is one thing in the yet unmanifested Universe and another in the phenomenal and Cosmic World. In the latter, he is that Occult, electric, vital power, which, under the Will of the Creative Logos, unites and brings together all forms, giving them the first impulse which becomes in time law. But in the unmanifested Universe, Fohat is no more this, than Eros is the later brilliant winged Cupid, or LOVE. Fohat has naught to do with Kosmos yet, since Kosmos is not born, and the gods still sleep in the bosom of "Father-Mother." He is an abstract philosophical idea. He produces nothing yet by himself; he is simply that potential creative power in virtue of whose action the NOUMENON of all future phenomena divides, so to speak, but to reunite in a mystic supersensuous act, and emit the creative ray. When the "Divine Son" breaks forth, then Fohat becomes the propelling force, the active Power which causes the ONE to become TWO and THREE -- on the Cosmic plane of manifestation. The triple One differentiates into the many, and then Fohat is transformed into that force which brings together the elemental atoms and makes them aggregate and combine. We find an echo of this primeval teaching in early Greek mythology. Erebos and Nux are born out of Chaos, and, under the action of Eros, give birth in their turn to Ether and Hemera, the light of the superior and the light of the inferior or terrestrial regions. Darkness generates light. See in the Puranas Brahma's "Will" or desire to create; and in the Phoenician Cosmogony of Sanchoniathon the doctrine that Desire, [[*pothos*]], is the principle of creation.

Fohat is closely related to the "ONE LIFE." From the Unknown One, the Infinite TOTALITY, the manifested ONE, or the periodical, Manvantaric Deity, emanates; and this is the Universal Mind, which, separated from its Fountain-Source, is the Demiurgos or the creative Logos of the Western Kabalists, and the four-faced Brahma of the Hindu religion. In its totality, viewed from the standpoint of manifested Divine Thought in the esoteric doctrine, it represents the Hosts of the higher creative Dhyan Chohans. Simultaneously with the evolution of the Universal Mind, the concealed Wisdom of Adi-Buddha -- the One Supreme and eternal -- manifests itself as Avalokiteshwara (or manifested Iswara), which is the Osiris of the Egyptians, the Ahura-Mazda of the Zoroastrians, the Heavenly Man of the Hermetic philosopher, the Logos of the Platonists, and the Atman of the Vedantins. By the action of the manifested Wisdom, or Mahat, represented by these innumerable centres of spiritual Energy in the Kosmos, the reflection of the Universal Mind, which is Cosmic Ideation and the intellectual Force accompanying such ideation, becomes objectively the Fohat of the Buddhist esoteric philosopher. Fohat, running along the seven principles of AKASA, acts upon manifested substance or the One Element, as declared above, and by differentiating it into various centres of Energy, sets in motion the law of Cosmic Evolution, which, in obedience to the Ideation of the Universal Mind, brings into existence all the various states of being in the manifested Solar System.

The Solar System, brought into existence by these agencies, consists of Seven Principles, like everything else within these centres. Such is the teaching of the trans-Himalayan Esotericism. Every philosophy, however, has its own way of dividing these principles.

Fohat, then, is the personified electric vital power, the transcendental binding Unity of all Cosmic Energies, on the unseen as on the manifested planes, the action of which resembles -- on an immense scale -- that of a living Force created by WILL, in those phenomena where the seemingly subjective acts on the seemingly objective and propels it to action. Fohat is not only the living Symbol and Container of that Force, but is looked upon by the Occultists as an Entity -- the forces he acts upon being cosmic, human and terrestrial, and exercising their influence on all those planes respectively. On the earthly plane his influence is felt in the magnetic and active force generated by the strong desire of the magnetizer. On the Cosmic, it is present in the constructive power that carries out, in the formation of things -- from the planetary system down to the glow-worm and simple daisy -- the plan in the mind of nature, or in the Divine Thought, with regard to the development and growth of that special thing. He is, metaphysically, the objectivised thought of the gods; the "Word made flesh," on a lower scale, and the messenger of Cosmic and human ideations: the active force in Universal Life. In his secondary aspect, Fohat is the Solar Energy, the electric vital fluid, and the preserving fourth principle, the animal Soul of Nature, so to say, or -- Electricity. In India, Fohat is connected with Vishnu and Surya in the early character of the (first) God; for Vishnu is not a high god in the Rig Veda. The name Vishnu is from the root *vish*, "to pervade," and Fohat is called the "Pervader" and the Manufacturer, because he shapes the atoms from crude material. In the sacred texts of the Rig Veda, Vishnu, also, is "a manifestation of the Solar Energy," and he is described as striding through the Seven regions of the Universe in three steps, the Vedic God having little in common with the Vishnu of later times. Therefore the two are identical in this particular feature, and one is the copy of the other.

The "three and seven" strides refer to the Seven spheres inhabited by man, of the esoteric Doctrine, as well as to the Seven regions of the Earth. Notwithstanding the frequent objections made by would-be Orientalists, the Seven Worlds or spheres of our planetary chain are distinctly referred to in the exoteric Hindu scriptures. But how strangely all these numbers are connected with like numbers in other Cosmogonies and with their symbols, can be seen from comparisons and parallelisms made by students of old religions. The "three strides of Vishnu" through the "seven regions of the Universe," of the Rig Veda, have been variously explained by commentators as meaning "fire, lightning and the Sun" cosmically; and as having been taken in the Earth, the atmosphere, and the sky; also as the "three steps" of the dwarf (Vishnu's incarnation), though more philosophically -- and in the astronomical sense, very correctly -- they are explained by Aurnavabha as being the various positions of the sun, rising, noon, and setting. Esoteric philosophy alone explains it clearly, and the Zohar laid it down very philosophically and comprehensively. It is said and plainly demonstrated therein that in the beginning the Elohim (Elhim) were called Echod, "one," or the "Deity is one in many," a very simple idea in a pantheistic conception (in its philosophical sense, of course). Then came the change, "Jehovah is Elohim," thus unifying the multiplicity and taking the first step towards Monotheism. Now to the query, "How is Jehovah Elohim?" the answer is, "By three Steps" from below.

The meaning is plain. They are all symbols, and emblematic, mutually and correlatively, of Spirit, Soul and Body (MAN); of the circle transformed into Spirit, the Soul of the World, and its body (or Earth). Stepping out of the Circle of Infinity, that no man comprehendeth, Ain-Soph (the Kabalistic synonym for Parabrahm, for the Zeroana Akerne, of the Mazdeans, or for any other "UNKNOWABLE") becomes "One" -- the ECHOD, the EKA, the AHU -- then he (or it) is transformed by evolution into the One in many, the Dhyani-Buddhas or the Elohim, or again the Amshaspends, his third Step being taken into generation of the flesh, or "Man." And from man, or Jah-Hova, "male female," the *inner* divine entity becomes, on the metaphysical plane, once more the Elohim.

The Kabalistic idea is identical with the Esotericism of the Archaic period. This esotericism is the common property of all, and belongs neither to the Aryan 5th Race, nor to any of its numerous Sub-races. It cannot be claimed by the Turanians, so-called, the Egyptians, Chinese, Chaldeans, nor any of the Seven divisions of the Fifth Root Race, but really belongs to the Third and Fourth Root Races, whose descendants we find in the Seed of the Fifth, the earliest Aryans. The Circle was with every nation the symbol of the Unknown -- "Boundless Space," the abstract garb of an ever present abstraction -- the Incognisable Deity. It represents limitless Time in Eternity. The Zeroana Akerne is also the "Boundless Circle of the Unknown Time," from which Circle issues the radiant light the Universal SUN, or Ormazd -- and the latter is identical with Kronos, in his Aeolian form, that of a Circle. For the circle is Sar, and Saros, or cycle, and was the Babylonian god whose circular horizon was the visible symbol of the invisible, while the sun was the ONE Circle from which proceeded the Cosmic orbs, and of which he was considered the leader. Zero-ana, is the Chakra or circle of Vishnu, the mysterious emblem which is, according to the definition of a mystic, "a curve of such a nature that as to any, the least possible part thereof, if the curve be protracted either way it will proceed and finally re-enter upon itself, and form one and the same curve -- or that which we call the circle." No better definition could thus be given of the natural symbol and the evident nature of Deity, which having its circumference everywhere (the boundless) has, therefore, its central point also everywhere; in other words, is in every point of the Universe. The invisible Deity is thus also the Dhyan Chohans, or the Rishis, the primitive seven, and the nine, without, and ten, including, their synthetical unit; from which IT steps into Man. Returning to the Commentary (4) of Stanza IV. the reader will understand why, while the

trans-Himalayan Chakra has inscribed within it △ | □ | ✵ (triangle, first line, cube second line, and a pentacle with a dot in the centre thus: ✵, and some other variations), the Kabalistic circle of the Elohim reveals, when the letters of the word

אלהים (Alhim or Elohim) are numerically read, the famous numerals 13514, or by anagram 31415 -- the astronomical (pi) number, or the hidden meaning of Dhyani-Buddhas, of the Gebers, the Geborim, the Kabeiri, and the Elohim, all signifying "great men," "Titans," "Heavenly Men," and, on earth, "the giants."

The Seven was a Sacred Number with every nation; but none applied it to more physiologically materialistic uses than the Hebrews. With these it was pre-eminently the generative number and 9 the male causative one, forming as shown by the Kabalists the

צ ע or *otz* -- "the Tree of the Garden of Eden," the "double hermaphrodite rod" of the fourth race. Whereas with the Hindus and Aryans generally, the significance was manifold, and related almost entirely to purely metaphysical and astronomical truths. Their Rishis and gods, their Demons and Heroes, have historical and ethical meanings, and the Aryans never made their religion rest solely on physiological symbols, as the old Hebrews have done. This is found in the exoteric Hindu Scriptures. That these accounts are blinds is shown by their contradicting each other, a different construction being found in almost every Purana and epic poem. Read esoterically -- they will all yield the same meaning. Thus one account enumerates Seven worlds, exclusive of the nether worlds, also seven in number; these fourteen upper and nether worlds have nothing to do with the classification of the septenary chain and belong to the purely aethereal, invisible worlds. These will be noticed elsewhere. Suffice for the present to show that they are purposely referred to as though they belonged to the chain. "Another enumeration calls the Seven worlds -- earth, sky, heaven, middle region, place of birth, mansion of the blest, and abode of truth; placing the 'Sons of Brahma' in the sixth division, and stating the fifth, or Jana Loka, to be that where animals destroyed in the general conflagration are born again." (see *Hindu Classical Dictionary.*) Some real esoteric teaching is given in the "Symbolism." He who is prepared for it will understand the hidden meaning.

3. **H**E IS THEIR GUIDING SPIRIT AND LEADER. **W**HEN HE COMMENCES WORK, HE SEPARATES THE SPARKS OF THE LOWER KINGDOM (*mineral atoms*) THAT FLOAT AND THRILL WITH JOY IN THEIR RADIANT DWELLINGS (*gaseous clouds*), AND FORMS THEREWITH THE GERMS OF WHEELS. **H**E PLACES THEM IN THE SIX DIRECTIONS OF SPACE AND ONE IN THE MIDDLE -- THE CENTRAL WHEEL (*a*).

(*a*) "Wheels," as already explained, are the centres of force, around which primordial Cosmic matter expands, and, passing through all the six stages of consolidation, becomes spheroidal and ends by being transformed into globes or spheres. It is one of the fundamental dogmas of Esoteric Cosmogony, that during the Kalpas (or aeons) of life, MOTION, which, during the periods of Rest "pulsates and thrills through every slumbering atom" (Commentary on Dzyan), assumes an evergrowing tendency, from the first awakening of Kosmos to a new "Day," to circular movement. The "Deity becomes a WHIRLWIND." They are also called Rotae -- the moving wheels of the celestial orbs participating in the world's creation -- when the meaning refers to the animating principle of the stars and planets; for in the Kabala, they are represented by the Ophanim, the Angels of the Spheres and stars, of which they are the informing Souls. (See *Kabala Denudata*, "*De Anima*," p. 113.)

This law of vortical movement in primordial matter, is one of the oldest conceptions of Greek philosophy, whose first historical Sages were nearly all Initiates of the Mysteries. The Greeks had it from the Egyptians, and the latter from the Chaldeans, who had been the pupils of Brahmins of the esoteric school. Leucippus, and Democritus of Abdera -- the pupil of the Magi -- taught that this gyratory movement of the atoms and spheres existed from eternity. Hicetas, Heraclides, Ecphantus, Pythagoras, and all his pupils, taught the rotation of the earth; and Aryabhata of India, Aristarchus, Seleucus, and Archimedes calculated its revolution as scientifically as the astronomers do now; while the theory of the Elemental Vortices was known to Anaxagoras, and maintained by him 500 years B.C., or nearly 2,000 before it was taken up by Galileo, Descartes, Swedenborg, and finally, with slight modifications, by Sir W. Thomson. (See his "*Vortical Atoms.*") All such knowledge, if justice be only done to it, is an echo of the archaic doctrine, an attempt to explain which is now being made. How men of the last few centuries have come to the same ideas and conclusions that were taught as axiomatic truths in the secrecy of the Adyta dozens of millenniums ago, is a question that is treated separately. Some were led to it by the natural progress in physical science and by independent observation; others -- such as

Copernicus, Swedenborg, and a few more -- their great learning notwithstanding, owed their knowledge far more to intuitive than to acquired ideas, developed in the usual way by a course of study. (See "A Mystery about Buddha.")

By the "Six directions of Space" is here meant the "Double Triangle," the junction and blending together of pure Spirit and Matter, of the Arupa and the Rupa, of which the Triangles are a Symbol. This double Triangle is a sign of Vishnu, as it is Solomon's seal, and the Sri-Antara of the Brahmins.

4. FOHAT TRACES SPIRAL LINES TO UNITE THE SIX TO THE SEVENTH -- THE CROWN (*a*); AN ARMY OF THE SONS OF LIGHT STANDS AT EACH ANGLE (*and*) THE LIPIKA -- IN THE MIDDLE WHEEL. THEY (*the Lipika*) SAY, "THIS IS GOOD" (*b*). THE FIRST DIVINE WORLD IS READY, THE FIRST (*is now*), THE SECOND (*world*), THEN THE "DIVINE ARUPA" (*the formless Universe of Thought*) REFLECTS ITSELF IN CHHAYALOKA (*the shadowy world of primal form, or the intellectual*) THE FIRST GARMENT OF (*the*) ANUPADAKA (*c*).

(*a*) This tracing of "Spiral lines" refers to the evolution of man's as well as Nature's principles; an evolution which takes place gradually (as will be seen in Book II., on "The origin of the Human Races"), as does everything else in nature. The Sixth principle in Man (Buddhi, the Divine Soul) though a mere breath, in our conceptions, is still something material when compared with divine "Spirit" (Atma) of which it is the carrier or vehicle. Fohat, in his capacity of DIVINE LOVE (*Eros*), the electric Power of affinity and sympathy, is shown allegorically as trying to bring the pure Spirit, the Ray inseparable from the ONE absolute, into union with the Soul, the two constituting in Man the MONAD, and in Nature the first link between the ever unconditioned and the manifested. "The first is now the second" (world) -- of the Lipikas -- has reference to the same.

(*b*) The "Army" at each angle is the Host of angelic Beings (Dhyan-Chohans) appointed to guide and watch over each respective region from the beginning to the end of Manvantara. They are the "Mystic Watchers" of the Christian Kabalists and Alchemists, and relate, symbolically as well as cosmogonically, to the numerical system of the Universe. The numbers with which these celestial Beings are connected are extremely difficult to explain, as each number refers to several groups of distinct ideas, according to the particular group of "Angels" which it is intended to represent. Herein lies the *nodus* in the study of symbology, with which, unable to untie by disentangling it, so many scholars have preferred dealing as Alexander dealt with the Gordian knot; hence erroneous conceptions and teachings, as a direct result.

The "First is the Second," because the "First" cannot really be numbered or regarded as the First, as that is the realm of noumena in its primary manifestation: the threshold to the World of Truth, or SAT, through which the direct energy that radiates from the ONE REALITY -- the Nameless Deity -- reaches us. Here again, the untranslateable term SAT (*Be-ness*) is likely to lead into an erroneous conception, since that which is manifested cannot be SAT, but is something phenomenal, not everlasting, nor, in truth, even sempiternal. It is coeval and coexistent with the One Life, "Secondless," but as a manifestation it is still a Maya -- like the rest. This "World of Truth" can be described only in the words of the Commentary as "A bright star dropped from the heart of Eternity; the beacon of hope on whose Seven Rays hang the Seven Worlds of Being." Truly so; since those are the Seven Lights whose reflections are the human immortal Monads -- the Atma, or the irradiating Spirit of every creature of the human family. First, this septenary Light; then: --

(*c*) The "Divine World" -- the countless Lights lit at the primeval Light -- the Buddhis, or formless divine Souls, of the last Arupa (formless) world; the "Sum Total," in the mysterious language of the old Stanza. In the Catechism, the Master is made to ask the pupil:

"*Lift thy head, oh Lanoo; dost thou see one, or countless lights above thee, burning in the dark midnight sky?*"

"*I sense one Flame, oh Gurudeva, I see countless undetached sparks shining in it.*"

"Thou sayest well. And now look around and into thyself. That light which burns inside thee, dost thou feel it different in anywise from the light that shines in thy Brother-men?"

"It is in no way different, though the prisoner is held in bondage by Karma, and though its outer garments delude the ignorant into saying, 'Thy Soul and My Soul.' "

The radical unity of the ultimate essence of each constituent part of compounds in Nature -- from Star to mineral Atom, from the highest Dhyan Chohan to the smallest infusoria, in the fullest acceptation of the term, and whether applied to the spiritual, intellectual, or physical worlds -- this is the one fundamental law in Occult Science. "The Deity is boundless and infinite expansion," says an Occult axiom; and hence, as remarked, the name of Brahma. There is a deep philosophy underlying the earliest worship in the world, that of the Sun and of Fire. Of all the Elements known to physical science, Fire is the one that has ever eluded definite analysis. It is confidently asserted that Air is a mixture containing the gases Oxygen and Nitrogen. We view the Universe and the Earth as matter composed of definite chemical molecules. We speak of the primitive ten Earths, endowing each with a Greek or Latin name. We say that water is, chemically, a compound of Oxygen and Hydrogen. But what is FIRE? It is the effect of combustion, we are gravely answered. It is heat and light and motion, and a correlation of physical and chemical forces in general. And this scientific definition is philosophically supplemented by the theological one in Webster's Dictionary, which explains fire as "the instrument of punishment, or the punishment of the impenitent in another state" -- the "state," by the bye, being supposed to be spiritual; but, alas! the presence of fire would seem to be a convincing proof of its material nature. Yet, speaking of the illusion of regarding phenomena as simple, because they are familiar, Professor Bain says (*Logic.* Part II.): "Very familiar facts seem to stand in no need of explanation themselves and to be the means of explaining whatever can be assimilated to them. Thus, the boiling and evaporation of a liquid is supposed to be a very simple phenomenon requiring no explanation, and a satisfactory explanation of rarer phenomena. That water should dry up is, to the uninstructed mind, a thing wholly intelligible; whereas to the man acquainted with physical science the liquid state is anomalous and inexplicable. The lighting of a fire by a flame is a GREAT SCIENTIFIC DIFFICULTY, yet few people think so" (p. 125).

What says the esoteric teaching with regard to fire? "Fire," it says, "is the most perfect and unadulterated reflection, in Heaven as on Earth, of the ONE FLAME. It is Life and Death, the origin and the end of every material thing. It is divine 'SUBSTANCE.' " Thus, not only the FIRE-WORSHIPPER, the Parsee, but even the wandering savage tribes of America, which proclaim themselves "born of fire," show more science in their creeds and truth in their superstitions, than all the speculations of modern physics and learning. The Christian who says: "God is a living Fire," and speaks of the Pentecostal "Tongues of Fire" and of the "burning bush" of Moses, is as much a fire-worshipper as any other "heathen." The Rosicrucians, among all the mystics and Kabalists, were those who defined Fire in the right and most correct way. Procure a sixpenny lamp, keep it only supplied with oil, and you will be able to light at its flame the lamps, candles, and fires of the whole globe without diminishing that flame. If the Deity, the radical One, is eternal and an infinite substance ("the Lord thy God is a consuming fire") and never consumed, then it does not seem reasonable that the Occult teaching should be held as unphilosophical when it says: "Thus were the Arupa and Rupa worlds formed: from ONE light seven lights; from each of the seven, seven times seven," etc., etc.

5. FOHAT TAKES FIVE STRIDES (*having already taken the first three*) (*a*), AND BUILDS A WINGED WHEEL AT EACH CORNER OF THE SQUARE FOR THE FOUR HOLY ONES . . . . . AND THEIR ARMIES (*hosts*) (*b*).

(*a*) The "strides," as already explained (see Commentary on Stanza **IV**.), refer to both the Cosmic and the Human principles -- the latter of which consist, in the exoteric division, of three (Spirit, Soul, and Body), and, in the esoteric calculation, of seven principles -- three rays of the Essence and four aspects. Those who have studied Mr. Sinnett's "*Esoteric Buddhism*" can easily grasp the nomenclature. There are two esoteric schools -- or rather one school, divided into two parts -- one for the inner Lanoos, the other for the outer or semi-lay chelas beyond the Himalayas; the first teaching a septenary, the other a six-fold division of human principles.

From a Cosmic point of view, Fohat taking "five strides" refers here to the five upper planes of Consciousness and Being, the sixth and the seventh (counting downwards) being the astral and the terrestrial, or the two lower planes.

(*b*) "Four winged wheels at each corner . . . . . for the four holy ones and their armies (hosts)" . . . . . These are the "four Maharajahs" or great Kings of the Dhyan-Chohans, the Devas who preside, each over one of the four cardinal points. They are the Regents or Angels who rule over the Cosmical Forces of North, South, East and West, Forces having each a distinct occult property. These BEINGS are also connected with Karma, as the latter needs physical and material agents to carry out her decrees, such as the four kinds of winds, for instance, professedly admitted by Science to have their respective evil and beneficent influences upon the health of Mankind and every living thing. There is occult philosophy in that Roman Catholic doctrine which traces the various public calamities, such as epidemics of disease, and wars, and so on, to the invisible "Messengers" from North and West. "The glory of God comes from the way of the East" says Ezekiel; while Jeremiah, Isaiah, and the Psalmist assure their readers that all the evil under the Sun comes from the North and the West -- which proposition, when applied to the Jewish nation, sounds like an undeniable prophecy for themselves. And this accounts also for St. Ambrose (On Amos, ch. iv.) declaring that it is precisely for that reason that "we curse the North-Wind, and that during the ceremony of baptism we begin by turning towards the West (Sidereal), to renounce the better him who inhabits it; after which we turn to the East."

Belief in the "Four Maharajahs" -- the Regents of the Four cardinal points -- was universal and is now that of Christians, who call them, after St. Augustine, "Angelic Virtues," and "Spirits" when enumerated by themselves, and "Devils" when named by Pagans. But where is the difference between the Pagans and the Christians in this cause? Following Plato, Aristotle explained that the term [[*stoicheia*]] was understood only as meaning the incorporeal principles placed at each of the four great divisions of our Cosmical world to supervise them. Thus, no more than the Christians did, do they *adore* and *worship* the Elements and the cardinal (imaginary) points, but the "gods" that ruled these respectively. For the Church there are two kinds of Sidereal beings, the Angels and the Devils. For the Kabalist and Occultist there is but one; and neither of them makes any difference between "the Rectors of Light" and the Cosmocratores, or "Rectores tenebrarum harum," whom the Roman Church imagines and discovers in a "Rector of Light" as soon as he is called by another name than the one she addresses him by. It is not the "Rector" or "Maharajah" who punishes or rewards, with or without "God's" permission or order, but man himself -- his deeds or Karma, attracting individually and collectively (as in the case of whole nations sometimes), every kind of evil and calamity. We produce CAUSES, and these awaken the corresponding powers in the sidereal world; which powers are magnetically and irresistibly attracted to -- and react upon -- those who produced these causes; whether such persons are practically the evil-doers, or simply Thinkers who brood mischief. Thought is matter, we are taught by modern Science; and "every particle of the existing matter must be a register of all that has happened," as in their "*Principles of Science*" Messrs. Jevons and Babbage tell the profane. Modern Science is drawn more every day into the maelstrom of Occultism; unconsciously, no doubt, still very sensibly. The two main theories of science -- *re* the relations between Mind and Matter -- are Monism and Materialism. These two cover the whole ground of negative psychology with the exception of the quasi-occult views of the pantheistic German schools.

The views of our present-day scientific thinkers as to the relations between mind and matter may be reduced to two hypotheses. These show that both views equally exclude the possibility of an independent Soul, distinct from the physical brain through which it functions. They are: --

(1.) **M**ATERIALISM, the theory which regards mental phenomena as the product of molecular change in the brain; *i.e.*, as the outcome of a transformation of motion into feeling (!). The cruder school once went so far as to identify mind with a "peculiar mode of motion" (!!), but this view is now happily regarded as absurd by most of the men of science themselves.

(2.) **M**ONISM, or the Single Substance Doctrine, is the more subtle form of negative psychology, which one of its advocates, Professor Bain, ably terms "guarded.

In the Egyptian temples, according to Clemens Alexandrinus, an immense curtain separated the tabernacle from the place for the congregation. The Jews had the same. In both, the curtain was drawn over five pillars (the Pentacle) symbolising our five senses and five Root-races esoterically, while the four colours of the curtain represented the four cardinal points and the four terrestrial elements. The whole was an allegorical symbol. It is through the four high Rulers over the four points and Elements that our five senses may become cognisant of the hidden truths of Nature; and not at all, as Clemens would have it, that it is the elements *per se* that furnished the Pagans with divine Knowledge or the knowledge of God. While the Egyptian emblem was spiritual, that of the Jews was purely materialistic, and, indeed, honoured only the blind Elements and the imaginary "Points." For what was the meaning of the square tabernacle raised by Moses in the wilderness, if it had not the same cosmical significance? "Thou shalt make an hanging . . . of blue, purple, and scarlet" and "five pillars of shittim wood for the hanging . . . four brazen rings in the four corners thereof . . . boards of fine wood for the four sides, North, South, West, and East . . . of the Tabernacle . . . with Cherubims of cunning work." (Exodus, ch. xxvi., xxvii.) The Tabernacle and the square courtyard, Cherubim and all, were precisely the same as those in the Egyptian temples. The square form of the Tabernacle meant just the same thing as it still means, to this day, in the exoteric worship of the Chinese and Tibetans -- the four cardinal points signifying that which the four sides of the pyramids, obelisks, and other such square erections mean. Josephus takes care to explain the whole thing. He declares that the Tabernacle pillars are the same as those raised at Tyre to the four Elements, which were placed on pedestals whose four angles faced the four cardinal points: adding that "the angles of the pedestals had equally the four figures of the Zodiac" on them, which represented the same orientation (*Antiquities I.,* VIII., ch. xxii.).

The idea may be traced in the Zoroastrian caves, in the rock-cut temples of India, as in all the sacred square buildings of antiquity that have survived to this day. This is shown definitely by Layard, who finds the four cardinal points, and the four primitive elements, in the religion of every country, under the shape of square obelisks, the four sides of the pyramids, etc., etc. Of these elements and their points the four Maharajahs were the regents and the directors.

If the student would know more of them, he has but to compare the Vision of Ezekiel (chap. i.) with what is known of Chinese Buddhism (even in its exoteric teachings); and examine the outward shape of these "Great Kings." In the opinion of the Rev. Joseph Edkins, they are "the Devas who preside each over one of the four continents into which the Hindus divide the world." Each leads an army of spiritual beings to protect mankind and Buddhism. With the exception of favouritism towards Buddhism, the four celestial beings are precisely this. They are the protectors of mankind and also the Agents of Karma on Earth, whereas the Lipika are concerned with Humanity's hereafter. At the same time they are the four living creatures "who have the likeness of a man" of Ezekiel's visions, called by the translators of the Bible, "Cherubim," "Seraphim," etc.; and by the Occultists, "the winged Globes," the "Fiery Wheels," and in the Hindu Pantheon by a number of different names. All these Gandharvas, the "Sweet Songsters," the Asuras, Kinnaras, and Nagas, are the allegorical descriptions of the "four Maharajahs." The Seraphim are the fiery Serpents of Heaven which we find in a passage describing Mount Meru as: "the exalted mass of glory, the venerable haunt of gods and heavenly choristers . . . . not to be reached by sinful men . . . . because guarded by Serpents." They are called the Avengers, and the "Winged Wheels."

Their mission and character being explained, let us see what the Christian Bible-interpreters say of the Cherubim: -- "The word signifies in Hebrew, fullness of knowledge; these angels are so called from their exquisite Knowledge, and were therefore used for the punishment of men who affected divine Knowledge." (Interpreted by Cruden in his Concordance, from Genesis iii., 24.) Very well; and vague as the information is, it shows that the Cherub placed at the gate of the garden of Eden after the "Fall," suggested to the venerable Interpreters the idea of punishment connected with forbidden Science or divine Knowledge -- one that generally leads to another "Fall," that of the gods, or "God," in man's estimation. But as the good old Cruden knew nought of Karma, he may be forgiven. Yet the allegory is suggestive. From Meru, the abode of gods, to Eden, the distance is very small, and from the Hindu Serpents to the Ophite Cherubim, the third out of the seven of which was the Dragon, the separation is still smaller, for both watched the entrance to the realm of Secret Knowledge. But Ezekiel plainly describes the four Cosmic Angels: "I looked, and behold, a whirlwind, a cloud and fire infolding it . . . also out of the midst thereof came the likeness of four living creatures . . . they had the likeness of a man. And every one had four faces and four wings . . . the face of a man, and the face of a lion, the face of an ox, and the face of an eagle . . . " ("Man" was here substituted for "Dragon." Compare the "*Ophite Spirits.*") . . . "Now as I beheld the living creatures behold one wheel upon the Earth with his four faces . . . as it were a wheel in the middle of a wheel . . . for the support of the living creature was in the wheel . . . their appearance was like coals of fire . . ." etc. (Ezekiel, ch. i.)

There are three chief groups of Builders and as many of the Planetary Spirits and the Lipika, each group being again divided into Seven sub-groups. It is impossible, even in such a large work as this, to enter into a minute examination of even the three principal groups, as it would demand an extra volume. The "Builders" are the representatives of the first "Mind-Born" Entities, therefore of the primeval Rishi-Prajapati: also of the Seven great Gods of Egypt, of which Osiris is the chief: of the Seven Amshaspends of the Zoroastrians, with Ormazd at their head: or the "Seven Spirits of the Face": the Seven Sephiroth separated from the first Triad, etc., etc.

They build or rather rebuild every "System" after the "Night." The Second group of the Builders is the Architect of our planetary chain exclusively; and the third, the progenitor of our Humanity -- the Macrocosmic prototype of the microcosm.

The Planetary Spirits are the informing spirits of the Stars in general, and of the Planets especially. They rule the destinies of men who are all born under one or other of their constellations; the second and third groups pertaining to other systems have the same functions, and all rule various departments in Nature. In the Hindu exoteric Pantheon they are the guardian deities who preside over the eight points of the compass -- the four cardinal and the four intermediate points -- and are called *Loka-Palas*, "Supporters or guardians of the World" (in our visible Kosmos), of which Indra (East), Yama (South), Varuna (West), and Kuvera (North) are the chief; their elephants and their spouses pertaining of course to fancy and afterthought, though all of them have an occult significance.

The Lipika (a description of whom is given in the Commentary on Stanza IV. No. 6) are the Spirits of the Universe, whereas the Builders are only our own planetary deities. The former belong to the most occult portion of Cosmogenesis, which cannot be given here. Whether the Adepts (even the highest) know this angelic order in the completeness of its triple degrees, or only the lower one connected with the records of our world, is something which the writer is unprepared to say, and she would incline rather to the latter supposition. Of its highest grade one thing only is taught: the Lipika are connected with Karma -- being its direct Recorders.

6. THE LIPIKA CIRCUMSCRIBE THE TRIANGLE, THE FIRST ONE (*the vertical line or the figure* 1.), THE CUBE, THE SECOND ONE, AND THE PENTACLE WITHIN THE EGG (*circle*) (*a*). IT IS THE RING CALLED "PASS NOT," FOR THOSE WHO DESCEND AND ASCEND (*as also for those*) WHO, DURING THE KALPA, ARE PROGRESSING TOWARD THE GREAT DAY "BE WITH US" (*b*). . . . THUS WERE FORMED THE ARUPA AND THE RUPA (*the Formless World*

and the World of Forms); FROM ONE LIGHT SEVEN LIGHTS; FROM EACH OF THE SEVEN SEVEN TIMES SEVEN LIGHTS. THE "WHEELS" WATCH THE RING.

The Stanza proceeds with a minute classification of the Orders of Angelic Hierarchy. From the group of Four and Seven emanates the "mind-born" group of Ten, of Twelve, of Twenty-one, etc., all these divided again into sub-groups of septenaries, novenaries, duodecimals, and so on, until the mind is lost in this endless enumeration of celestial hosts and Beings, each having its distinct task in the ruling of the visible Kosmos during its existence.

(*a*) The esoteric meaning of the first sentence of the Sloka is, that those who have been called Lipikas, the Recorders of the Karmic ledger, make an impassible barrier between the personal EGO and the impersonal SELF, the Noumenon and Parent-Source of the former. Hence the allegory. They circumscribe the manifested world of matter within the RING "Pass-Not." This world is the symbol (objective) of the ONE divided into the many, on the planes of Illusion, of Adi (the "First") or of Eka (the "One"); and this One is the collective aggregate, or totality, of the principal Creators or Architects of this visible universe. In Hebrew Occultism their name is both Achath, feminine, "One," and Achod, "One" again, but masculine. The monotheists have taken (and are still taking) advantage of the profound esotericism of the Kabala to apply the name by which the One Supreme Essence is known to ITS manifestation, the Sephiroth-Elohim, and call it Jehovah. But this is quite arbitrary and against all reason and logic, as the term Elohim is a plural noun, identical with the plural word *Chiim,* often compounded with the Elohim. Moreover, in Occult metaphysics there are, properly speaking, two "ONES" -- the One on the unreachable plane of Absoluteness and Infinity, on which no speculation is possible, and the Second "One" on the plane of Emanations. The former can neither emanate nor be divided, as it is eternal, absolute, and immutable. The Second, being, so to speak, the reflection of the first One (for it is the Logos, or Iswara, in the Universe of Illusion), can do all this.   It emanates from itself -- as the upper Sephirothal Triad emanates the lower seven Sephiroth -- the seven Rays or Dhyan Chohans; in other words, the Homogeneous becomes the Heterogeneous, the "Protyle" differentiates into the Elements. But these, unless they return into their primal Element, can never cross beyond the Laya, or zero-point.

Hence the allegory. The Lipika separate the world (or plane) of pure spirit from that of Matter. Those who "descend and ascend" -- the incarnating Monads, and men striving towards purification and "ascending," but still not having quite reached the goal -- may cross the "circle of the Pass-Not," only on the day "Be-With-Us"; that day when man, freeing himself from the trammels of ignorance, and recognising fully the non-separateness of the Ego within his personality -- erroneously regarded as his own -- from the UNIVERSAL EGO (Anima Supra-Mundi), merges thereby into the One Essence to become not only one "with us" (the manifested universal lives which are "ONE" LIFE), but that very life itself.

Astronomically, the "Ring PASS-NOT" that the Lipika trace around the Triangle, the First One, the Cube, the Second One, and the Pentacle to circumscribe these figures, is thus shown to contain the symbol of 31415 again, or the coefficient constantly used in mathematical tables (the value of , pi), the geometrical figures standing here for numerical figures. According to the general philosophical teachings, this ring is beyond the region of what are called nebulae in astronomy. But this is as erroneous a conception as that of the topography and the descriptions, given in Puranic and other exoteric Scriptures, about the 1008 worlds of the Devaloka worlds and firmaments. There are worlds, of course, in the esoteric as well as in the profane scientific teachings, at such incalculable distances that the light of the nearest of them which has just reached our modern Chaldees, had left its luminary long before the day on which the words "Let there be Light" were pronounced; but these are no worlds on the Devaloka plane, but in our Kosmos.

The chemist goes to the *laya* or zero point of the plane of matter with which he deals, and then stops short. The physicist or the astronomer counts by billions of miles beyond the nebulae, and then they also stop short; the semi-initiated Occultist will represent this laya-point to himself as existing on some plane which, if not physical, is still conceivable to the human intellect. But the full Initiate *knows* that the ring "Pass-Not" is neither a locality nor can it be measured by distance, but that it exists in the absoluteness of infinity. In this "Infinity" of the full Initiate there is neither height, breadth nor thickness, but all is fathomless profundity, reaching down from the physical to the "para-para-metaphysical." In using the word "down," essential depth -- "nowhere and everywhere" -- is meant, not depth of physical matter.

If one searches carefully through the exoteric and grossly anthropomorphic allegories of popular religions, even in these the doctrine embodied in the circle of "Pass-Not" thus guarded by the Lipika, may be dimly perceived. Thus one finds it even in the teachings of the Vedantin sect of the Visishtadwaita, the most tenaciously anthropomorphic in all India. For we read of the released soul that: --

After reaching Moksha (a state of bliss meaning "release from Bandha" or bondage), bliss is enjoyed by it in a place called PARAMAPADHA, which place is not material, but made of Suddasatwa (the essence, of which the body of Iswara -- "the Lord" -- is formed). There, Muktas or Jivatmas (Monads) who have attained Moksha, are never again subject to the qualities of either matter or Karma. "But if they choose, *for the sake of doing good to the world*, they may incarnate on Earth." The way to Paramapadha, or the immaterial worlds, from this world, is called Devayana. When a person has attained Moksha and the body dies:

"The Jiva (Soul) goes with Sukshma Sarira from the heart of the body, to the Brahmarandra in the crown of the head, traversing Sushumna, a nerve connecting the heart with the Brahmarandra. The Jiva breaks through the Brahmarandra and goes to the region of the Sun (Suryamandala) through the solar Rays. Then it goes, through a dark spot in the Sun, to Paramapadha. The Jiva is directed on its way by the Supreme Wisdom acquired by Yoga. The Jiva thus proceeds to Paramapadha by the aid of Athivahikas (bearers in transit), known by the names of Archi-Ahas . . . Aditya, Prajapati, etc. The Archis here mentioned are certain pure Souls, etc., etc." (Visishtadwaita Catechism, by Pundit Bhashyacharya, **F.T.S.**)

No Spirit except the "Recorders" (Lipika) has ever crossed its forbidden line, nor will any do so until the day of the next Pralaya, for it is the boundary that separates the finite -- however infinite in man's sight -- from the truly INFINITE. The Spirits referred to, therefore, as those who "ascend and descend" are the "Hosts" of what we loosely call "celestial Beings." But they are, in fact, nothing of the kind.

the right Path. Note well, "Christos" with the Gnostics meant the impersonal principal, the Atman of the Universe, and the Atma within every man's soul -- not Jesus; though in the old Coptic **MSS.** in the British Museum "Christos" is almost constantly replaced by "Jesus."

They are Entities of the higher worlds in the hierarchy of Being, so immeasurably high that, to us, they must appear as Gods, and collectively -- **GOD**. But so we, mortal men, must appear to the ant, which reasons on the scale of its special capacities. The ant may also, for all we know, see the avenging finger of a personal God in the hand of the urchin who, in one moment, under the impulse of mischief, destroys its anthill, the labour of many weeks -- long years in the chronology of insects. The ant, feeling it acutely, and attributing the undeserved calamity to a combination of Providence and sin, may also, like man, see in it the result of the sin of its first parent. Who knows and who can affirm or deny? The refusal to admit in the whole Solar system of any other reasonable and intellectual beings on the human plane, than ourselves, is the greatest conceit of our age. All that science has a right to affirm, is that there are no invisible Intelligences living under the same conditions as we do. It cannot deny point-blank the possibility of there being worlds within worlds, under totally different conditions to those that constitute the nature of our world; nor can it deny that there may be a certain limited communication between some of those worlds and our own. To the highest, we are taught, belong the seven orders of the purely divine Spirits; to the six lower ones belong hierarchies that can occasionally be seen and heard by men, and who do communicate with their progeny of the Earth; which progeny is indissolubly linked with them, each principle in man having its direct source in the nature of those great Beings, who furnish us with the respective invisible elements in us. Physical Science is welcome to speculate upon the physiological mechanism of living beings, and to continue her fruitless efforts in trying to resolve our feelings, our sensations, mental and spiritual, into functions of their inorganic vehicles. Nevertheless, all that will ever be accomplished in this direction has already been done, and Science will go no farther.

STANZA VI.

COMMENTARY

1. BY THE POWER OF THE MOTHER OF MERCY AND KNOWLEDGE (*a*), KWAN YIN, THE "TRIPLE" OF KWAN-SHAI-YIN, RESIDING IN KWAN-YIN-TIEN (*b*), FOHAT, THE BREATH OF THEIR PROGENY, THE SON OF THE SONS, HAVING CALLED FORTH FROM THE LOWER ABYSS (*chaos*) THE ILLUSIVE FORM OF SIEN-TCHAN (*our Universe*) AND THE SEVEN ELEMENTS: --

(*a.*) The Mother of Mercy and Knowledge is called "the triple" of Kwan-Shai-Yin because in her correlations, metaphysical and cosmical, she is the "Mother, the Wife and the Daughter" of the *Logos*, just as in the later theological translations she became "the Father, Son and (the female) Holy Ghost" -- the *Sakti* or Energy -- the Essence of the three. Thus in the Esotericism of the Vedantins, *Daiviprakriti*, the Light manifested through Eswara, the *Logos,* is at one and the same time the Mother and also the Daughter of the Logos or Verbum of Parabrahmam; while in that of the trans-Himalayan teachings it is -- in the hierarchy of allegorical and metaphysical theogony -- "the MOTHER" or abstract, ideal matter, Mulaprakriti, the Root of Nature; -- from the metaphysical standpoint, a correlation of Adi-Bhuta, manifested in the Logos, Avalokiteshwara; -- and from the purely occult and Cosmical, Fohat, the "Son of the Son," the androgynous energy resulting from this "Light of the Logos," and which manifests in the plane of the objective Universe as the hidden, as much as the revealed, Electricity -- which is LIFE.

(*b*) *Kwan-Yin-Tien* means the "melodious heaven of Sound," the abode of Kwan-Yin, or the "*Divine Voice*" literally. This "Voice" is a synonym of the *Verbum* or the Word: "Speech," as the expression of thought. Thus may be traced the connection with, and even the origin of the Hebrew *Bath-Kol,* the "daughter of the Divine Voice," or *Verbum,* or the male and female Logos, the "Heavenly Man" or Adam Kadmon, who is at the same time Sephira. The latter was surely anticipated by the Hindu Vach, the goddess of Speech, or of the Word. For Vach -- the daughter and the female portion, as is stated, of Brahma, one "generated by the gods" -- is, in company with Kwan-Yin, with Isis (also the *daughter,* wife and *sister* of Osiris) and other goddesses, the female *Logos,* so to speak, the goddess of the *active* forces in Nature, the Word, Voice or Sound, and Speech. If Kwan-Yin is the "melodious Voice," so is Vach; "the melodious cow who milked forth sustenance and water" (the female principle) -- "who yields us nourishment and sustenance," as Mother-Nature. She is associated in the work of creation with the Prajapati. She is male and female *ad libitum,* as Eve is with Adam. And she is a form of Aditi -- the principle higher than *Ether* -- in Akasa, the synthesis of all the forces in Nature; thus Vach and Kwan-Yin are both the magic potency of Occult sound in Nature and Ether -- which "Voice" calls forth Sien-Tchan, the illusive form of the Universe out of Chaos and the Seven Elements.

Thus in Manu Brahma (the *Logos* also) is shown dividing his body into two parts, male and female, and creating in the latter, who is Vach, Viraj, who is himself, or Brahma again -- it is in this way a learned Vedantin Occultist speaks of that "goddess," explaining the reason why Eswara (or Brahma) is called *Verbum* or *Logos*; why in fact it is called Sabda Brahmam: --

"The explanation I am going to give you will appear thoroughly mystical; but if mystical, it has a tremendous significance when properly understood. Our old writers said that *Vach* is of four kinds (see Rig Veda and the Upanishads). *Vaikhari-Vach* is what we utter. Every kind of *Vaikhari-Vach* exists in its *Madhyama,* further in its *Pasyanti,* and ultimately in its *Para* form. The reason why this Pranava is called Vach is this, that the four principles of the great Kosmos correspond to these four forms of *Vach*. Now the whole manifested solar System exists in its *Sukshma* form in the light or energy of the *Logos*, because its energy is caught up and transferred to Cosmic matter. . . . The whole Kosmos in its objective form is *Vaikhari-Vach*, the light of the *Logos* is the *Madhyama* form, and the Logos itself the *Pasyanti* form, and Parabrahm the *Para* form or aspect of that Vach. It is by the light of this explanation that we must try to understand certain statements made by various philosophers to the effect that the manifested Kosmos is the *Verbum* manifested as Kosmos" (see Lecture on the Bhagavadgita, referred to above).

2. THE **S**WIFT AND THE **R**ADIANT **O**NE PRODUCES THE SEVEN *Layu* (*a*) CENTRES, AGAINST WHICH NONE WILL PREVAIL TO THE GREAT DAY "**B**E WITH US" -- AND SEATS THE UNIVERSE ON THESE ETERNAL FOUNDATIONS, SURROUNDING **S**IEN-**T**CHAN WITH THE **E**LEMENTARY **G**ERMS (*b*).

(*a*.) The seven *Layu* centres are the seven Zero points, using the term Zero in the same sense that Chemists do, to indicate a point at which, in Esotericism, the scale of reckoning of differentiation begins. From the Centres -- beyond which Esoteric philosophy allows us to perceive the dim metaphysical outlines of the "Seven Sons" of Life and Light, the Seven Logoi of the Hermetic and all other philosophers -- begins the differentiation of the elements which enter into the constitution of our Solar System. It has often been asked what was the exact definition of Fohat and his powers and functions, as he seems to exercise those of a Personal God as understood in the popular religions. The answer has just been given in the comment on Stanza V. As well said in the Bhagavadgita Lectures, "The whole Kosmos must necessarily exist in the One Source of energy from which this light (*Fohat*) emanates." Whether we count the principles in Kosmos and man as seven or only as four, the forces of, and in, physical Nature are Seven; and it is stated by the same authority that "*Pragna*, or the capacity of perception, exists in seven different aspects corresponding to the seven conditions of matter" (*Personal and impersonal God*). For, "just as a human being is composed of seven principles, differentiated matter in the Solar System exists in seven different conditions" (*ibid*). So does Fohat. He is One and Seven, and on the Cosmic plane is behind all such manifestations as light, heat, sound, adhesion, etc., etc., and is the "spirit" of ELECTRICITY, which is the **L**IFE of the Universe. As an abstraction, we call it the **O**NE LIFE; as an objective and evident Reality, we speak of a septenary scale of manifestation, which begins at the upper rung with the One Unknowable **C**AUSALITY, and ends as Omnipresent Mind and Life immanent in every atom of Matter. Thus, while science speaks of its evolution through brute matter, blind force, and senseless motion, the Occultists point to *intelligent* LAW and *sentient* LIFE, and add that Fohat is the guiding Spirit of all this. Yet he is no personal god at all, but the emanation of those other Powers behind him whom the Christians call the "Messengers" of their God (who is in reality only the Elohim, or rather one of the Seven Creators called Elohim), and we, the "Messenger of the primordial Sons of Life and Light."

(*b*.) The "Elementary Germs" with which he fills Sien-Tchan (the "Universe") from Tien-Sin (the "Heaven of Mind," literally, or that which is absolute) are the Atoms of Science and the Monads of Leibnitz.

3. **O**F THE SEVEN (*elements*) -- FIRST ONE MANIFESTED, SIX CONCEALED; TWO MANIFESTED -- FIVE CONCEALED; THREE MANIFESTED -- FOUR CONCEALED; FOUR PRODUCED -- THREE HIDDEN; FOUR AND ONE TSAN (*fraction*) REVEALED -- TWO AND ONE HALF CONCEALED; SIX TO BE MANIFESTED -- ONE LAID ASIDE (*a*). LASTLY, SEVEN SMALL WHEELS REVOLVING; ONE GIVING BIRTH TO THE OTHER (*b*).

(*a*.) Although these Stanzas refer to the whole Universe after a Mahapralaya (universal destruction), yet this sentence, as any student of Occultism may see, refers also by analogy to the evolution and final formation of the primitive (though compound) Seven Elements on our Earth. Of these, four elements are now fully manifested, while the fifth -- Ether -- is only partially so, as we are hardly in the second half of the Fourth Round, and consequently the fifth Element will manifest fully only in the Fifth Round. The Worlds, including our own, were of course, as germs, primarily evolved from the ONE Element in its second stage ("Father-Mother," the differentiated World's Soul, not what is termed the "Over-Soul" by Emerson), whether we call it, with modern Science, Cosmic dust and Fire Mist, or with Occultism -- Akasa, Jivatma, divine Astral Light, or the "Soul of the World." But this first stage of Evolution was in due course of time followed by the next. No world, as no heavenly body, could be constructed on the objective plane, had not the Elements been sufficiently differentiated already from their primeval *Ilus*, resting in *Laya.* The latter term is a synonym of Nirvana. It is, in fact, the Nirvanic dissociation of all substances, merged after a life-cycle into the latency of their primary conditions. It is the luminous but bodiless shadow of the matter *that was*, the realm of negativeness -- wherein lie latent during their period of rest the active Forces of the Universe. Now, speaking of Elements, it is made the standing reproach of the Ancients, that they "supposed their Elements simple and undecomposable." Once more this is an unwarrantable statement; as, at any rate, their initiated philosophers can hardly come under such an imputation, since it is they who have invented allegories and religious myths from the beginning. Had they been ignorant of the Heterogeneity of their Elements they would have had no personifications of Fire, Air, Water, Earth, and AEther; their Cosmic gods and goddesses would never have been blessed with such posterity, with so many sons and daughters, elements born *from* and *within each respective Element.* Alchemy and occult phenomena would have been a delusion and a snare, even in theory, had the Ancients been ignorant of the potentialities and correlative functions and attributes of every element that enters into the composition of Air, Water, Earth, and even *Fire* -- the latter a terra incognita to this day to modern Science, which is obliged to call it Motion, evolution of light and heat, state of ignition, -- defining it by its outward aspects in short, and remaining ignorant of its nature. But that which modern Science seems to fail to perceive is that, differentiated as may have been those simple chemical atoms -- which archaic philosophy called "the creators of their respective Parents," fathers, brothers, husbands of their mothers, and those mothers the daughters of their own sons, like Aditi and Daksha, for example -- differentiated as these elements were in the beginning, still, they were not the compound bodies known to science, as they are now. Neither Water, Air, Earth (synonym for solids generally) existed in their present form, representing the three states of matter alone recognised by Science; for all these are the productions already recombined by the atmospheres of globes completely formed -- even to fire -- so that in the first periods of the earth's formation they were something quite *sui generis.* Now that the conditions and laws ruling our solar system are fully developed; and that the atmosphere of our earth, as of every other globe, has become, so to say, a crucible of its own, Occult Science teaches that there is a perpetual exchange taking place in space of molecules, or of atoms rather, correlating, and thus changing their combining equivalents on every planet. Some men of Science, and those among the greatest physicists and chemists, begin to suspect this fact, which has been known for ages to the Occultists. The spectroscope only shows the probable similarity (on external evidence) of terrestrial and sidereal substance; it is unable to go any farther, or to show whether atoms gravitate towards one another in the same way and under the same conditions as they are supposed to do on our planet, physically and chemically. The scale of temperature, from the highest degree to the lowest that can be conceived of, may be imagined to be one and the same in and for the whole Universe; nevertheless, its properties, other than those of dissociation and reassociation, differ on every planet; and thus atoms enter into new forms of existence, undreamt of, and incognizable to, physical Science. As already expressed in "Five Years of Theosophy," the essence of Cometary matter, for instance, "is totally different from any of the chemical or physical characteristics with which the greatest chemists and physicists of the earth are acquainted" (p. 242). And even that matter, during rapid passage through our atmosphere, undergoes a certain change in its nature. Thus not alone the elements of our planets, but even those of all its sisters in the Solar System, differ as widely from each other in their combinations, as from the Cosmic elements beyond our Solar limits. Therefore, they cannot be taken as a standard for comparison with the same in other worlds. Enshrined in their virgin, pristine state within the bosom of the Eternal Mother, every atom born beyond the threshold of her realm is doomed to incessant differentiation. "The Mother sleeps, yet is ever breathing." And every breath sends out into the plane of manifestation her Protean products, which, carried on by the wave of the efflux, are scattered by Fohat, and driven toward and beyond this or another planetary atmosphere. Once caught by the latter, the atom is lost; its pristine purity is gone for ever, unless Fate dissociates it by leading it to "a current of EFFLUX" (an occult term meaning quite a different process from that which the ordinary term implies); when it may be carried once more to the borderland where it had perished, and taking its flight, not into Space *above* but into Space *within*, it will be brought under a state of differential equilibrium and happily re-absorbed. Were a truly learned Occultist-alchemist to write the "Life and Adventures of an Atom" he would secure thereby the eternal scorn of the modern chemist, perchance also his subsequent gratitude. However it may be, "*The Breath of the Father-Mother issues cold and radiant and gets hot and corrupt, to cool once more, and be purified in the eternal bosom of inner Space*," says the Commentary. Man absorbs cold pure air on the mountain-top, and throws it out impure, hot and transformed. Thus -- the higher atmosphere being the mouth, and the lower one the lungs of every globe -- the man of our planet breathes only the refuse of "Mother"; therefore, "he is doomed to die on it."

(*b*) The process referred to as "the small wheels giving birth, one to the other," takes place in the sixth region from above, and on the plane of the most material world of all in the manifested Kosmos -- our terrestrial plane. These "Seven Wheels" are our planetary chain (see Commentary Nos. 5 and 6). By "Wheels" the various spheres and centres of forces are generally meant; but in this case they refer to our septenary ring.

4. HE BUILDS THEM IN THE LIKENESS OF OLDER WHEELS (*worlds*), PLACING THEM ON THE IMPERISHABLE CENTRES (*a*).

HOW DOES FOHAT BUILD THEM? HE COLLECTS THE FIERY DUST. HE MAKES BALLS OF FIRE, RUNS THROUGH THEM AND ROUND THEM, INFUSING LIFE THEREINTO; THEN SETS THEM INTO MOTION, SOME ONE, SOME THE OTHER WAY. THEY ARE COLD -- HE MAKES THEM HOT. THEY ARE DRY -- HE MAKES THEM MOIST. THEY SHINE -- HE FANS AND COOLS THEM (*b*).

THUS ACTS FOHAT FROM ONE *Twilight* TO THE OTHER DURING SEVEN ETERNITIES.

(*a*) The Worlds are built "in the likeness of older Wheels" -- *i.e.*, those that existed in preceding Manvantaras and went into Pralaya, because the LAW for the birth, growth, and decay of everything in Kosmos, from the Sun to the glow-worm in the grass, is ONE. It is an everlasting work of perfection with every new appearance, but the Substance-Matter and Forces are all one and the same. But this LAW acts on every planet through minor and varying laws. The "imperishable Laya Centres" have a great importance, and their meaning must be fully understood if we would have a clear conception of the Archaic Cosmogony, whose theories have now passed into Occultism. At present, one thing may be stated. The worlds are built neither *upon*, nor *over*, nor *in* the *Laya* centres, the zero-point being a condition, not any mathematical point.

(*b*) Bear in mind that Fohat, the constructive Force of Cosmic Electricity, is said, metaphorically, to have sprung like Rudra from Brahma "from the brain of the Father and the bosom of the Mother," and then to have metamorphosed himself into a male and a female, *i.e.*, polarity, into positive and negative electricity. He has *seven sons* who are *his brothers;* and Fohat is forced to be born time after time whenever any two of his son-brothers indulge *in too close contact* -- whether an embrace or a fight. To avoid this, he binds together and unites those of unlike nature and separates those of similar temperaments. This, of course, relates, as any one can see, to electricity generated by friction and to the law involving attraction between two objects of unlike, and repulsion between those of like polarity. The Seven "Sons-brothers," however, represent and personify the seven forms of Cosmic magnetism called in *practical Occultism* the "Seven Radicals," whose co-operative and active progeny are, among other energies, Electricity, Magnetism, Sound, Light, Heat, Cohesion, etc. Occult Science defines all these as Super-sensuous effects in their hidden behaviour, and as objective phenomena in the world of senses; the former requiring abnormal faculties to perceive them -- the latter, our ordinary physical senses. They all pertain to, and are the emanations of, still more supersensuous spiritual qualities, not personated by, but belonging to, real and conscious CAUSES. To attempt a description of such ENTITIES would be worse than useless. The reader must bear in mind that, according to our teaching which regards this phenomenal Universe as a great *Illusion*, the nearer a body is to the UNKNOWN SUBSTANCE, the more it approaches *reality*, as being removed the farther from this world of *Maya*. Therefore, though the molecular constitution of their bodies is not deducible from their manifestations on this plane of consciousness, they nevertheless (from the standpoint of the adept Occultist) possess a distinctive objective if not material structure, in the relatively noumenal -- as opposed to the phenomenal -- Universe. Men of science may term them Force or Forces generated by matter, or "modes of its motion," if they will; Occultism sees in the effects "Elemental" (forces), and, in the direct causes producing them, intelligent DIVINE Workmen. The intimate connection of those Elementals (guided by the unerring hand of the Rulers) -- their correlation we might call it -- with the elements of pure Matter, results in our terrestrial phenomena, such as light, heat, magnetism, etc., etc. Of course we shall never agree with the American Substantialists who call every Force and Energy -- whether Light, Heat, Electricity or Cohesion -- an "Entity"; for this would be equivalent to calling the noise produced by the rolling of the wheels of a vehicle an *Entity* -- thus confusing and identifying that "noise" with the driver *outside*, and the guiding Master Intelligence *within* the vehicle. But we certainly give that name to the "drivers" and to these guiding Intelligences -- the ruling Dhyan Chohans, as shown. The "Elementals," the Nature-Forces, are the acting, though invisible, or rather imperceptible, secondary Causes and in themselves the effects of primary Causes behind the Veil of all terrestrial phenomena. Electricity, light, heat, etc., have been aptly termed the "Ghost or Shadow of Matter in Motion," *i.e.*, supersensuous states of matter whose effects only we are able to cognize. To expand, then, the simile given above. The sensation of light is like the sound of the rolling wheels -- a purely phenomenal effect, having no existence outside the observer; the proximate exciting cause of the sensation is comparable to the driver -- a supersensuous state of matter in motion, a Nature-Force or Elemental. But, behind even this, stand -- just as the owner of the carriage directs the driver from within -- the higher and *noumenal* causes, the *Intelligences* from whose essence radiate these States of "*Mother*," generating the countless milliards of Elementals or psychic Nature-Spirits, just as every drop of water generates its physical infinitesimal Infusoria. (See "Gods, Monads, and Atoms," in Part III.) It is Fohat who guides the transfer of the principles from one planet to the other, from one star to another -- child-star. When a planet dies, its informing principles are transferred to a *laya* or sleeping centre, with potential but latent energy in it, which is thus awakened into life and begins to form itself into a new sidereal body. (*Vide infra*, "A Few Theosophical Misconceptions, etc.")

It is most remarkable that, while honestly confessing their entire ignorance of the true Nature of even terrestrial matter -- primordial substance being regarded more as a dream than as a sober reality -- the physicists should set themselves up as judges, nevertheless, of that matter, and claim to know what it is able and is not able to do, in various combinations. Scientists know it (matter) hardly skin-deep, and yet they will dogmatise. It is "a mode of motion" and nothing else. But the *force* that is inherent in a living person's breath, when blowing a speck of dust from the table, is also, and undeniably, "a mode of motion"; and it is as undeniably not a quality of the matter, or the particles of that speck, and it emanates from the living and thinking Entity that breathed, whether the impulse originated consciously or unconsciously. Indeed, to endow matter -- something of which nothing is known so far -- with an inherent quality called Force, of the nature of which still less is known, is to create a far more serious difficulty than that which lies in the acceptation of the intervention of our "Nature-Spirits" in every natural phenomenon.

The Occultists, who do not say -- if they would express themselves correctly -- that *matter*, but only the *substance* or *essence* of matter, is indestructible and eternal, (*i.e.*, the Root of all, *Mulaprakriti*): assert that all the so-called Forces of Nature, Electricity, Magnetism, Light, Heat, etc., etc., far from being modes of motion of material particles, are *in esse*, *i.e.*, in their ultimate constitution, the differentiated aspects of that Universal Motion which is discussed and explained in the first pages of this volume (*See Proem*). When Fohat is said to produce "Seven Laya Centres," it means that for formative or creative purposes, the GREAT LAW (Theists may call it God) stops, or rather modifies its perpetual motion on seven invisible points within the area of the manifested Universe. "*The great Breath digs through Space seven holes into Laya to cause them to circumgyrate during Manvantara*" (Occult Catechism). We have said that Laya is what Science may call the Zero-point or line; the realm of absolute negativeness, or the one real absolute Force, the NOUMENON of the Seventh State of that which we ignorantly call and recognise as "Force"; or again the Noumenon of Undifferentiated Cosmic Substance which is itself an unreachable and unknowable object to finite perception; the root and basis of all states of objectivity and subjectivity too; the neutral axis, not one of the many aspects, but its centre. It may serve to elucidate the meaning if we attempt to imagine a neutral centre -- the dream of those who would discover perpetual motion. A "neutral centre" is, in one aspect, the limiting point of any given set of senses. Thus, imagine two consecutive planes of matter as already formed; each of these corresponding to an appropriate set of perceptive organs. We are forced to admit that between these two planes of matter an incessant circulation takes place; and if we follow the atoms and molecules of (say) the lower in their transformation upwards, these will come to a point where they pass altogether beyond the range of the faculties we are using on the lower plane. In fact, to us the matter of the lower plane there vanishes from our perception into nothing -- or rather it passes on to the higher plane, and the state of matter corresponding to such a point of transition must certainly possess special and not readily discoverable properties. Such "Seven Neutral Centres," then, are produced by Fohat, who, when, as Milton has it --

"Fair foundations (are) laid whereon to build . . ."
quickens matter into activity and evolution.

The *Primordial Atom* (*anu*) cannot be multiplied either in its pregenetic state, or its primogeneity; therefore it is called "SUM TOTAL," figuratively, of course, as that "SUM TOTAL" is boundless. (See Addendum to this Book.) That which is the abyss of nothingness to the physicist, who knows only the world of visible causes and effects, is the boundless Space of the Divine *Plenum* to the Occultist. Among many other objections to the doctrine of an endless evolution and re-involution (or re-absorption) of the Kosmos, a process which, according to the Brahminical and Esoteric Doctrine, is without a beginning or an end, the Occultist is told that it cannot be, since "by all the admissions of modern scientific philosophy it is a necessity of Nature to run down." If the tendency of Nature "to run down" is to be considered so forcible an objection to Occult Cosmogony, "How," we may ask, "do your Positivists and Free-thinkers and Scientists account for the phalanx around us of active stellar systems?" They had eternity to "run down" in; why, then, is not the Kosmos a huge inert mass? Even the moon is only hypothetically believed to be a dead planet, "run down," and astronomy does not seem to be acquainted with many such dead planets. The query is unanswerable. But apart from this it must be noted that the idea of the amount of "transformable energy" in our little system coming to an end is based purely on the fallacious conception of a "white-hot, incandescent Sun" perpetually radiating away his heat without compensation into Space. To this we reply that nature runs down and disappears from the objective plane, only to re-emerge after a time of rest out of the subjective and to reascend once more. Our Kosmos and Nature will run down only to reappear on a more perfect plane after every PRALAYA. The *matter* of the Eastern philosophers is not the "matter" and Nature of the Western metaphysicians. For what is Matter? And above all, what is our scientific philosophy but that which was so justly and so politely defined by Kant as "the Science of the *limits* to our Knowledge"? Where have the many attempts made by Science to bind, to connect, and define all the phenomena of organic life by mere physical and chemical manifestations, brought it to? To speculation generally -- mere soap-bubbles, that burst one after the other before the men of Science were permitted to discover real facts. All this would have been avoided, and the progress of knowledge would have proceeded with gigantic strides, had only Science and its philosophy abstained from accepting hypotheses on the mere one-sided Knowledge of *their* Matter.

If no physical intellect is capable of counting the grains of sand covering a few miles of sea-shore; or to fathom the ultimate nature and essence of those grains, palpable and visible on the palm of the naturalist, how can any materialist limit the laws changing the conditions and being of the atoms in primordial chaos, or know anything certain about the capabilities and potency of their atoms and molecules before and after their formation into worlds? These changeless and eternal molecules -- far thicker in space than the grains on the ocean shore -- may differ in their constitution along the line of their planes of existence, as the soul-substance differs from its vehicle, the body. Each atom has seven planes of being or existence, we are taught; and each plane is governed by its specific laws of evolution and absorption. Ignorant of any, even approximate, chronological data from which to start in attempting to decide the age of our planet or the origin of the solar system, astronomers, geologists, and physicists are drifting with each new hypothesis farther and farther away from the shores of fact into the fathomless depths of speculative ontology. The Law of Analogy in the plan of structure between the trans-Solar systems and the intra-Solar planets, does not necessarily bear upon the finite conditions to which every visible body is subject, in this our plane of being. In Occult Science this law is the first and most important key to Cosmic physics; but it has to be studied in its minutest details and, "to be turned seven times," before one comes to understand it. Occult philosophy is the only science that can teach it. How, then, can anyone hang the truth or the untruth of the Occultist's proposition that "the Kosmos is eternal in its unconditioned collectivity, and finite but in its conditioned manifestations" on this one-sided physical enunciation that "it is a necessity of Nature to run down?"

With these verses -- the 4th Sloka of Stanza VI. -- ends that portion of the Stanzas which relates to the Universal Cosmogony after the last Mahapralaya or Universal destruction, which, when it comes, sweeps out of Space every differentiated thing, Gods as atoms, like so many dry leaves. From this verse onwards, the Stanzas are concerned only with our Solar System in general, with the planetary chains therein, inferentially, and with the history of our globe (the 4th and its chain) especially. All the Stanzas and verses which follow in this Book I. refer only to the evolution of, and on, our Earth. With regard to the latter, a strange tenet -- strange from the modern scientific stand-point only, of course -- is held, which ought to be made known.

But before entirely new and rather startling theories are presented to the reader, they must be prefaced by a few words of explanation. This is absolutely necessary, as these theories clash not only with modern science, but contradict, on certain points, earlier statements made by other Theosophists, who claim to base their explanations and renderings of these teachings on the same authority as we do.

This may give rise to the idea that there is a decided contradiction between the expounders of the same doctrine; whereas the difference, in reality, arises from the incompleteness of the information given to earlier writers, who thus drew some erroneous conclusions and indulged in premature speculations, in their endeavour to present a complete system to the public. Thus the reader, who is already a student of Theosophy, must not be surprised to find in these pages the rectification of certain statements made in various Theosophical works, and also the explanation of certain points which have remained obscure, because they were necessarily left incomplete. Many are the questions upon which even the author of "Esoteric Buddhism" (the best and most accurate of all such works) has not touched. On the other hand, even he has introduced several mistaken notions which must now be presented in their true mystic light, as far as the present writer is capable of doing so.

Let us then make a short break between the Slokas just explained and those which follow, for the Cosmic periods which separate them are of immense duration. This will afford us ample time to take a bird's eye view of some points pertaining to the Secret Doctrine, which have been presented to the public under a more or less uncertain and sometimes mistaken light.

A FEW EARLY THEOSOPHICAL MISCONCEPTIONS
CONCERNING PLANETS, ROUNDS, AND MAN

Among the eleven Stanzas omitted there is one which gives a full description of the formation of the planetary chains one after another, after the first Cosmic and Atomic differentiation had commenced in the primitive *Acosmism*. It is idle to speak of "laws arising when Deity prepares to create" for (*a*) laws or rather LAW is eternal and uncreated; and (*b*) that Deity is Law, and *vice versa*. Moreover, the one eternal LAW unfolds everything in the (to be) manifested Nature on a sevenfold principle; among the rest, the countless circular chains of worlds, composed of seven globes, graduated on the four lower planes of the world of formation (the three others belonging to the Archetypal Universe). Out of these seven only *one, the lowest and the most material of those globes*, is within our plane or means of perception, the six others lying outside of it and being therefore invisible to the terrestrial eye. Every such chain of worlds is the progeny and creation of another, *lower*, and *dead* chain -- *its reincarnation*, so to say. To make it clearer: we are told of the planets -- of which *seven only* were held as sacred, as being ruled by the highest regents or gods, and not at all because the ancients knew nothing of the others   -- that each of these, whether known or unknown, is a septenary, as is the chain to which the Earth belongs (see "Esoteric Buddhism"). For instance, all such planets as Mercury, Venus, Mars, Jupiter, Saturn, etc., etc., or our Earth, are as visible to us as our globe, probably, is to the inhabitants of the other planets, if any, because they are all on the same plane; while the superior fellow-globes of these planets are on other planes quite outside that of our terrestrial senses. As their relative position is given further on, and also in the diagram appended to the Comments on Verse 7 of Stanza VI., a few words of explanation is all that is needed at present. These invisible companions correspond curiously to that which we call "the principles in Man." The seven are on three material planes and one spiritual plane, answering to the three *Upadhis* (material bases) and one spiritual vehicle (*Vahan*) of our seven principles in the human division. If, for the sake of a clearer mental conception, we imagine the human principles to be arranged as in the following scheme, we shall obtain the annexed diagram of correspondences: --

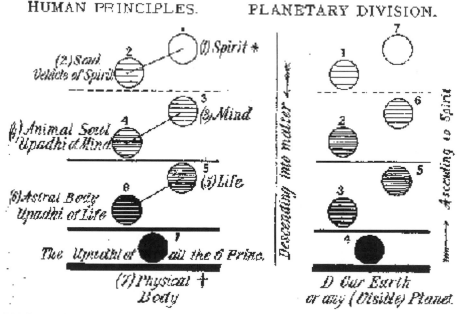

DIAGRAM I.

The dark horizontal lines of the lower planes are the Upadhis in one case, and the planes in the case of the planetary chain. Of course, as regards the human principles, the diagram does not place them quite in order, yet it shows the correspondence and analogy to which attention is now drawn. As the reader will see, it is a case of descent into matter, the adjustment -- in both the mystic and the physical senses -- of the two, and their interblending for the great coming "struggle of life" that awaits both the *entities*. "Entity" may be thought a strange term to use in the case of a globe; but the ancient philosophers, who saw in the earth a huge "animal," were wiser in their generation than our modern geologists are in theirs; and Pliny, who called the Earth our kind nurse and mother, the only element which is not inimical to man, spoke more truly than Watts, who fancied that he saw in her the footstool of God. For Earth is only the footstool of man in his ascension to higher regions; the vestibule --

".   .   .   .   .   .   . *to glorious mansions,*
Through which a moving crowd for ever press."

But this only shows how admirably the occult philosophy fits everything in Nature, and how much more logical are its tenets than the lifeless hypothetical speculations of physical science.

Having learned thus much, the mystic will be better prepared to understand the occult teaching, though every formal student of modern science may, and probably will, regard it as preposterous nonsense. The student of occultism, however, holds that the theory at present under discussion is far more philosophical and probable than any other. It is more logical, at any rate, than the theory recently advanced which made of the moon the projection of a portion of our Earth extruded when the latter was but a globe in fusion, a molten plastic mass.

It is said that the planetary chains having their "Days" and their "Nights" -- *i.e.*, periods of activity or life, and of inertia or death -- and behave in heaven as do men on Earth: they generate their likes, get old, and become personally extinct, their spiritual principles only living in their progeny as a survival of themselves.

Without attempting the very difficult task of giving out the whole process in all its cosmic details, enough may be said to give an approximate idea of it. When a planetary chain is in its last Round, its Globe 1 or A, before finally *dying out*, sends all its energy and "principles" into a neutral centre of latent force, a "laya centre," and thereby informs a new nucleus of undifferentiated substance or matter, *i.e.*, calls it into activity or gives it life. Suppose such a process to have taken place in the lunar "planetary" chain; suppose again, for argument's sake (though Mr. Darwin's theory quoted below has lately been upset, even if the fact has not yet been ascertained by mathematical calculation) that the moon is far older than the Earth. Imagine the six fellow-globes of the moon -- aeons before the first globe of our seven was evolved -- just in the same position in relation to each other as the fellow-globes of our chain occupy in regard to our Earth now. (See in "Esoteric Buddhism," "The Constitution of Man," and the "Planetary Chain.") And now it will be easy to imagine further Globe A of the lunar chain informing Globe A of the terrestrial chain, and -- dying; Globe B of the former sending after that its energy into Globe B of the new chain; then Globe C of the lunar, creating its progeny sphere C of the terrene chain; then the Moon (our Satellite) pouring forth into SEPTENARY DIVISION IN DIFFERENT INDIAN SYSTEMS.

"We give below in a tabular form the classifications adopted by the Buddhist and Vedantic teachers of the principles of man: --

Classification in Esoteric Buddhism.	Vedantic Classification.	Classification in Taraka Raja Yoga.
1. Sthula Sarira.	Annamaya kosa.*	Sthulopadhi.§
2. Prana.†		
3. The vehicle of Prana.‡	Pranamaya kosa.	
4. Kama Rupa.		
5. Mind (a) Volitions and feelings, etc.	Manomaya kosa.	Sukshmopadhi.
(b) Vignanam.	Vignanamaya kosa.	
6. Spiritual Soul.‖	Anandamaya kosa.	Karanopadhi.
7. Atma.	Atma.	Atma.

Kosa (kosha) is "Sheath" literally, the sheath of every principle.
† "Life."
‡ The astral body or Linga Sarira.
§ Sthula-Upadhi, or basis of the principle.
‖ Buddhi.

From the foregoing table it will be seen that the third principle in the Buddhist classification is not separately mentioned in the Vedantic division, as it is merely the vehicle of Prana. It will also be seen that the Fourth principle is included in the third Kosa (Sheath), as the same principle is but the vehicle of will-power, which is but an energy of the mind. It must also be noticed that the Vignanamaya Kosa is considered to be distinct from the Manomaya Kosa, as a division is made after death between the lower part of the mind, as it were, which has a closer affinity with the fourth principle than with the sixth; and its higher part, which attaches itself to the latter, and which is, in fact, the basis for the higher spiritual individuality of man.

We may also here point out to our readers that the classification mentioned in the last column is, for all practical purposes, connected with Raja Yoga, the best and simplest. Though there are seven principles in man, there are but three distinct Upadhis (bases), in each of which his Atma may work independently of the rest. These three Upadhis can be separated by an Adept without killing himself. He cannot separate the seven principles from each other without destroying his constitution."

The student will now be better prepared to see that between the three Upadhis of the Raja Yoga and its Atma, and our three Upadhis, Atma, and the additional three divisions, there is in reality but very little difference. Moreover, as every adept in cis-Himalayan or trans-Himalayan India, of the Patanjali, the Aryasanga or the Mahayana schools, has to become a Raja Yogi, he must, therefore, accept the Taraka Raja classification in principle and theory whatever classification he resorts to for practical and occult purposes. Thus, it matters very little whether one speaks of the *three Upadhis with their three aspects* and Atma, the eternal and immortal synthesis, or calls them the "seven principles."

For the benefit of those who may not have read, or, if they have, may not have clearly understood, in Theosophical writings, the doctrine of the septenary chains of worlds in the Solar Kosmos, the teaching is briefly thus: --

1. Everything in the metaphysical as in the physical Universe is septenary. Hence every sidereal body, every planet, whether visibleor invisible, is credited with six companion globes. (See Diagram No. 3, after verse 6 of this commentary.) The evolution of life proceeds on these seven globes or bodies from the 1st to the 7th in Seven **ROUNDS** or Seven Cycles.

2. These globes are formed by a process which the Occultists call the "rebirth of planetary chains (or rings)." When the seventh and last Round of one of such rings has been entered upon, the highest or first globe "A," followed by all the others down to the last, instead of entering upon a certain time of rest -- or "obscuration," as in their previous Rounds -- begins to die out. The "planetary" dissolution (*pralaya*) is at hand, and its hour has struck; each globe has to transfer its life and energy to another planet. (See diagram No. 2 *infra*, "The Moon and the Earth.")

3. Our Earth, as the visible representative of its invisible superior fellow globes, its "lords" or "principles" (see diagram No. 1), has to live, as have the others, through seven Rounds. During the first three, it forms and consolidates; during the fourth it settles and hardens; during the last three it gradually returns to its first ethereal form: it is spiritualised, so to say.

4. Its Humanity develops fully only in the Fourth -- our present Round. Up to this fourth Life-Cycle, it is referred to as "humanity" only for lack of a more appropriate term. Like the grub which becomes chrysalis and butterfly, Man, or rather that which becomes man, passes through all the forms and kingdoms during the first Round and through all the human shapes during the two following Rounds. Arrived on our Earth at the commencement of the Fourth in the present series of life-cycles and races, MAN is the first form that appears thereon, being preceded only by the mineral and vegetable kingdoms -- even the latter *having to develop and continue its further evolution through man*. This will be explained in Book II. During the three Rounds to come, Humanity, like the globe on which it lives, will be ever tending to reassume its primeval form, that of a Dhyan Chohanic Host. Man tends to become a God and then -- **G**OD, like every other atom in the Universe.

"Beginning so early as with the 2nd round, Evolution proceeds already on quite a different plan. It is only during the 1st round that (heavenly) man becomes a human being on globe A (rebecomes) a mineral, a plant, an animal, on globe B and C, etc. The process changes entirely from the second round -- but you have learned prudence . . . and I advise you *to say nothing before the time for saying it has come. . .*" (Extract from the Teacher's letters on various topics.)

5. Every life-cycle on Globe D (our Earth) is composed of seven root-races. They commence with the Ethereal and end with the spiritual on the double line of physical and moral evolution -- from the beginning of the terrestrial round to its close. (One is a "planetary round" from Globe A to Globe G, the seventh; the other, the "globe round," or the *terrestrial*).

This is very well described in "Esoteric Buddhism" and needs no further elucidation for the time being.

6. The first root-race, *i.e.*, the first "men" on earth (irrespective of form) were the progeny of the "celestial men," called rightly in Indian philosophy the "Lunar Ancestors" or the Pitris, of which there are seven classes or Hierarchies. As all this will be sufficiently explained in the following sections and in Book II., no more need be said of it here.

But the two works already mentioned, both of which treat of subjects from the occult doctrine, need particular notice. "Esoteric Buddhism" is too well known in Theosophical circles, and even to the outside world, for it to be necessary to enter at length upon its merits here. It is an excellent book, and has done still more excellent work. But this does not alter the fact that it contains some mistaken notions, and that it has led many Theosophists and lay-readers to form an erroneous conception of the Secret Eastern Doctrines. Moreover it seems, perhaps, a little too materialistic.

"MAN," which came later, was an attempt to present the archaic doctrine from a more ideal standpoint, to translate some visions in and from the Astral Light, to render some teachings partly gathered from a Master's thoughts, but unfortunately misunderstood. This work also speaks of the evolution of the early Races of men on Earth, and contains some excellent pages of a philosophical character. But so far it is only an interesting little mystical romance. It has failed in its mission, because the conditions required for a correct translation of these visions were not present. Hence the reader must not wonder if our Volumes contradict these earlier descriptions in several particulars.

Esoteric "Cosmogony" in general, and the evolution of the human Monad especially, differ so essentially in these two books and in other Theosophical works written independently by *beginners*, that it becomes impossible to proceed with the present work without special mention of these two earlier volumes, for both have a number of admirers -- "Esoteric Buddhism" especially. The time has arrived for the explanation of some matters in this direction. Mistakes have now to be checked by the original teachings and corrected. If one of the said works has too pronounced a bias toward materialistic science, the other is decidedly too idealistic, and is, at times, fantastic.

From the doctrine -- rather incomprehensible to western minds -- which deals with the periodical "obscurations" and successive "Rounds" of the Globes along their circular chains, were born the first perplexities and misconceptions. One of such has reference to the "*Fifth-*" and even "*Sixth*-Rounders." Those who knew that a Round was preceded and followed by a long *Pralaya*, a pause of rest which created an impassable gulf between two Rounds until the time came for a renewed cycle of life, could not understand the "fallacy" of talking about "*fifth* and *sixth* Rounders" in our *Fourth* Round. Gautama Buddha, it was held, was a Sixth-Rounder, Plato and some other great philosophers and minds, "Fifth-Rounders." How could it be? One Master taught and affirmed that there were such "Fifth-Rounders" even now on Earth; and though *understood to say* that mankind was yet "in the Fourth Round," in another place he *seemed* to say that we were in the Fifth. To this an "apocalyptic answer" was returned by another Teacher: -- "A few drops of rain do not make a Monsoon, though they presage it." . . . "No, we are not in the Fifth Round, but Fifth Round men have been coming in for the last few thousand years." This was worse than the riddle of the Sphinx! Students of Occultism subjected their brains to the wildest work of speculation. For a considerable time they tried to outvie OEdipus and reconcile the two statements. And as the Masters kept as silent as the stony Sphinx herself, they were accused of inconsistency, "contradiction," and "discrepancies." But they were simply allowing the speculations to go on, in order *to teach a lesson* which the Western mind sorely needs. In their conceit and arrogance, as in their habit of materializing every metaphysical conception and term without allowing any margin for Eastern metaphor and allegory, the Orientalists have made a jumble of the Hindu exoteric philosophy, and the Theosophists were now doing the same with regard to esoteric teachings. To this day it is evident that the latter have utterly failed to understand the meaning of the term "Fifth and Sixth Rounders." But it is simply this: every "Round" brings about a new development and even an entire change in the mental, psychic, spiritual and physical constitution of man, all these principles evoluting on an ever ascending scale. Thence it follows that those persons who, like Confucius and Plato, belonged psychically, mentally and spiritually to the higher planes of evolution, were in our Fourth Round as the average man will be in the Fifth Round, whose mankind is destined to find itself, on this scale of Evolution, immensely higher than is our present humanity. Similarly Gautama Buddha -- Wisdom incarnate -- was still higher and greater than all the men we have mentioned, who are called Fifth Rounders, while Buddha and Sankaracharya are termed Sixth Rounders, allegorically. Thence again the concealed wisdom of the remark, pronounced at the time "evasive" -- that a few drops of rain do not make the Monsoon, *though they presage it.*"

And now the truth of the remark made in "Esoteric Buddhism" by its author will be fully apparent: --

"It is impossible, *when the complicated facts of an entirely unfamiliar science are being presented to untrained minds for the first time*, to put them forward with all their appropriate qualifications . . . and abnormal developments. . . . We must be content to take the broad rules first and deal with the exceptions afterwards, and especially is this the case with study, in connection with which *the traditional methods of teaching, generally followed, aim at impressing every fresh idea on the memory by provoking the perplexity it at last relieves.*"

As the author of the remark was himself, as he says, "an untrained mind" in Occultism, his own inferences, and his better knowledge of modern astronomical speculations than of archaic doctrines led him quite naturally, and as unconsciously to himself, to commit a few mistakes of detail rather than of any "broad rule." One such will now be noticed. It is a trifling one, still it is calculated to lead many a beginner into erroneous conceptions. But as the mistaken notions of the earlier editions were corrected in the *annotations* of the fifth edition, so the sixth may be revised and perfected. There were several reasons for such mistakes. (1) They were due to the necessity under which the teachers laboured of giving what were considered as "evasive answers": the questions being too persistently pressed to be left unnoticed, while, on the other hand, they *could only be partially answered.* (2) This position notwithstanding, the confession that "half a loaf is better than no bread" was but too often misunderstood and hardly appreciated as it ought to have been. As a result thereof gratuitous speculations were sometimes indulged in by the European lay-chelas. Among such were (a) the "Mystery of the Eighth Sphere" in its relation to the Moon; and (b) the erroneous statement that two of the superior Globes of the terrestrial chain were two of our well-known planets: "besides the Earth . . . there are *only two other worlds of our chain which are visible. . . .* Mars and Mercury. . . ." (*Esoteric Buddhism*; p. 136.)

This was a great mistake. But the blame for it is to be attached as much to the vagueness and incompleteness of the Master's answer as to the question of the learner itself, which was equally vague and indefinite.

It was asked: "What planets, of those known to ordinary science, besides Mercury, belong to our system of worlds?" Now if by "System of Worlds" our *terrestrial chain* or "string" was intended in the mind of the querist, instead of the "Solar System of Worlds," as it should have been, then of course the answer was likely to be misunderstood. For the reply was: "Mars, etc., and four other planets of which astronomy knows nothing. Neither A, B, nor YZ are known nor can they be seen through physical means however perfected." This is plain: (a) Astronomy as yet knows nothing in reality of the planets, neither the ancient ones, nor those discovered in modern times. (b) No *companion* planets from A to Z, *i.e.*, no upper globes of any chain in the Solar System, can be seen. As to Mars, Mercury, and "the four other planets," they bear a relation to Earth of which no master or high Occultist will ever speak, much less explain the nature.

Let it now be distinctly stated, then, that the theory broached is impossible, with or without the additional evidence furnished by modern Astronomy. Physical Science can supply corroborative, though still very uncertain, evidence, but only as regards heavenly bodies on the same plane of materiality as our objective Universe. Mars and Mercury, Venus and Jupiter, like every hitherto discovered planet (or those still to be discovered), are all, *per se*, the representatives on our plane of such chains. As distinctly stated in one of the numerous letters of Mr. Sinnett's "Teacher," "there are other and innumerable Manvantaric chains of globes which bear intelligent Beings both in and outside our solar system." But neither Mars nor Mercury belong *to our chain*. They are, along with the other planets, septenary *Units* in the great host of "chains" of our system, and all are as visible as their *upper* globes are invisible.

If it is still argued that certain expressions in the Teacher's letters were liable to mislead, the answer comes: -- Amen; so it was. The author of "Esoteric Buddhism" understood it well when he wrote that such are "the traditional modes of teaching . . . by provoking the perplexity" . . . they *do*, or *do not relieve* -- as the case may be. At all events, if it is urged that this might have been explained earlier, and the true nature of the planets given out as they now are, the answer comes that: "it was not found expedient to do so at the time, as it would have opened the way to a series of additional questions *which could never be answered on account of their esoteric nature*, and thus would only become embarrassing." It had been declared from the first and has been repeatedly asserted since that (1st) no Theosophist, *not even as an accepted chela* -- let alone lay *students -- could expect to have the secret teachings explained to him thoroughly and completely*, before *he had irretrievably pledged himself to the Brotherhood and passed through at least one initiation*, because no figures and numbers could be given to the public, for figures and numbers are the key to the esoteric system. (2.) That what was revealed was merely the esoteric lining of that which is contained in almost all the exoteric Scriptures of the world-religions -- pre-eminently in the Brahmanas, and the

Upanishads of the Vedas and even in the Puranas. It was a small portion of what is divulged far more fully now in the present volumes; and even this is very incomplete and fragmentary.

When the present work was commenced, the writer, feeling sure that the speculation about Mars and Mercury was a mistake, applied to the Teachers *by letter* for explanation and an authoritative version. Both came in due time, and *verbatim* extracts from these are now given.

" . . . . . *It is quite correct that Mars is in a state of obscuration at present, and Mercury just beginning to get out of it. You might add that Venus is in her last Round. . . . . If neither Mercury nor Venus have satellites, it is because of the reasons . . .* (vide footnote supra, where those reasons are given), *and also because Mars has two satellites to which he has no right. . . . . Phobos, the supposed* INNER *satellite, is no satellite at all. As remarked long ago by Laplace and now by Faye (see* COMPTES RENDUS, *Tome* **XC.**, *p. 569), Phobos keeps a too short periodic time, and therefore there 'must exist some defect in the mother idea of the theory' as Faye justly observes. . . . . Again, both (Mars and Mercury) are septenary chains, as independent of the Earth's sidereal lords and superiors as you are independent of the 'principles' of Daumling (Tom Thumb) -- which were perhaps his six brothers, with or without night-caps. . . . . 'Gratification of curiosity is the end of knowledge for some men,' was said by Bacon, who was as right in postulating this truism, as those who were familiar with it before him were right in hedging off* **WISDOM** *from Knowledge, and tracing limits to that which is to be given out at one time. . . .*

Remember: --

'. . . . . *knowledge dwells*
In heads replete with thoughts of other men,
Wisdom in minds attentive to their own. . . .'
You can never impress it too profoundly on the minds of those to whom you impart some of the esoteric teachings. . ."

Again, here are more extracts from another letter written by the same authority. This time it is in answer to some objections laid before the Teachers. They are based upon extremely scientific, and as futile, reasonings about the advisability of trying to reconcile the Esoteric theories with the speculations of Modern Science, and were written by a young Theosophist as a warning against the "Secret Doctrine" and in reference to the same subject. He had declared that if there were such companion Earths "they must be only a wee bit less material than our globe." How then was it that they could not be seen? The answer was: --

" . . . . *Were psychic and spiritual teachings more fully understood, it would become next to impossible to even imagine such an incongruity. Unless less trouble is taken to reconcile the irreconcileable -- that is to say, the metaphysical and spiritual sciences with physical or natural philosophy, 'natural' being a synonym to them (men of science) of that matter which falls under the perception of their corporeal senses -- no progress can be really achieved. Our Globe, as taught from the first, is at the bottom of the arc of descent, where the matter of our perceptions exhibits itself in its grossest form. . . . . . . Hence it only stands to reason that the globes which overshadow our Earth must be on different and superior planes. In short, as Globes, they are in* CO-ADUNITION *but not* IN CONSUBSTANTIALITY WITH OUR EARTH *and thus pertain to quite another state of consciousness. Our planet (like all those we see) is adapted to the peculiar state of its human stock, that state which enables us to see with our naked eye the sidereal bodies which are co-essential with our terrene plane and substance, just as their respective inhabitants, the Jovians, Martians and others can perceive our little world: because our planes of consciousness, differing as they do in degree but being the same in kind, are on the same layer of differentiated matter. . . . . What I wrote was 'The minor Pralaya concerns only our little STRINGS OF GLOBES.' (We called chains 'Strings' in those days of lip-confusion.) . . . 'To such a string our Earth belongs.' This ought to have shown plainly that the other planets were also 'strings' or* **CHAINS.** . . . *If he (meaning the objector) would perceive even the dim silhouette of one of* such 'planets' on the higher planes, he has to first throw off even the thin clouds of the astral matter that stands between him and the next plane. . . . ."

It becomes patent why we could not perceive, even with the help of the best earthly telescopes, that which is outside our world of matter. Those alone, whom we call adepts, who know how to direct their mental vision and to transfer their consciousness -- physical and psychic both --to other planes of being, are able to speak with authority on such subjects. And they tell us plainly: --

"Lead the life necessary for the acquisition of such knowledge and powers, and Wisdom will come to you naturally. Whenever your are able to attune your consciousness to any of the seven chords of 'Universal Consciousness,' those chords that run along the sounding-board of Kosmos, vibrating from one Eternity to another; when you have studied thoroughly 'the music of the Spheres,' then only will you become quite free to share your knowledge with those with whom it is safe to do so. Meanwhile, be prudent. Do not give out the great Truths that are the inheritance of the future Races, to our present generation. Do not attempt to unveil the secret of being and non-being to those unable to see the hidden meaning of Apollo's HEPTACHORD -- the lyre of the radiant god, in each of the seven strings of which dwelleth the Spirit, Soul and Astral body of the Kosmos, whose shell only has now fallen into the hands of Modern Science. . . . . . Be prudent, we say, prudent and wise, and above all take care what those who learn from you believe in; lest by deceiving themselves they deceive others . . . . . for such is the fate of every truth with which men are, as yet, unfamiliar. . . . Let rather the planetary chains and other super- and sub-cosmic mysteries remain a dreamland for those who can neither see, nor yet believe that others can. . . ."

It is to be regretted that few of us have followed the wise advice; and that many a priceless pearl, many a jewel of wisdom, has been cast to an enemy unable to understand its value and who has turned round and rent us.

" '*Let us imagine,*' wrote the same Master to his two 'lay chelas,' as he called the author of 'Esoteric Buddhism' and another gentleman, his co-student for some time -- '*let us imagine* THAT OUR EARTH IS ONE OF A GROUP OF SEVEN PLANETS OR MAN-BEARING WORLDS. . . . . . (*The* SEVEN *planets are the sacred planets of antiquity, and are all septenary.*) *Now the life-impulse reaches A, or rather that which is destined to become A, and which so far is but cosmic dust* (a "laya centre") . . *etc.*' "

In these early letters, in which the terms had to be invented and words coined, the "Rings" very often became "Rounds," and the "Rounds" life-cycles, and *vice versa.* To a correspondent who called a "Round" a "World Ring," the Teacher wrote. "I believe this will lead to a further confusion. A Round we are agreed to call the passage of a monad from Globe A to Globe G or Z. . . The 'World-Ring' is correct. . . Advise Mr. . . . strongly, to agree upon a nomenclature before going any further. . . "

Notwithstanding this agreement, many mistakes, owing to this confusion, crept into the earliest teachings. The Races even were occasionally mixed up with the "Rounds" and "Rings," and led to similar mistakes in "Man." From the first the Master had written --

"Not being permitted to give you *the whole truth*, or divulge the number of isolated fractions . . . I am unable to satisfy you."

This in answer to the questions, "If we are right, then the total existence prior to the man-period is 637," etc., etc. To all the queries relating to figures, the reply was, "Try to solve the problem of 777 incarnations. . . . *Though I am obliged to withhold information . . . yet if you should work out the problem by yourself, it will be my duty to tell you so.*"

But they never were so worked out, and the results were -- never-ceasing perplexity and mistakes.

Even the teaching about the Septenary constitution of the sidereal bodies and of the macrocosm -- from which the septenary division of the microcosm, or Man -- has until now been among the most esoteric. In olden times it used to be divulged only at the Initiation and along with the most sacred figures of the cycles. Now, as stated in one of the Theosophical journals, the revelation of the whole system of Cosmogony had not been contemplated, nor even thought for one moment possible, at a time when a few bits of information were sparingly given out in answer to letters written by the author of "Esoteric Buddhism," in which he put forward a multiplicity of questions. Among these were questions on such problems *as no* **MASTER**, *however high and independent he might be, would have the right to answer, thus divulging to the world the most time-honoured and archaic of the mysteries of the ancient college-temples.* Hence only a few of the doctrines were revealed in their broad outlines, while details were constantly withheld, and all the efforts made to elicit more information about them were systematically eluded from the beginning. This is perfectly natural. Of the four Vidyas -- out of the seven branches of Knowledge mentioned in the Puranas -- namely, "Yajna-Vidya" (the performance of religious rites in order to produce certain results); "Maha-Vidya," the great (Magic) knowledge, now degenerated into Tantrika worship; "Guhya-Vidya," the science of Mantras and their true rhythm or chanting, of mystical incantations, etc. -- it is only the last one, "Atma-Vidya," or the true *Spiritual* and *Divine wisdom*, which can throw absolute and final light upon the teachings of the three first named. Without the help of Atma-Vidya, the other three remain no better than *surface* sciences, geometrical magnitudes having length and breadth, but no thickness. They are like the soul, limbs, and mind of a sleeping man: capable of mechanical motions, of chaotic dreams and even sleep-walking, of producing visible effects, but stimulated by instinctual not intellectual causes, least of all by fully conscious spiritual impulses. A good deal can be given out and explained from the three first-named sciences. But unless the key to their teachings is furnished by Atma-Vidya, they will remain for ever like the fragments of a mangled text-book, like the adumbrations of great truths, dimly perceived by the most spiritual, but distorted out of all proportion by those who would nail every shadow to the wall.

Then, again, another great perplexity was created in the minds of students by the incomplete exposition of the doctrine of the evolution of the Monads. To be fully realised, both this process and that of the birth of the Globes must be examined far more from their metaphysical aspect than from what one might call a statistical standpoint, involving figures and numbers which are rarely permitted to be broadly used. Unfortunately, there are few who are inclined to handle these doctrines only metaphysically. Even the best of the Western writers upon our doctrine declares in his work that "on pure metaphysics of that sort we are not now engaged," when speaking of the evolution of the Monads ("Esoteric Buddhism," p. 46). And in such case, as the Teacher remarks in a letter to him, "Why this preaching of our doctrines, all this uphill work and swimming *in adversum flumen?* Why should the West . . . learn . . . from the East . . . that which can never meet the requirements of the special tastes of the aesthetics?" And he draws his correspondent's attention "to the formidable difficulties encountered by us (the Adepts) in every attempt we make to explain our metaphysics to the Western mind."

And well he may; for *outside* of metaphysics no occult philosophy, no esotericism is possible. It is like trying to explain the aspirations and affections, the love and hatred, the most private and sacred workings in the soul and mind of the living man, by an anatomical description of the chest and brain of his dead body.

Let us now examine two tenets mentioned above and hardly alluded to in "Esoteric Buddhism," and supplement them as far as lies in our power.

ADDITIONAL FACTS AND EXPLANATIONS CONCERNING THE GLOBES AND THE MONADS

Two statements made in "Esoteric Buddhism" must be noticed and the author's opinions quoted. On p. 47 (fifth edition) it is said: --

" . . . the spiritual monads . . . do not fully complete their mineral existence on Globe A, then complete it on Globe B, and so on. They pass several times round the whole circle as minerals, and then again several times round as vegetables, and several times as animals. We purposely refrain for the present from going into figures," etc., etc.

This was a wise course to adopt in view of the great secrecy maintained with regard to figures and numbers. This reticence is now partially relinquished; but it would perhaps have been better had the real numbers concerning Rounds and evolutional gyrations been either entirely divulged at the time, or as entirely withheld. Mr. Sinnett understood this difficulty well when saying (p. 140) that: "For reasons which are not easy for the outsider to divine, the possessors of occult knowledge are especially reluctant to give out facts relating to Cosmogony, though it is hard for the uninitiated to understand why they should be withheld."

That there were such reasons is evident. Nevertheless, it is to this reticence that most of the confused ideas of some Eastern as well as Western pupils are due. The difficulties in the way of the acceptance of the two particular tenets under consideration seemed great, just because of the absence of any data to go upon. But there it was. For the figures belonging to the Occult calculations cannot be given -- as the Masters have many times declared -- outside the circle of pledged chelas, and not even these can break the rules.

To make things plainer, without touching upon the mathematical aspects of the doctrine, the teaching given may be expanded and some obscure points solved. As the evolution of the Globes and that of the Monads are so closely interblended, we will make of the two teachings one. In reference to the Monads, the reader is asked to bear in mind that Eastern philosophy rejects the Western theological dogma of a newly-created soul for every baby born, as being as unphilosophical as it is impossible in the economy of Nature. There must be a limited number of Monads evolving and growing more and more perfect through their assimilation of many successive personalities, in every new Manvantara. This is absolutely necessary in view of the doctrines of Rebirth, Karma, and the gradual return of the human Monad to its source -- *absolute* Deity. Thus, although the hosts of more or less progressed Monads are almost incalculable, they are still finite, as is everything in this Universe of differentiation and finiteness.

As shown in the double diagram of the human "principles" and the ascending Globes of the world-chains, there is an eternal concatenation of causes and effects, and a perfect analogy which runs through, and links together, all the lines of evolution. One begets the other -- globes as personalities. But, let us begin at the beginning.

The general outline of the process by which the successive planetary chains are formed has just been given. To prevent future misconceptions, some further details may be offered which will also throw light on the history of humanity on our own chain, the progeny of that of the Moon.

In the diagrams on p. 172, Fig. 1 represents the "lunar-chain" of seven planets at the outset of its seventh or last Round; while Fig. 2 represents the "earth-chain" which will be, but is not yet in existence. The seven Globes of each chain are distinguished in their cyclic order by the letters A to G, the Globes of the Earth-chain being further marked by a cross -- + -- the symbol of the Earth.

Now, it must be remembered that the Monads cycling round any septenary chain are divided into seven classes or hierarchies according to their respective stages of evolution, consciousness, and merit. Let us follow, then, the order of their appearance on planet A, in the first Round. The time-spaces between the appearances of these hierarchies on any one Globe are so adjusted that when Class 7, the last, appears on Globe A, Class 1, the first, has just passed on to Globe B, and so on, step by step, all round the chain.

Again, in the Seventh Round on the Lunar chain, when Class 7, the last, quits Globe A, that Globe, instead of falling asleep, as it had done in previous Rounds, begins to die (to go into its planetary pralaya); and in dying it transfers successively, as just said, its "principles," or life-elements and energy, etc., one after the other to a new "laya-centre," which commences the formation of Globe A of the Earth Chain. A similar process takes place for each of the Globes of the "lunar chain" one after the other, each forming a fresh Globe of the "earth-chain." Our Moon was the fourth Globe of the series, and was

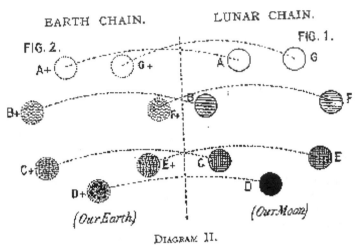

EARTH CHAIN.   LUNAR CHAIN.

FIG. 2.   FIG. 1.

DIAGRAM II.

on the same plane of perception as our Earth. But Globe A of the lunar chain is not fully "dead" till the first Monads of the first class have passed from Globe G or Z, the last of the "lunar chain," into the Nirvana which awaits them between the two chains; and similarly for all the other Globes as stated, each giving birth to the corresponding globe of the "earth-chain."

Further, when Globe A of the new chain is ready, the first class or Hierarchy of Monads from the Lunar chain incarnate upon it in the lowest kingdom, and so on successively. The result of this is, that it is only the first class of Monads which attains the human state of development during the first Round, since the second class, on each planet, arriving later, has not time to reach that stage. Thus the Monads of Class 2 reach the incipient human stage only in the Second Round, and so on up to the middle of the Fourth Round. But at this point -- and on this Fourth Round in which the human stage will be *fully* developed -- the "Door" into the human kingdom closes; and henceforward the number of "human" Monads, *i.e.*, Monads in the human stage of development, is complete. For the Monads which had not reached the human stage by this point will, owing to the evolution of humanity itself, find themselves so far behind that they will reach the human stage only at the close of the seventh and last Round. They will, therefore, not be men on this chain, but will form the humanity of a future Manvantara and be rewarded by becoming "Men" on a higher chain altogether, thus receiving their Karmic compensation. To this there is *but one solitary exception*, for very good reasons, of which we shall speak farther on. But this accounts for the difference in the races.

It thus becomes apparent how perfect is the analogy between the processes of Nature in the Kosmos and in the individual man. The latter lives through his life-cycle, and dies. His "higher principles," corresponding in the development of a planetary chain to the cycling Monads, pass into Devachan, which corresponds to the "Nirvana" and states of rest intervening between two chains. The Man's lower "principles" are disintegrated in time and are used by Nature again for the formation of new human principles, and the same process takes place in the disintegration and formation of Worlds. Analogy is thus the surest guide to the comprehension of the Occult teachings.

This is one of the "seven mysteries of the Moon," and it is now revealed. The seven "mysteries" are called by the Japanese *Yamaboosis*, the mystics of the Lao-Tze sect and the ascetic monks of Kioto, the Dzenodoo -- the "seven jewels." Only the Japanese and the Chinese

Buddhist ascetics and Initiates are, if possible, even more reticent in giving out their "Knowledge" than are the Hindus.

But the reader must not be allowed to lose sight of the Monads, and must be enlightened as to their nature, as far as permitted, without trespassing upon the highest mysteries, of which the writer does not in any way pretend to know the last or final word.

The Monadic Host may be roughly divided into three great classes:

1. The most developed Monads (the Lunar Gods or "Spirits," called, in India, the Pitris), whose function it is to pass in the first Round through the whole triple cycle of the mineral, vegetable, and animal kingdoms in their most ethereal, filmy, and rudimentary forms, in order to clothe themselves in, and assimilate, the nature of the newly formed chain. They are those who first reach the human form (if there can be any form in the realm of the almost subjective) on Globe A in the first Round. It is they, therefore, who lead and represent the human element during the second and third Rounds, and finally evolve their shadows at the beginning of the Fourth Round for the second class, or those who come behind them.

2. Those Monads that are the first to reach the human stage during the three and a half Rounds, and to become men.

3. The laggards; the Monads which are retarded, and which will not reach, by reason of Karmic impediments, the human stage at all during this cycle or Round, save one exception which will be spoken of elsewhere as already promised.

Now the evolution of the *external* form or body round the *astral* is produced by the terrestrial forces, just as in the case of the lower kingdoms; but the evolution of the internal or real MAN is purely spiritual. It is now no more a passage of the impersonal Monad through many and various forms of matter -- endowed at best with instinct and consciousness on quite a different plane -- as in the case of external evolution, but a journey of the "pilgrim-soul" through various *states* of *not only matter* but Self-consciousness and self-perception, or of *perception* from apperception (See "*Gods, Monads and Atoms.*")

The MONAD emerges from its state of spiritual and intellectual unconsciousness; and, skipping the first two planes -- too near the ABSOLUTE to permit of any correlation with anything on a lower plane -- it gets direct into the plane of Mentality. But there is no plane in the whole universe with a wider margin, or a wider field of action in its almost endless gradations of perceptive and apperceptive qualities, than this plane, which has in its turn an appropriate smaller plane for every "form," from the "mineral" monad up to the time when that monad blossoms forth by evolution into the DIVINE MONAD. But all the time it is still one and the same Monad, differing only in its incarnations, throughout its ever succeeding cycles of partial or total obscuration of spirit, or the partial or total obscuration of matter -- two polar antitheses -- as it ascends into the realms of mental spirituality, or descends into the depths of materiality.

To return to "Esoteric Buddhism." It is there stated with regard to the enormous period intervening between the mineral epoch on Globe A, and the man-epoch, that: "The full development of the mineral epoch on Globe A, prepares the way for the vegetable development, and, as soon as this begins, the mineral life-impulse overflows into Globe B. Then, when the vegetable development on Globe A is complete and the animal development begins, the vegetable life-impulse overflows to Globe B, and the mineral impulse passes on to Globe C. Then finally comes the human life-impulse on Globe A." (Page 49.)

And so it goes on for three Rounds, when it slackens, and finally stops at the threshold of our Globe, at the Fourth Round; because the human period (of the true physical men to be), the seventh, is now reached. This is evident, for as said, " . . . there are processes of evolution which precede the mineral kingdom, and thus a wave of evolution, indeed several waves of evolution, precede the mineral wave in its progress round the spheres" (*ibid*).

And now we have to quote from another article, "The Mineral Monad" in "*Five Years of Theosophy*," p. 273 *et seq.*

"There are seven kingdoms. The first group comprises three degrees of elementals, or nascent centres of forces -- from the first stage of differentiation of (from) Mulaprakriti (or rather Pradhana, primordial homogeneous matter) to its third degree -- *i.e.*, from full unconsciousness to semi-perception; the second or higher group embraces the kingdoms from vegetable to man; the mineral kingdom thus forming the central or turning point in the degrees of the "Monadic Essence," considered as an evoluting energy. Three stages (sub-physical) on the elemental side; the mineral kingdom; three stages on the objective physical side -- these are the (first or preliminary) seven links of the evolutionary chain."

"Preliminary" because they are preparatory, and though belonging in fact to the natural, they yet would be more correctly described as sub-natural evolution. This process makes a halt in its stages at the Third, at the threshold of the Fourth stage, when it becomes, on the plane of the natural evolution, the first really manward stage, thus forming with the three elemental kingdoms, the ten, the Sephirothal number. It is at this point that begins: -- evolution; a re-ascent from the deepest depths of materiality (the mineral) towards its *status quo ante*, with a corresponding dissipation of concrete organism -- up to Nirvana, the vanishing point of differentiated matter." ("*Five Years of Theosophy*," p. 276.)

Therefore it becomes evident why that which is pertinently called in *Esoteric Buddhism* "Wave of Evolution," and mineral-, vegetable-, animal- and man-"impulse," stops at the door of our Globe, at its Fourth cycle or Round. It is at this point that the Cosmic Monad (Buddhi) will be wedded to and become the vehicle of the Atmic Ray, *i.e.*, it (Buddhi) will awaken to an apperception of it (Atman); and thus enter on the first step of a new septenary ladder of evolution, which will lead it eventually to the tenth (counting from the lowest upwards) of the Sephirothal tree, the Crown.

Everything in the Universe follows analogy. "As above, so below"; Man is the microcosm of the Universe. That which takes place on the spiritual plane repeats itself on the Cosmic plane. Concretion follows the lines of abstraction; corresponding to the highest must be the lowest; the material to the spiritual. Thus, corresponding to the Sephirothal Crown (or upper triad) there are the three elemental Kingdoms, which precede the Mineral (see diagram on p. 277 in *Five Years of Theosophy*), and which, using the language of the Kabalists, answer in the Cosmic differentiation to the worlds of Form and Matter from the Super-Spiritual to the Archetypal.

Now what is a "Monad?" And what relation does it bear to an Atom? The following reply is based upon the explanations given in answer to these questions in the above-cited article: "The Mineral Monad," written by the author.

"None whatever," is answered to the second question, "to the atom or molecule as existing in the scientific conception at present. It can neither be compared with the microscopic organism, once classed among polygastric infusoria, and now regarded as vegetable, and classed among Algae; nor is it quite the Monas of the Peripatetics. Physically or constitutionally the mineral monad differs, of course, from the human monad, which is neither physical nor can its constitution be rendered by chemical symbols and elements." In short, as the spiritual Monad is One, Universal, Boundless and Impartite, whose rays, nevertheless, form what we, in our ignorance, call the "Individual Monads" of men, so the Mineral Monad -- being at the opposite point of the circle -- is also One -- and from it proceed the countless physical atoms, which Science is beginning to regard as individualized.

Otherwise how could one account for and explain mathematically the evolutionary and spiral progress of the Four Kingdoms? The "Monad" is the combination of the last two "principles" in man, the 6th and the 7th, and, properly speaking, the term "human monad" applies only to the dual soul (Atma-Buddhi), not to its highest spiritual vivifying Principle, Atma, alone. But since the Spiritual Soul, if divorced from the latter (Atma) could have no existence, no being, it has thus been called . . . . Now the Monadic, or rather Cosmic, Essence (if such a term be permitted) in the mineral, vegetable, and animal, though the same throughout the series of cycles from the lowest elemental up to the Deva Kingdom, yet differs in the scale of progression. It would be very misleading to imagine a Monad as a separate Entity trailing its slow way in a distinct path through the lower Kingdoms, and after an incalculable series of transformations flowering into a human being; in short, that the Monad of a Humboldt dates back to the Monad of an atom of horneblende. Instead of saying a "Mineral Monad," the more correct phraseology in physical Science, which differentiates every atom, would of course have been to call it "the Monad manifesting in that form of Prakriti called the Mineral Kingdom." The atom, as represented in the ordinary scientific hypothesis, is not a particle of something, animated by a psychic something, destined after aeons to blossom as a man. But it is a concrete manifestation of the Universal Energy which itself has not yet become individualized; a sequential manifestation of the one Universal Monas. The ocean (of matter) does not divide into its potential and constituent drops until the sweep of the life-impulse reaches the evolutionary stage of man-birth. The tendency towards segregation into individual Monads is gradual, and in the higher animals comes almost to the point. The Peripatetics applied the word Monas to the whole Kosmos, in the pantheistic sense; and the Occultists, while accepting this thought for convenience sake, distinguish the progressive stages of the evolution of the concrete from the abstract by terms of which the "Mineral, Vegetable, Animal, (etc.), Monad" are examples. The term merely means that the tidal wave of spiritual evolution is passing through that arc of its circuit. The "Monadic Essence" begins to imperceptibly differentiate towards individual consciousness in the Vegetable Kingdom. As the Monads are uncompounded things, as correctly defined by Leibnitz, it is the spiritual essence which vivifies them in their degrees of differentiation, which properly constitutes the Monad -- not the atomic aggregation, which is only the vehicle and the substance through which thrill the lower and the higher degrees of intelligence.

Leibnitz conceived of the Monads as elementary and indestructible units endowed with the power *of giving and receiving* with respect to other units, and thus of determining all spiritual and physical phenomena. It is he who invented the term apperception, which together with nerve- (not perception, but rather) -- sensation, expresses the state of the Monadic consciousness through all the Kingdoms up to Man.

Thus it may be wrong on strictly metaphysical lines to call Atma-Buddhi a MONAD, since in the materialistic view it is dual and therefore compound. But as Matter is Spirit, and *vice versa;* and since the Universe and the Deity which informs it are unthinkable apart from each other; so in the case of Atma-Buddhi. The latter being the vehicle of the former, Buddhi stands in the same relation to Atma, as Adam-Kadmon, the Kabalistic Logos, does to En-Soph, or Mulaprakriti to Parabrahm.

A few words more of the Moon.

What, it may be asked, are the "Lunar Monads," just spoken of? The description of the seven classes of Pitris will come later, but now some general explanations may be given. It must be plain to everyone that they are Monads, who, having ended their life-cycle on the lunar chain, which is inferior to the terrestrial chain, have incarnated on this one. But there are some further details which may be added, though they border too closely on forbidden ground to be treated of fully. The last word of the mystery is divulged only to the adepts, but it may be stated that our satellite is only the gross body of its invisible principles. Seeing then that there are 7 Earths, so there are 7 Moons, the last one alone being visible; the same for the Sun, whose visible body is called a Maya, a reflection, just as man's body is. "The real Sun and the real Moon are as invisible as the real man," says an occult maxim.

And it may be remarked *en passant* that those ancients were not so foolish after all who first started the idea of "the seven moons." For though this conception is now taken solely as an astronomical measure of time, in a very materialised form, yet underlying the husk there can still be recognised the traces of a profoundly philosophical idea.

In reality the Moon is only the satellite of the Earth in one respect, viz., that physically the Moon revolves round the Earth. But in every other respect it is the Earth which is the satellite of the Moon, and not *vice versa.* Startling as the statement may seem it is not without confirmation from scientific knowledge. It is evidenced by the tides, by the cyclic changes in many forms of disease which coincide with the lunar phases; it can be traced in the growth of plants, and is very marked in the phenomena of human gestation and conception. The importance of the Moon and its influence on the Earth were recognized in every ancient religion, notably the Jewish, and have been remarked by many observers of psychical and physical phenomena. But, so far as Science knows, the Earth's action on the Moon is confined to the physical attraction, which causes her to circle in her orbit. And should an objector insist that this fact alone is sufficient evidence that the Moon is truly the Earth's satellite on other planes of action, one may reply by asking whether a mother, who walks round and round her child's cradle keeping watch over the infant, is the subordinate of her child or dependent upon it; though in one sense she is its satellite, yet she is certainly older and more fully developed than the child she watches.

It is, then, the Moon that plays the largest and most important part, as well in the formation of the Earth itself, as in the peopling thereof with human beings. The "Lunar Monads" or Pitris, the ancestors of man, become in reality man himself. They are the "Monads" who enter on the cycle of evolution on Globe A, and who, passing round the chain of planets, evolve the human form as has just been shown. At the beginning of the human stage of the Fourth Round on this Globe, they "ooze out" their astral doubles from the "ape-like" forms which they had evolved in Round III. And it is this subtle, finer form, which serves as the model round which Nature builds physical man. These "Monads" or "divine sparks" are thus the "Lunar" ancestors, the Pitris themselves. For these "Lunar Spirits" have to become "Men" in order that their "Monads" may reach a higher plane of activity and self-consciousness, *i.e.,* the plane of the Manasa-Putras, those who endow the "senseless" shells, created and informed by the Pitris, with "mind" in the latter part of the Third Root-Race.

In the same way the "Monads" or Egos of the men of the seventh Round of our Earth, after our own Globes A, B, C, D, *et seq.,* parting with their life-energy, will have informed and thereby called to life other laya-centres destined to live and act on a still higher plane of being -- in the same way will the Terrene "Ancestors" create those who will become their superiors.

It now becomes plain that there exists in Nature a triple evolutionary scheme, for the formation of the three *periodical Upadhis;* or rather three separate schemes of evolution, which in our system are inextricably interwoven and interblended at every point. These are the Monadic (or spiritual), the intellectual, and the physical evolutions. These three are the finite aspects or the reflections on the field of Cosmic Illusion of ATMA, the seventh, the ONE REALITY.

1. The Monadic is, as the name implies, concerned with the growth and development into still higher phases of activity of the Monad in conjunction with: --

2. The Intellectual, represented by the Manasa-Dhyanis (the Solar Devas, or the Agnishwatta Pitris) the "givers of intelligence and consciousness" to man and: --

3. The Physical, represented by the Chhayas of the lunar Pitris, round which Nature has concreted the present physical body. This body serves as the vehicle for the "growth" (to use a misleading word) and the transformations through Manas and -- owing to the accumulation of experiences -- of the finite into the INFINITE, of the transient into the Eternal and Absolute.

Each of these three systems has its own laws, and is ruled and guided by different sets of the highest Dhyanis or "Logoi." Each is represented in the constitution of man, the Microcosm of the great Macrocosm; and it is the union of these three streams in him which makes him the complex being he now is.

"Nature," the physical evolutionary Power, could never evolve intelligence unaided -- she can only create "senseless forms," as will be seen in our "ANTHROPOGENESIS." The "Lunar Monads" cannot progress, for they have not yet had sufficient touch with the forms created by "Nature" to allow of their accumulating experiences through its means. It is the

Manasa-Dhyanis who fill up the gap, and they represent the evolutionary power of Intelligence and Mind, the link between "Spirit" and "Matter" -- in this Round.

Also it must be borne in mind that the Monads which enter upon the evolutionary cycle upon Globe A, in the first Round, are in very different stages of development. Hence the matter becomes somewhat complicated. . . . Let us recapitulate.

The most developed Monads (the lunar) reach the human germ-stage in the first Round; become terrestrial, though very ethereal human beings towards the end of the Third Round, remaining on it (the globe) through the "obscuration" period as the seed for future mankind in the Fourth Round, and thus become the pioneers of Humanity at the beginning of this, the Fourth Round. Others reach the Human stage only during later Rounds, *i.e.*, in the second, third, or first half of the Fourth Round. And finally the most retarded of all, *i.e.*, those still occupying animal forms after the middle turning-point of the Fourth Round -- will not become men at all during this Manwantara. They will reach to the verge of humanity only at the close of the seventh Round to be, in their turn, ushered into a new chain after *pralaya* -- by older pioneers, the progenitors of humanity, or the Seed-Humanity (*Sishta*), viz., the men who will be at the head of all at the end of these Rounds.

The student hardly needs any further explanation on the part played by the fourth Globe and the fourth Round in the scheme of evolution.

From the preceding diagrams, which are applicable, *mutatis mutandis*, to Rounds, Globes or Races, it will be seen that the fourth member of a series occupies a unique position. Unlike the others, the Fourth has no "sister" Globe on the same plane as itself, and it thus forms the fulcrum of the "balance" represented by the whole chain. It is the sphere of final evolutionary adjustments, the world of Karmic scales, the Hall of Justice, where the balance is struck which determines the future course of the Monad during the remainder of its incarnations in the cycle. And therefore it is, that, after this central turning-point has been passed in the Great Cycle, -- *i.e.*, after the middle point of the Fourth Race in the Fourth Round on our Globe -- no more Monads can enter the human kingdom. The door is closed for this Cycle and the balance struck. For were it otherwise -- had there been a new soul created for each of the countless milliards of human beings that have passed away, and had there been no reincarnation -- it would become difficult indeed to provide room for the disembodied "Spirits;" nor could the origin and cause of suffering ever be accounted for. It is the ignorance of the occult tenets and the enforcement of false conceptions under the guise of religious education, which have created materialism and atheism as a protest against the asserted divine order of things.

The only exceptions to the rule just stated are the "dumb races," whose Monads are already within the human stage, in virtue of the fact that these "animals" are later than, and even half descended from man, their last descendants being the anthropoid and other apes. These "human presentments" are in truth only the distorted copies of the early humanity. But this will receive full attention in the next Book.

As the Commentary, broadly rendered, says: --

1. "*Every form on earth, and every speck (atom) in Space strives in its efforts towards self-formation to follow the model placed for it in the* ' HEAVENLY MAN.' . . . *Its (the atom's) involution and evolution, its external and internal growth and development, have all one and the same object -- man; man, as the highest physical and ultimate form on this earth; the* MONAD, *in its absolute totality and awakened condition -- as the culmination of the divine incarnations on Earth.*"

2. "*The Dhyanis (Pitris) are those who have evolved their* BHUTA (*doubles*) *from themselves, which* RUPA (*form*) *has become the vehicle of monads (seventh and sixth principles) that had completed their cycle of transmigration in the three preceding Kalpas (Rounds). Then, they (the astral doubles) became the men of the first Human Race of the Round. But they were not complete, and were senseless.*"

This will be explained in the Books that follow. Meanwhile man -- or rather his Monad -- has existed on the earth from the very beginning of this Round. But, up to our own Fifth Race, the external shapes which covered those divine astral doubles changed and consolidated with every sub-race; the form and physical structure of the fauna changing at the same time, as they had to be adapted to the ever-changing conditions of life on this globe during the geological periods of its formative cycle. And thus shall they go on changing with every Root Race and *every chief sub-race* down to the last one of the Seventh in this Round.

3. "*The inner, now concealed, man, was then (in the beginnings) the external man. The progeny of the Dhyanis (Pitris), he was 'the son like unto his father.' Like the lotus, whose external shape assumes gradually the form of the model within itself, so did the form of man in the beginning evolve from within without. After the cycle in which man began to procreate his species after the fashion of the present animal kingdom, it became the reverse. The human foetus follows now in its transformations all the forms that the physical frame of man had assumed throughout the three Kalpas (Rounds) during the tentative efforts at Plastic formation around the monad by senseless, because imperfect, matter, in her blind wanderings. In the present age, the physical embryo is a plant, a reptile, an animal, before it finally becomes man, evolving within himself his own ethereal counterpart, in his turn. In the beginning it was that counterpart (astral man) which, being senseless, got entangled in the meshes of matter.*"

But this "man" belongs to the fourth Round. As shown, the MONAD had passed through, journeyed and been imprisoned in, every transitional form throughout every kingdom of nature during the three preceding Rounds. But the monad which becomes human *is not the Man.* In this Round -- with the exception of the highest mammals after man, the anthropoids destined to die out in this our race, when their monads will be liberated and pass into the astral human forms (or the highest elementals) of the Sixth and the Seventh Races, and then into lowest human forms in the fifth Round -- no units of either of the kingdoms are animated any longer by monads destined to become human in their next stage, but only by the lower Elementals of their respective realms.

The last human Monad incarnated before the beginning of the 5th Root-Race. The cycle of *metempsychosis* for the human monad is closed, for we are in the Fourth Round and the Fifth Root-Race. The reader will have to bear in mind -- at any rate one who has made himself acquainted with "Esoteric Buddhism" -- that the Stanzas which follow in this Book and Book II speak of the evolution in our Fourth Round only. The latter is the cycle of the turning-point, after which, matter, having reached its lowest depths, begins to strive onward and to get spiritualized with every new Race and with every fresh cycle. Therefore the student must take care not to see contradiction where there is none, as in "Esoteric Buddhism" Rounds are spoken of in general, while here only the Fourth, or our present Round, is meant. Then it was the work of formation; now it is that of reformation and evolutionary perfection.

Finally, to close this chapter anent various, but unavoidable misconceptions, we must refer to a statement in "Esoteric Buddhism" which has produced a very fatal impression upon the minds of many Theosophists. One unfortunate sentence from the work just referred to is constantly brought forward to prove the materialism of the doctrine. On p. 48, 5th Edition, the Author, referring to the progress of organisms on the Globes, says that "the mineral kingdom will no more develop the vegetable . . . than the Earth was able to develop man from the ape, till it received an impulse."

Whether this sentence renders literally the thought of the author, or is simply (as we believe it is) a *lapsus calami*, may remain an open question.

It is really with surprise that we have ascertained the fact that "Esoteric Buddhism" was so little understood by some Theosophists, as to have led them into the belief that it thoroughly supported Darwinian evolution, and especially the theory of the descent of man from a pithecoid ancestor. As one member writes: "I suppose you realise that three-fourths of Theosophists and even outsiders imagine that, as far as the evolution of man is concerned, Darwinism and Theosophy kiss one another." Nothing of the kind was ever realised, nor is there any great warrant for it, so far as we know, in "Esoteric Buddhism." It has been repeatedly stated that evolution as taught by Manu and Kapila was the groundwork of the modern teachings, but neither Occultism nor Theosophy has ever supported the wild theories of the present Darwinists -- least of all the descent of man from an ape. Of this, more hereafter. But one has only to turn to p. 47 of "Esoteric Buddhism," 5th edition, to find there the statement that "Man belongs to a kingdom distinctly separate from that of the animals." With such a plain and unequivocal statement before him, it is very strange that any careful student should have been so misled unless he is prepared to charge the author with a gross contradiction.

Every Round repeats on a higher scale the evolutionary work of the preceding Round. With the exception of some higher anthropoids, as just mentioned, the Monadic inflow, or inner evolution, is at an end till the next Manvantara. It can never be too often repeated, that the full-blown human Monads have to be first disposed of, before the new crop of candidates appears on this Globe at the beginning of the next cycle. Thus there is a lull; and this is why, during the Fourth Round, man appears on Earth earlier than any animal creation, as will be described.

But it is still urged that the author of "Esoteric Buddhism" has "preached Darwinism" all along. Certain passages would undoubtedly seem to lend countenance to this inference. Besides which the Occultists themselves are ready to concede *partial* correctness to the Darwinian hypothesis, in later details, bye-laws of Evolution, and after the midway point of the Fourth Race. Of that which has taken place, physical science can really know nothing, for such matters lie entirely outside of its sphere of investigation. But what the Occultists have never admitted, nor will they ever admit, is that man was *an ape in this or in any other Round;* or that he ever could be one, however much he may have been "ape-like." This is vouched for by the very authority from whom the author of "Esoteric Buddhism" got his information.

Thus to those who confront the Occultists with these lines from the above-named volume: "It is enough to show that we may as reasonably -- and that we must, if we would talk about these matters at all -- conceive a life-impulse giving birth to mineral form, as of the same sort of impulse concerned to *raise a race of apes into a race of rudimentary men.*" To those who bring this passage forward as showing "decided Darwinism," the Occultists answer by pointing to the explanation of the Master (Mr. Sinnett's "teacher") which would contradict these lines, were they written in the spirit attributed to them. A copy of this letter was sent to the writer, together with others, two years ago (1886), with additional marginal remarks, to quote from, in the "*Secret Doctrine.*" It begins by considering the difficulty experienced by the Western student, in reconciling some facts, previously given, with the evolution of man from the animal, *i.e.,* from the mineral, vegetable and animal kingdoms, and advises the student to hold to the doctrine of analogy and correspondences. Then it touches upon the mystery of the Devas, and even Gods, having to pass through states which it was agreed to refer to as "Inmetallization, Inherbation, Inzoonization and finally Incarnation," and explains this by hinting at the necessity of failures even in the ethereal races of Dhyan Chohans. Concerning this it says:

"Still, as these 'failures' are too far progressed and spiritualized to be thrown back forcibly from Dhyan Chohanship into the vortex of a new primordial evolution through the lower kingdoms. . . . ." After which only a hint is given about the mystery contained in the allegory of the fallen Asuras, which will be expanded and explained in Book II. When Karma has reached them at the stage of human evolution, "they will have to drink it to the last drop in the bitter cup of retribution. Then they become an active force and commingle with the Elementals, the progressed entities of the pure animal kingdom, to develop little by little the full type of humanity."

These Dhyan Chohans, as we see, do not pass through the three kingdoms as do the lower Pitris; nor do they incarnate in man until the Third Root Race. Thus, as the teaching stands:

"*Man in the First Round and First Race on Globe D, our Earth, was an ethereal being (a Lunar Dhyani, as man), non-intelligent but superspiritual; and correspondingly, on the law of analogy, in the First Race of the Fourth Round. In each of the subsequent races and sub-races . . . he grows more and more into an encased or incarnate being, but still preponderatingly ethereal. . . . He is sexless, and, like the animal and vegetable he develops monstrous bodies correspondential with his coarser surroundings.*

"II. Round. He (Man) is still gigantic and ethereal but growing firmer and more condensed in body, a more physical man. Yet still less intelligent than spiritual (1), for mind is a slower and more difficult evolution than is the physical frame . . .

"III. Round. He has now a perfectly concrete or compacted body, at first the form of a giant-ape, and now more intelligent, or rather cunning, than spiritual. For, on the downward arc, he has now reached a point where his primordial spirituality is eclipsed and overshadowed by nascent mentality (2). In the last half of the Third Round his gigantic stature decreases, and his body improves in texture, and he becomes a more rational being, though still more an ape than a

Deva. . . . (All this is almost exactly repeated in the third Root-Race of the Fourth Round.)

"IV. Round. Intellect has an enormous development in this Round. The (hitherto) dumb races acquire our (present) human speech on this globe, on which, from the Fourth Race, language is perfected and knowledge increases. At this half-way point of the Fourth Round (as of the Fourth Root, or Atlantean, race) humanity passes the axial point of the minor Manvantara cycle . . . . the world teeming with the results of intellectual activity and spiritual decrease . . . ."

This is from the authentic letter; what follows are the later remarks and additional explanations traced by the same hand in the form of footnotes.

(1.) " . . . The original letter contained general teaching -- a 'bird's eye view' -- and particularized nothing. . . . To speak of 'physical man' while limiting the statement to the early Rounds would be drifting back to the miraculous and instantaneous 'coats of skin.' . . . The first 'Nature,' the first 'body,' the first 'mind' on the first plane of perception, on the first Globe in the first Round, is what was meant. For Karma and evolution have --

' . . . centred in our make such strange extremes!

From different Natures marvellously mixed . . .'

(2.) "Restore: he has now reached the point (by analogy, and as the Third Root Race in the Fourth Round) where his ("the angel"-man's) primordial spirituality is eclipsed and overshadowed by nascent human mentality, and you have the true version on your thumbnail. . . ."

These are the words of the Teacher. It stands to reason that there must be an enormous difference in such terms as "objectivity" and "subjectivity," "materiality" and "spirituality," when the same terms are applied to different planes of being and perception. All this must be taken in its relative sense. And therefore there is little to be wondered at, if, left to his own speculations, an author, however eager to learn, yet quite inexperienced in these abstruse teachings, has fallen into an error. Neither was the difference between the "Rounds" and the "Races" sufficiently defined in the letters received, nor was there anything of the kind required before, as the ordinary Eastern disciple would have found out the difference in a moment. Moreover, to quote from a letter of the Master's (188-), "the teachings were imparted under protest. . . . They were, so to say, smuggled goods . . . and when I remained face to face with only one correspondent, the other, Mr. . . . ., had so far tossed all the cards into confusion, that little remained to be said without trespassing upon law." Theosophists, "whom it may concern," will understand what is meant.

The outcome of all this is that nothing had ever been said in the "letters" to warrant the assurance that the Occult doctrine has ever taught, or any Adept believed in, the preposterous modern theory of the descent of man from a common ancestor with the ape -- an anthropoid of the actual animal kind, unless metaphorically. To this day the world is more full of "ape-like men" than the woods are of "men-like apes." The ape is sacred in India because its origin is well known to the Initiates, though concealed under a thick veil of allegory. Hanuman is the son of Pavana (Vayu, "the god of the wind") by Anjana, a monster called Kesari, though his genealogy varies. The reader who bears this in mind will find in Book II. *passim*, the whole explanation of this ingenious allegory. The "Men" of the Third Race (who separated) were "Gods" by their spirituality and purity, though senseless, and as yet destitute of mind, as men.

These "Men" of the Third Race -- the ancestors of the Atlanteans -- were just such ape-like, intellectually senseless giants as were those beings, who, during the Third Round, represented Humanity. Morally irresponsible, it was these third Race "men" who, through promiscuous connection with animal species lower than themselves, created that missing link which became ages later (in the tertiary period only) the remote ancestor of the real ape as we find it now in the pithecoid family.

Thus the earlier teachings, however unsatisfactory, vague and fragmentary, did not teach the evolution of "man" from the "ape." Nor does the author of "Esoteric Buddhism" assert it anywhere in his work in so many words; but, owing to his inclination towards modern science, he uses language which might perhaps justify such an inference. The man who preceded the Fourth, the Atlantean race, however much he may have looked physically like a "gigantic ape" -- "the counterfeit of man who hath not the life of a man" -- was still a thinking and already a speaking man. The "Lemuro-Atlantean" was a highly civilized race, and if one accepts tradition, which is better history than the speculative fiction which now passes under that name, he was higher than we are with all our sciences and the degraded civilization of the day: at any rate, the Lemuro-Atlantean of the closing Third Race was so.

And now we may return to the Stanzas.

5. AT THE FOURTH (*Round, or revolution of life and being around "the seven smaller wheels"*) (*a*), THE SONS ARE TOLD TO CREATE THEIR IMAGES. ONE THIRD REFUSES. TWO (*thirds*) OBEY.

The full meaning of this sloka can be fully comprehended only after reading the detailed additional explanations in the "Anthropogenesis" and its commentaries, in Book II. Between this Sloka and the last, Sloka 4 in this same Stanza, extend long ages; and there now gleams the dawn and sunrise of another aeon. The drama enacted on our planet is at the beginning of its fourth act, but for a clearer comprehension of the whole play the reader will have to turn back before he can proceed onward. For this verse belongs to the general Cosmogony given in the archaic volumes, whereas Book II. will give a detailed account of the "Creation" or rather the formation, of the first human beings, followed by the second humanity, and then by the third; or, as they are called, "the first, second, and the third Root-Races." As the solid Earth began by being a ball of liquid fire, of fiery dust and its protoplasmic phantom, so did man.

(*a*) That which is meant by the qualification the "Fourth" is explained as the "fourth Round" only on the authority of the Commentaries. It can equally mean fourth "Eternity" as "Fourth Round," or even the fourth (our) Globe. For, as will repeatedly be shown, it is the fourth Sphere on the fourth or lowest plane of material life. And it so happens that we are in the Fourth Round, at the middle point of which the perfect equilibrium between Spirit and Matter had to take place. Says the Commentary explaining the verse: --

"*The holy youths (the gods) refused to multiply and create species after their likeness, after their kind. They are not fit forms (rupas) for us. They have to grow. They refuse to enter the chhayas (shadows or images) of their inferiors. Thus had selfish feeling prevailed from the beginning, even among the gods, and they fell under the eye of the Karmic Lipikas.*"

They had to suffer for it in later births. How the punishment reached the gods will be seen in the second volume.

6. THE CURSE IS PRONOUNCED (*a*): THEY WILL BE BORN IN THE FOURTH (*Race*), SUFFER AND CAUSE SUFFERING (*b*). THIS IS THE FIRST WAR (*c*).

(*a*) It is a universal tradition that, before the physiological "Fall," propagation of one's kind, whether human or animal, took place through the WILL of the Creators, or of their progeny. It was the Fall of Spirit into generation, not the Fall of mortal man. It has already been stated that, to become a Self-Conscious Spirit, the latter must pass through every cycle of being, culminating in its highest point on earth in Man.

(*b*) "The curse is pronounced" does not mean, in this instance, that any personal Being, god, or superior Spirit, pronounced it, but simply that the cause which could but create bad results had been generated, and that the effects of a Karmic cause could lead the "Beings" that counteracted the laws of Nature, and thus impeded her legitimate progress, only to bad incarnations, hence to suffering.

(c) "There were many wars" refers to several struggles of adjustment, spiritual, cosmical, and astronomical, but chiefly to the mystery of the evolution of man as he is now. Powers -- pure Essences -- "that were told to create" is a sentence that relates to a mystery explained, as already said, elsewhere. It is not only one of the most hidden secrets of Nature -- that of generation, over whose solution the Embryologists have vainly put their heads together -- but likewise a divine function that involves that other religious, or rather dogmatic, mystery, the "Fall" of the Angels, as it is called. Satan and his rebellious host would thus prove, when the meaning of the allegory is explained, to have refused to create physical man, only to become the direct Saviours and the Creators of "*divine* Man." The symbolical teaching is more than mystical and religious, it is purely scientific, as will be seen later on. For, instead of remaining a mere blind, functioning medium, impelled and guided by fathomless LAW, the "rebellious" Angel claimed and enforced his right of independent judgment and will, his right of free-agency and responsibility, since man and angel are alike under Karmic Law.

"And there was war in Heaven. . . . Michael and his angels fought against the Dragon; and the Dragon fought and his angels, and prevailed not; neither was their place found any more in Heaven. And the Dragon was cast out, that old serpent, called the devil and Satan, which deceiveth the whole world."

The Kabalistic version of the same story is given in the Codex Nazareus, the scripture of the Nazarenes, the real mystic Christians of John the Baptist and the Initiates of Christos. Bahak-Zivo, the "Father of the Genii," is ordered to construct creatures (to create). But, as he is "ignorant of Orcus," he fails to do so, and calls in Fetahil, a still purer spirit, to his aid, who fails still worse. This is a repetition of the failure of the "Fathers," the lords of light who fail one after the other. (Book II, Sloka 17.)

We will now quote from our earlier Volumes: --

"Then steps on the stage of creation the spirit   (of the Earth so-called, or the Soul, Psyche, which St. James calls 'devilish') the lower portion the *Anima Mundi* or Astral Light. (See the close of this Sloka). With the Nazarenes and the Gnostics this Spirit was *feminine.* Thus the spirit of the Earth perceiving that for Fetahil, the *newest man* (the latest), the splendour was 'changed,' and that for splendour existed 'decrease and damage,' she awakes Karabtanos, 'who was frantic and *without sense and judgment*,' and says to him: -- 'Arise, see, the splendour (light) of the *newest* man (Fetahil) has failed (to produce or create men), the decrease of this splendour is visible. Rise up, come with thy MOTHER (the Spiritus) and free thee from limits by which thou art held, and those more ample than the whole world.' After which follows the union of the frantic and blind matter, guided by the insinuations of the spirit (not the *Divine* breath but the *Astral* spirit, which by its double essence is already tainted with matter); and the offer of the MOTHER being accepted, the Spiritus conceives "Seven Figures," and the seven *stellars* (planets) which represent also the *seven capital sins*, the progeny of an astral soul separated from its divine source (spirit) and *matter*, the blind demon of concupiscence. Seeing this, Fetahil extends his hand towards the abyss of matter, and says: -- 'Let the Earth exist, just as the abode of the powers has existed.' Dipping his hand in the chaos, which he condenses, he creates our planet. "

"Then the Codex proceeds to tell how Bahak-Zivo was separated from the Spiritus, and the Genii or angels from the rebels.   Then Mano   (the greatest), who dwells with the greatest FERHO, call Kebar-Zivo (known also by the name of Nebat-Iavar bar Iufin Ifafin), Helm and *Vine* of the food of life,   he being the third life, and commiserating the rebellious and foolish Genii, on account of the magnitude of their ambition, says: 'Lord of the Genii   (AEons), see what the Genii, the rebellious angels do, and about what they are consulting.   They say, 'Let us call for the world, and let us call the 'powers' into existence." The Genii are the *Principes*, the "Sons of Light," but thou art the "*Messenger of Life.*"

And in order to counteract the influence of the seven "badly disposed" principles, the progeny of *Spiritus*, CABAR-ZIO, the mighty Lord of Splendor, produces *seven other lives* (the cardinal virtues) who shine in their own form and light "from on high"   and thus re-establish the balance between good and evil, light and darkness.

Here one finds a repetition of the early *allegorical*, dual systems, as the Zoroastrian, and detects a germ of the dogmatic and dualistic religions of the future, a germ which has grown into such a luxuriant tree in ecclesiastical Christianity. It is already the outline of the two "Supremes" -- God and Satan. But in the Stanzas no such idea exists.

Most of the Western Christian Kabalists -- pre-eminently Eliphas Levi -- in their desire to reconcile the Occult Sciences with Church dogmas, did their best to make of the "Astral Light" only and preeminently the *Pleroma* of early Church Fathers, the abode of the Hosts of the Fallen Angels, of the "Archons" and "Powers." But the Astral Light, while only the lower aspect of the Absolute, is yet dual. It is the *Anima Mundi*, and ought never to be viewed otherwise, except for Kabalistic purposes. The difference which exists between its "light" and its "Living Fire" ought to be ever present in the mind of the Seer and the "Psychic." The higher aspect, without which only creatures of matter from that Astral Light can be produced, is this Living Fire, and it is the Seventh Principle. It is said in "Isis Unveiled," in a complete description of it: --

"The Astral Light or *Anima Mundi* is dual and bisexual. The (ideal) male part of it is purely divine and spiritual, it is the *Wisdom*, it is Spirit or Purusha; while the female portion (the Spiritus of the Nazarenes) is tainted, in one sense, with matter, *is* indeed matter, and therefore is evil already. It is the life-principle of every living creature, and furnishes the astral soul, the fluidic *perisprit*, to men, animals, fowls of the air, and everything living. Animals have only the latent germ of the highest immortal soul in them. . . . . This latter will develop only after a series of countless evolutions; the doctrine of which evolution is contained in the Kabalistic axiom: 'A stone becomes a plant; a plant, a beast; a beast, a man; a man, a spirit; and the spirit, a god.'" (Vol. I., p. 301, note.)

The seven principles of the Eastern Initiates had not been explained when "Isis" was written, but only the three *Kabalistic Faces* of the semi-exoteric Kabala. But these contain the description of the mystic natures of the first group of Dhyan Chohans in the *regimen ignis*, the region and "rule (or government) of fire," which group is divided into three classes, synthesized by the first, which makes *four* or the "Tetraktis." (*See Comments on Stanza VII. Book I.*) If one studies the Comments attentively he will find the same progression in the angelic natures, viz., from the *passive* down to the *active*, the last of these Beings being as near to the *Ahamkara* element (the region or plane wherein *Egoship* or the feeling of *I-am-ness* is beginning to be defined) as the first ones are near to the undifferentiated essence. The former are *Arupa*, incorporeal; the latter, Rupa, corporeal.

In Volume II. of *Isis* (*p.* 183 *et seq.*) the philosophical systems of the Gnostics and the primitive Jewish Christians, the Nazarenes and the Ebionites, are fully considered. They show the views held in those days -- outside the circle of Mosaic Jews -- about Jehovah. He was identified by all the Gnostics with the evil, rather than with the good principle. For them, he was *Ilda-Baoth*, "the son of Darkness," whose mother, Sophia Achamoth, was the daughter of Sophia, the Divine Wisdom (the female Holy Ghost of the early Christians) -- Akasa;   while Sophia Achamoth personified the lower Astral Light or *Ether*. Ilda-Baoth, or Jehovah, is simply one of the Elohim, the seven creative Spirits, and one of the lower Sephiroth. He produces from himself seven other Gods, "Stellar Spirits" (or the lunar ancestors), for they are all the same.   They are all *in his own image* (the "Spirits of the Face"), and the reflections one of the other, and have become darker and more material as they successively receded from their originator. They also inhabit seven regions disposed like a ladder, as its rungs slope up and down the scale of spirit and matter.   With Pagans and Christians, with Hindus and Chaldeans, with the Greek as with the Roman Catholics -- with a slight variation of the texts in their interpretations -- they all were the Genii of the seven planets, as of the seven planetary spheres of our septenary chain, of which Earth is the lowest. (See *Isis*, Vol. II. *p.* 186.) This connects the "Stellar" and "Lunar" Spirits with the higher planetary Angels and the *Saptarishis* (the seven Rishis of the Stars) of the Hindus -- as subordinate Angels (Messengers) to these "Rishis," the emanations, on the descending scale, of the former. Such, in the opinion of the philosophical Gnostics, were the God and the Archangels now worshipped by the Christians! The "Fallen Angels" and the legend of the "War in Heaven" is thus purely pagan in its origin and comes from India *via* Persia and

Chaldea. The only reference to it in the Christian canon is found in Revelations xii., as quoted a few pages back.

Thus "SATAN," once he ceases to be viewed in the superstitious, dogmatic, unphilosophical spirit of the Churches, grows into the grandiose image of one who made of *terrestrial a divine* MAN; who gave him, throughout the long cycle of Maha-kalpa the law of the Spirit of Life, and made him free from the Sin of Ignorance, hence of death. (See the Section *On Satan* in Part II. Vol. II.)

6. **T**HE OLDER WHEELS ROTATED DOWNWARD AND UPWARD (*a*). . . . THE **M**OTHER'S SPAWN FILLED THE WHOLE (*Kosmos*). **T**HERE WERE BATTLES FOUGHT BETWEEN THE **C**REATORS AND THE **D**ESTROYERS, AND BATTLES FOUGHT FOR **S**PACE; THE SEED APPEARING AND REAPPEARING CONTINUOUSLY (*b*).

(*a*) Here, having finished for the time being with our side-issues -- which, however they may break the flow of the narrative, are necessary for the elucidation of the whole scheme -- the reader must return once more to Cosmogony. The phrase "Older wheels" refers to the worlds or Globes of our chain as they were during the "previous Rounds." The present Stanza, when explained esoterically, is found embodied entirely in the Kabalistic works. Therein will be found the very history of the evolution of those countless Globes which evolve after a periodical Pralaya, rebuilt from old material into new forms. The previous Globes disintegrate and reappear transformed and perfected for a new phase of life. In the Kabala, worlds are compared to sparks which fly from under the hammer of the great Architect -- LAW, the law which rules all the smaller Creators.

The following comparative diagram shows the identity between the two systems, the Kabalistic and the Eastern. The three upper are the three higher planes of consciousness, revealed and explained in both schools only to the Initiates, the lower ones represent the four lower planes -- the lowest being our plane, or the visible Universe.

These seven *planes* correspond to the seven *states* of consciousness in man. It remains with him to attune the three higher states in himself to the three higher planes in Kosmos. But before he can attempt to attune, he must awaken the three "seats" to life and activity. And how many are capable of bringing themselves to even a superficial comprehension of *Atma-Vidya* (Spirit-Knowledge), or what is called by the Sufis, *Rohanee!* In Section the **VII**th of this Book, in Sub-section 3, the reader will find a still clearer explanation of the above in the Commentary upon *Saptaparna* -- the man-plant. See also the Section of that name in Part II.

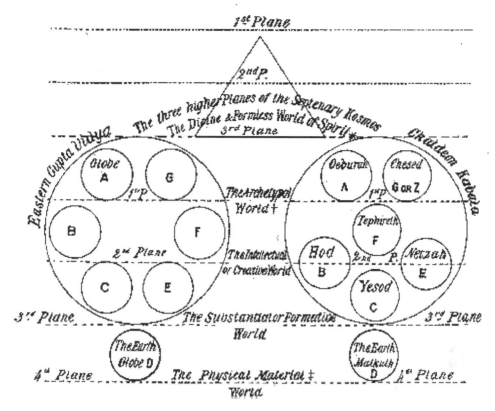

The *Arupa* or "formless," there where form ceases to exist, on the objective plane.

† The word "Archetypal" must not be taken here in the sense that the Platonists gave to it, *i.e.*, the world as it existed *in the Mind* of the Deity; but in that of a world made as a first model, to be followed and improved upon by the worlds which succeed it physically -- though deteriorating in purity.

‡ These are the four lower planes of Cosmic Consciousness, the three higher planes being inaccessible to human intellect as developed at present. The seven states of human consciousness pertain to quite another question.

(*b*) "The Seed appears and disappears continuously." Here "Seed" stands for "the World-germ," viewed by Science as material particles in a highly attenuated condition, but in Occult physics as "Spiritual particles," *i.e.*, supersensuous matter existing in a state of primeval differentiation. In theogony, every Seed is an ethereal organism, from which evolves later on a celestial being, a God.

In the "beginning," that which is called in mystic phraseology "Cosmic *Desire*" evolves into absolute Light. Now light without any shadow would be absolute light -- in other words, absolute darkness -- as physical science seeks to prove. That shadow appears under the form of primordial matter, allegorized -- if one likes -- in the shape of the Spirit of Creative Fire or Heat. If, rejecting the poetical form and allegory, science chooses to see in this the primordial Fire-Mist, it is welcome to do so. Whether one way or the other, whether Fohat or the famous FORCE of Science, nameless, and as difficult of definition as our Fohat himself, that Something "caused the Universe to move with circular motion," as Plato has it; or, as the Occult teaching expresses it:

"*The Central Sun causes Fohat to collect primordial dust in the form of balls, to impel them to move in converging lines and finally to approach each other and aggregate.*" (*Book of Dzyan*) . . . . . "*Being scattered in Space, without order or system, the world-germs come into frequent collision until their final aggregation, after which they become wanderers*

(Comets). Then the battles and struggles begin. The older (bodies) attract the younger, while others repel them. Many perish, devoured by their stronger companions. Those that escape become worlds."

We have been assured that there exist several modern works of speculative fancy upon such struggles for life in sidereal heaven, especially in the German language. We rejoice to hear it, for ours is an Occult teaching lost in the darkness of archaic ages. We have treated of it fully in "*Isis Unveiled*," and the idea of Darwinian-like evolution, of struggle for life and supremacy, and of the "survival of the fittest" among the Hosts above as the Hosts below, runs throughout both the volumes of our earlier work, written in 1876 (*See Index in "Isis Unveiled" at the words "Evolution" -- "Darwin" -- "Kapila" -- "Battle of Life*," etc. etc.) But the idea was not ours, it is that of antiquity.

Even the Puranic writers have ingeniously interwoven allegory with Cosmic facts and human events. Any symbologist may discern the astro-cosmical allusion even though he be unable to grasp the whole meaning. The great "Wars in Heaven," in the Puranas; the wars of the Titans, in Hesiod and other classical writers; the "struggles," also in the Egyptian legend between Osiris and Typhon, and even those in the Scandinavian legends, all refer to the same subject. Northern Mythology refers to it as the battle of the Flames, the sons of Muspel who fought on the field of Wigred. All these relate to Heaven and Earth, and have a double and often even a triple meaning, and esoteric application to things above as to things below. They relate severally to astronomical, theogonical and human struggles; to the adjustment of orbs, and the supremacy among nations and tribes. The "Struggle for Existence" and the "Survival of the Fittest" reigned supreme from the moment that Kosmos manifested into being, and could hardly escape the observant eye of the ancient Sages. Hence the incessant fights of Indra, the god of the Firmament, with the Asuras -- degraded from high gods into Cosmic demons; and with Vritri or Ah-hi; the battles fought between stars and constellations, between Moon and planets -- later on incarnated as kings and mortals. Hence also the War in Heaven of Michael and his Host against the Dragon (Jupiter and Lucifer-Venus), when a third of the stars of the rebellious host was hurled down into Space, and "its place was found no more in Heaven." As said long ago -- "This is the basic and fundamental stone of the secret cycles. It shows that the Brahmins and Tanaim . . . speculated on the creation and development of the world quite in a Darwinian way, both anticipating him and his school in the natural selection of species, the survival of the fittest, and transformation. . . . There were old worlds that perished conquered by the new," etc., etc. ("*Isis Unveiled*," Vol. II., *p.* 260.) The assertion that all the worlds (Stars, planets, etc.) -- as soon as a nucleus of primordial substance in the *laya* (undifferentiated) state is informed by the freed principles, of a just *deceased* sidereal body -- become first comets, and then Suns to cool down to inhabitable worlds, is a teaching as old as the Rishis.

Thus the Secret Books distinctly teach, as we see, an astronomy that would not be rejected even by modern speculation could the latter thoroughly understand its teachings.

For, archaic astronomy, and the ancient, physical and mathematical sciences, expressed views identical with those of modern science, and many of far more momentous import. A "struggle for life" as a "survival of the fittest" in the worlds above, as on our planet here below, are distinctly taught. This teaching, however, although it would not be "entirely rejected" by Science, is sure to be repudiated as an integral whole. For it avers that there are only seven Self-born primordial "gods" emanated from the trinitarian ONE. In other words, it means that all the worlds or sidereal bodies (always on strict analogy) are formed one from the other, after the primordial manifestation at the beginning of the "Great Age" is accomplished. The birth of the celestial bodies in Space is compared to a crowd or multitude of "pilgrims" at the festival of the "Fires." Seven ascetics appear on the threshold of the temple with seven lighted sticks of incense. At the light of these the first row of pilgrims light their incense sticks. After which every ascetic begins whirling his stick around his head in space, and furnishes the rest with fire. Thus with the heavenly bodies. A laya-centre is lighted and awakened into life by the fires of another "pilgrim," after which the new "centre" rushes into space and becomes a comet. It is only after losing its velocity, and hence its fiery tail, that the "Fiery Dragon" settles down into quiet and steady life as a regular respectable citizen of the sidereal family. Therefore it is said: --

Born in the unfathomable depths of Space, out of the homogeneous Element called the World-Soul, every nucleus of Cosmic matter, suddenly launched into being, begins life under the most hostile circumstances. Through a series of countless ages, it has to conquer for itself a place in the infinitudes. It circles round and round between denser and already fixed bodies, moving by jerks, and pulling towards some given point or centre that attracts it, trying to avoid, like a ship drawn into a channel dotted with reefs and sunken rocks, other bodies that draw and repel it in turn; many perish, their mass disintegrating through stronger masses, and, when born within a system, chiefly within the insatiable stomachs of various Suns. (*See Comm. to Stanza IV*). Those which move slower and are propelled into an elliptic course are doomed to annihilation sooner or later. Others moving in parabolic curves generally escape destruction, owing to their velocity.

Some very critical readers will perhaps imagine that this teaching, as to the cometary stage passed through by all heavenly bodies, is in contradiction with the statements just made as to the moon being the mother of the earth. They will perhaps fancy that intuition is needed to harmonize the two. But no intuition is in truth required. What does Science know of Comets, their genesis, growth, and ultimate behaviour? Nothing -- absolutely nothing! And what is there so impossible that a laya centre -- a lump of cosmic protoplasm, homogeneous and latent, when suddenly animated or fired up -- should rush from its bed in Space and whirl throughout the abysmal depths in order to strengthen its homogeneous organism by an accumulation and addition of differentiated elements? And why should not such a comet settle in life, live, and become an inhabited globe!

"The abodes of Fohat are many," it is said. "He places his four fiery (electro-positive) Sons in the "Four circles"; these *Circles* are the Equator, the Ecliptic, and the two parallels of declination, or the tropics -- to preside over the *climates* of which are placed the Four mystical Entities. Then again: "Other seven (sons) are commissioned to preside over the seven hot, and seven cold *lokas* (the hells of the orthodox Brahmins) at the two ends of the Egg of Matter (our Earth and its poles). The seven *lokas* are also called the "Rings," elsewhere, and the "Circles." The ancients made the polar circles *seven* instead of two, as Europeans do; for Mount Meru, which is the North Pole, is said to have seven gold and seven silver steps leading to it.

The strange statement made in one of the Stanzas: "The Songs of Fohat and his Sons were *radiant* as the noon-tide Sun and the Moon combined;" and that the four Sons on the *middle* four-fold Circle "*saw* their father's songs and *heard* his Solar-selenic radiance;" is explained in the Commentary in these words: "The agitation of *the Fohatic* Forces at the two cold ends (North and South Poles) of the Earth which resulted in a multicoloured radiance at night, have in them several of the properties of Akasa (Ether) *colour* and sound as well." . . . . . . "Sound is the characteristic of Akasa (Ether): it generates air, the property of which is Touch; which (by friction) becomes productive of Colour and Light." . . . . . . (Vishnu Purana.)

Perhaps the above will be regarded as archaic nonsense, but it will be better comprehended, if the reader remembers the Aurora Borealis and Australis, both of which take place at the very centres of terrestrial electric and magnetic forces. The two poles are said to be the store-houses, the receptacles and liberators, at the same time, of Cosmic and terrestrial Vitality (Electricity); from the surplus of which the Earth, had it not been for these two natural "safety-valves," would have been rent to pieces long ago. At the same time it is now a theory that has lately become an axiom, that the phenomenon of polar lights is accompanied by, and productive of, strong sounds, like whistling, hissing, and cracking. (But see Professor Trumholdt's works on the Aurora Borealis, and his correspondence regarding this moot question.)

7. MAKE THY CALCULATIONS, O LANOO, IF THOU WOULDST LEARN THE CORRECT AGE OF THY SMALL WHEEL (*chain*). ITS FOURTH SPOKE IS OUR MOTHER (*Earth*) (*a*). REACH THE FOURTH "FRUIT" OF THE FOURTH PATH OF KNOWLEDGE THAT LEADS TO NIRVANA, AND THOU SHALT COMPREHEND, FOR THOU SHALT SEE (*b*).

(*a*) The "small wheel" is our chain of spheres, and the fourth spoke is our Earth, the fourth in the chain. It is one of those on which the "hot (positive) breath of the Sun" has a direct effect.

To calculate its age, however, as the pupil is asked to do in the Stanza, is rather difficult, since we are not given the figures of the Great Kalpa, and are not allowed to publish those of our small Yugas, except as to the approximate duration of these. "The older wheels rotated for one Eternity and one half of an Eternity," it says. We know that by "Eternity" the seventh part of 311,040,000,000,000 years, or an age of Brahma is meant. But what of that? We also know that, to begin with, if we take for our basis the above figures, we have first of all to eliminate from the 100 years of Brahma (or 311,040,000,000,000 years) two *years* taken up by the Sandhyas (twilights), which leaves 98, as we have to bring it to the mystical combination 14 x 7. But *we* have no knowledge at what time precisely the evolution and formation of our little earth began. Therefore it is impossible to calculate its age, unless the time of its birth is given -- which the TEACHERS refuse to do, so far. At the close of this Book and in Book II., however, some chronological hints will be given. We must remember, moreover, that the law of Analogy holds good for the worlds, as it does for man; and that as "The ONE (Deity) becomes Two (Deva or Angel) and *Two* becomes *Three* (or man)," etc., etc., so we are taught that the *Curds* (world-stuff) become wanderers, (Comets), these become stars, and the stars (the centres of vortices) *our sun and planets* -- to put it briefly.

(*b*) There are four grades of initiation mentioned in exoteric works, which are known respectively in Sanskrit as "Srotapanna," "Sagardagan," "Anagamin," and "Arhan" -- the four paths to Nirvana, in this, our fourth Round, bearing the same appellations. The Arhan, though he can see the Past, the Present, and the Future, is not yet the highest Initiate; for the Adept himself, the *initiated* candidate, becomes chela (pupil) to a higher Initiate. Three further higher grades have to be conquered by the Arhan who would reach the apex of the ladder of Arhatship. There are those who have reached it even in this fifth race of ours, but the faculties necessary for the attainment of these higher grades will be fully developed in the average ascetic only at the end of this Root-Race, and in the Sixth and Seventh. Thus there will always be Initiates and the Profane till the end of this minor Manvantara, the present *life-cycle.* The *Arhats* of the "fire-mist" of the 7th rung are but one remove from the Root-Base of their Hierarchy -- the highest on Earth, and our Terrestrial chain. This "Root-Base" has a name which can only be translated by several compound words into English" -- "the ever-living-human-Banyan." This "Wondrous Being" descended from a "high region," they say, in the early part of the Third Age, before the separation of the sexes of the Third Race.

This Third Race is sometimes called collectively "the Sons of *Passive Yoga,*" i.e., it was produced unconsciously by the second Race, which, as it was intellectually inactive, is supposed to have been constantly plunged in a kind of blank or abstract contemplation, as required by the conditions of the Yoga state. In the first or earlier portion of the existence of this third race, while it was yet in its state of purity, the "Sons of Wisdom," who, as will be seen, incarnated in this Third Race, produced by *Kriyasakti* a progeny called the "Sons of Ad" or "of the Fire-Mist," the "Sons of Will and Yoga," etc. They were a conscious production, as a portion of the race was already animated with the divine spark of spiritual, superior intelligence. It was not a Race, this progeny. It was at first a wondrous Being, called the "Initiator," and after him a group of semi-divine and semi-human beings. "*Set apart*" in Archaic *genesis* for certain purposes, they are those in whom are said to have incarnated the highest Dhyanis, "Munis and Rishis from previous Manvantaras" -- *to form the nursery for future human adepts*, on this earth and during the present cycle. These "Sons of Will and Yoga" born, so to speak, in an immaculate way, remained, it is explained, entirely apart from the rest of mankind.

The "BEING" just referred to, which has to remain nameless, is the *Tree* from which, in subsequent ages, all the great *historically* known Sages and Hierophants, such as the Rishi Kapila, Hermes, Enoch, Orpheus, etc., etc., have branched off. As objective *man*, he is the mysterious (to the profane -- the ever invisible) yet ever present Personage about whom legends are rife in the East, especially among the Occultists and the students of the Sacred Science. It is he who changes form, yet remains ever the same. And it is he again who holds spiritual sway over the *initiated* Adepts throughout the whole world. He is, as said, the "Nameless One" who has so many names, and yet whose names and whose very nature are unknown. He is *the* "Initiator," called the "GREAT SACRIFICE." For, sitting at the threshold of LIGHT, he looks into it from within the circle of Darkness, which he will not cross; nor will he quit his post till the last day of this life-cycle. Why does the solitary Watcher remain at his self-chosen post? Why does he sit by the fountain of primeval Wisdom, of which he drinks no longer, as he has naught to learn which he does not know -- aye, neither on this Earth, nor in its heaven? Because the lonely, sore-footed pilgrims on their way back to their *home* are never sure to the last moment of not losing their way in this limitless desert of illusion and matter called Earth-Life. Because he would fain show the way to that region of freedom and light, from which he is a voluntary exile himself, to every prisoner who has succeeded in liberating himself from the bonds of flesh and illusion. Because, in short, he has sacrificed himself for the sake of mankind, though but a few Elect may profit by the GREAT SACRIFICE.

It is under the direct, silent guidance of this MAHA -- (great) -- GURU that all the other less divine Teachers and instructors of mankind became, from the first awakening of human consciousness, the guides of early Humanity. It is through these "Sons of God" that infant humanity got its first notions of all the arts and sciences, as well as of spiritual knowledge; and it is they who have laid the first foundation-stone of those ancient civilizations that puzzle so sorely our modern generation of students and scholars.

Although these matters were barely hinted at in "*Isis Unveiled*," it will be well to remind the reader of what was said in Vol. I., pp. 587 to 593, concerning a certain Sacred Island in Central Asia, and to refer him for further details to the chapter in Book II. on "The Sons of God and the Sacred Island." A few more explanations, however, though thrown out in a fragmentary form, may help the student to obtain a glimpse into the present mystery.

To state at least one detail concerning these mysterious "Sons of God" in plain words. It is from them, these Brahmaputras, that the high Dwijas, the initiated Brahmins of old justly claimed descent, while the modern Brahmin would have the lowest castes believe literally that they issued direct from the mouth of Brahma. This is the esoteric teaching, which adds moreover that, although these descendants (spiritually of course) from the "sons of Will and Yoga," became in time divided into opposite sexes, as their "*Kriyasakti*" progenitors did themselves, later on; yet even their degenerate descendants have down to the present day retained a veneration and respect for the creative function, and still regard it in the light of a religious ceremony, whereas the more civilized nations consider it as a mere animal function. Compare the western views and practice in these matters with the Institutions of Manu in regard to the laws of Grihasta and married life. The true Brahmin is thus indeed "he whose seven forefathers have drunk the juice of the moon-plant (Soma)," and who is a "Trisuparna," for he has understood the secret of the Vedas.

And, to this day, such Brahmins know that, during its early beginnings, psychic and physical intellect being dormant and consciousness still undeveloped, the spiritual conceptions of that race were quite unconnected with its physical surroundings. That *divine* man dwelt in his animal -- though externally human -- form; and, if there was instinct in him, no self-consciousness came to enlighten the darkness of the latent fifth principle. When, moved by the law of Evolution, the Lords of Wisdom infused into him the spark of consciousness, the first feeling it awoke to life and activity was a sense of solidarity, of one-ness with his spiritual creators. As the child's first feeling is for its mother and nurse, so the first aspirations of the awakening consciousness in primitive man were for those whose element he felt within himself, and who yet were outside, and independent of him. DEVOTION arose out of that feeling, and became the first and foremost motor in his nature; for it is the only one which is natural in our heart, which is innate in us, and which we find alike in human babe and the young of the animal. This feeling of irrepressible, instinctive aspiration in primitive man is beautifully, and one may say intuitionally, described by Carlyle. "The great antique heart," he exclaims, "how like a child's in its simplicity, like a man's in its earnest solemnity and depth! heaven lies over him wheresoever he goes or stands on the earth; making all the earth a mystic temple to him, the earth's business all a kind of worship. Glimpses of bright creatures flash in the common sunlight; angels yet hover, doing God's messages among men . . . . . Wonder, miracle, encompass the man; he lives in an element of miracle . . . . A great law of duty, high as these two infinitudes (heaven and hell), dwarfing all else, annihilating all else -- it was a reality, and it is one: the garment only of it is dead; the essence of it lives through all times and all eternity!"

It lives undeniably, and has settled in all its ineradicable strength and power in the Asiatic Aryan heart from the Third Race direct through its first "mind-born" sons, -- the fruits of *Kriyasakti*. As time rolled on the holy caste of Initiates produced but rarely, and from age to age, such perfect creatures: beings apart, inwardly, though the same as those who produced them, outwardly.

While in the infancy of the third primitive race:

> "*A creature of a more exalted kind*
> *Was wanting yet, and therefore was designed;*
> *Conscious of thought, of more capacious breast*
> *For empire formed and fit to rule the rest. . . . .*"

It was called into being, a ready and perfect vehicle for the incarnating denizens of higher spheres, who took forthwith their abodes in these forms born of *Spiritual* WILL and the natural divine power in man. It was a child of pure Spirit, mentally unalloyed with any tincture of earthly element. Its physical frame alone was of time and of life, as it drew its intelligence direct from above. It was the living tree of divine wisdom; and may therefore be likened to the Mundane Tree of the Norse Legend, which cannot wither and die until the last battle of life shall be fought, while its roots are gnawed all the time by the dragon Nidhogg; for even so, the first and holy Son of Kriyasakti had his body gnawed by the tooth of time, but the roots of his inner being remained for ever undecaying and strong, because they grew and expanded in heaven not on earth. He was the first of the FIRST, and he was the seed of all the others. There were other "Sons of Kriyasakti" produced by a second Spiritual effort, but the first one has remained to this day the Seed of divine Knowledge, the One and the Supreme among the terrestrial "Sons of Wisdom." Of this subject we can say no more, except to add that in every age -- aye, even in our own -- there have been great intellects who have understood the problem correctly.

How comes our physical body to the state of perfection it is found in now? Through millions of years of evolution, of course, yet never through, or from, animals, as taught by materialism. For, as Carlyle says: -- ". . . The essence of our being, the mystery in us that calls itself 'I,' -- what words have we for such things? -- it is a breath of Heaven, the highest Being reveals himself in man. This body, these faculties, this life of ours, is it not all as a vesture for the UNNAMED?"

The *breath* of heaven, or rather the breath of life, called in the Bible *Nephesh*, is in every animal, in every animate speck as in every mineral atom. But none of these has, like man, the consciousness of the nature of that highest Being, as none has that divine harmony in its form which man possesses. It is, as Novalis said, and no one since has said it better, as repeated by Carlyle: --

"There is but one temple in the universe, and that is the body of man. Nothing is holier than that high form . . . . We touch heaven when we lay our hand on a human body!" "This sounds like a mere flourish of rhetoric," adds Carlyle, "but it is not so. If well meditated it will turn out to be a scientific fact; the expression . . . of the actual truth of the thing. We are the miracle of miracles, -- the great inscrutable Mystery."

STANZA VII.

1. BEHOLD THE BEGINNING OF SENTIENT FORMLESS LIFE (*a*).
FIRST, THE DIVINE (*vehicle*) (*b*), THE ONE FROM THE MOTHER-SPIRIT (*Atman*); THEN THE SPIRITUAL -- (*Atma-Buddhi, Spirit-soul*) (*c*); (*again*) THE THREE FROM THE ONE (*d*), THE FOUR FROM THE ONE (*e*), AND THE FIVE (f), FROM WHICH THE THREE, THE FIVE AND THE SEVEN (*g*) -- THESE ARE THE THREE-FOLD AND THE FOUR-FOLD DOWNWARD; THE "MIND-BORN SONS OF THE FIRST LORD (*Avalokiteswara*) THE SHINING SEVEN (*the "Builders"*). IT IS THEY WHO ARE THOU, ME, HIM, O LANOO; THEY WHO WATCH OVER THEE AND THY MOTHER, BHUMI (*the Earth*).

(*a*) The hierarchy of Creative Powers is divided into seven (or 4 and 3) esoteric, within the twelve great Orders, recorded in the twelve signs of the Zodiac; the seven of the manifesting scale being connected, moreover, with the Seven Planets. All this is subdivided into numberless groups of divine Spiritual, semi-Spiritual, and ethereal Beings.

The Chief Hierarchies among these are hinted at in the great Quaternary, or the "four bodies and the three faculties" of Brahma exoterically, and the Panchasyam, the five Brahmas, or the five Dhyani-Buddhas in the Buddhist system.

The highest group is composed of the divine Flames, so-called, also spoken of as the "Fiery Lions" and the "Lions of Life," whose esotericism is securely hidden in the Zodiacal sign of Leo. It is the *nucleole* of the superior divine World (see *Commentary* in first pages of Addendum). They are the formless Fiery Breaths, identical in one aspect with the upper Sephirothal TRIAD, which is placed by the Kabalists in the "Archetypal World."

The same hierarchy, with the same numbers, is found in the Japanese system, in the "Beginnings" as taught by both the Shinto and the Buddhist sects. In this system, Anthropogenesis precedes Cosmogenesis, as the Divine merges into the human, and creates -- midway in its descent into matter -- the visible Universe. The legendary personages remarks reverentially Omoie -- "having to be understood as the stereotyped embodiment of the higher (secret) doctrine, and its sublime truths." To state it at full length, however, would occupy too much of our space, but a few words on this old system cannot be out of place. The following is a short synopsis of this Anthropo-Cosmogenesis, and it shows how closely the most separated notions echoed one and the same Archaic teaching.

When all was as yet Chaos (*Kon-ton*) three spiritual Beings appeared on the stage of future creation: (1) *Ame no ani naka nushi no Kami*, "Divine Monarch of the Central Heaven"; (2) *Taka mi onosubi no Kami*, "Exalted, imperial Divine offspring of Heaven and the Earth"; and (3) *Kamu mi musubi no Kami*, "Offspring of the Gods," simply.

These were without form or substance (our *arupa* triad), as neither the celestial nor the terrestrial substance had yet differentiated, "nor had the essence of things been formed."

In the Zohar -- which, as now arranged and re-edited by Moses de Leon, with the help of Syrian and Chaldean Christian Gnostics in the XIIth century, and corrected and revised still later by many Christian hands, is only a little less exoteric than the Bible itself -- this divine "Vehicle" no longer appears as it does in the "Chaldean Book of Numbers." True enough, Ain-Soph, the ABSOLUTE ENDLESS NO-THING, uses also the form of the ONE, the manifested "Heavenly man" (the FIRST CAUSE) as its chariot (*Mercabah*, in Hebrew; *Vahan*, in Sanskrit) or vehicle to descend into, and manifest through, in the phenomenal world. But the Kabalists neither make it plain how the ABSOLUTE can use anything, or exercise any attribute whatever, since, as the Absolute, it is devoid of attributes; nor do they explain that in reality it is the First Cause (Plato's *Logos*) the original and eternal IDEA, that manifests through Adam Kadmon, the *Second* Logos, so to speak. In the "Book of Numbers" it is explained that EN (or *Ain*, Aior) is the only self-existent, whereas its

"Depth" (*Bythos* or *Buthon* of the Gnostics, called *Propator*) is only periodical. The latter is Brahm as differentiated from Brahma or Parabrahm. It is the Depth, the Source of Light, or Propator, which is the *unmanifested* Logos or the abstract *Idea*, and not Ain-Soph, *whose ray* uses Adam-Kadmon or the *manifested* Logos (the objective Universe) "male and female" -- as a chariot through which to manifest. But in the Zohar we read the following incongruity: "*Senior occultatus est et absconditus; Microprosopus manifestus est, et non manifestus.*" (*Rosenroth; Liber Mysterii*, IV., 1.) This is a fallacy, since *Microprosopus* or the *microcosm*, can only exist during its manifestations, and is destroyed during the Maha-Pralayas. Rosenroth's Kabala is no guide, but very often a puzzle.

(*b*) As in the Japanese system, in the Egyptian, and every old cosmogony -- at this divine FLAME, The "One," are lit the three descending groups. Having their potential being in the higher group, they now become distinct and separate Entities. These are called the "Virgins of Life," the "Great Illusion," etc., etc., and collectively the "Six-pointed Star." The latter is the symbol, in almost every religion, of the *Logos* as the first emanation. It is that of Vishnu in India (the *Chakra*, or wheel), and the glyph of the Tetragrammaton, the "He of the four letters" or -- metaphorically -- "the limbs of Microprosopos" in the Kabala, which are ten and six respectively. The later Kabalists however, especially the Christian mystics, have played sad havoc with this magnificent symbol. For the "*ten* limbs" of the Heavenly Man are the ten Sephiroth; but the first Heavenly Man is the unmanifested Spirit of the Universe, and ought never to be degraded into Microprosopus -- the lesser Face or Countenance, the prototype of man on the terrestrial plane. Of this, however, later on. The six-pointed Star refers to the six Forces or Powers of Nature, the six planes, principles, etc., etc., all synthesized by the seventh, or the central point in the Star. All these, the upper and lower hierarchies included, emanate from the "Heavenly or Celestial Virgin," the great mother in all religions, the Androgyne, the Sephira-Adam-Kadmon. In its *Unity*, primordial light is the seventh, or highest, principle, *Daivi-prakriti*, the light of the unmanifested Logos. But in its differentiation it becomes *Fohat*, or the "Seven Sons." The former is symbolised by the Central point in the double-Triangle; the latter by the hexagon itself, or the "six limbs" of the Microprosopus the Seventh being Malkuth, the "Bride" of the Christian Kabalists, or our Earth. Hence the expressions:

"*The first after the 'One' is divine Fire; the second, Fire and AEther; the third is composed of Fire, AEther and Water; the fourth of Fire, AEther, Water, and Air.*" *The One is not concerned with Man-bearing globes, but with the inner invisible Spheres.* "*The 'First-Born' are the* LIFE, *the heart and pulse of the Universe; the Second are its* MIND *or Consciousness*," as said in the Commentary.

(*c*) The second Order of Celestial Beings, those of Fire and AEther (corresponding to Spirit and Soul, or the Atma-Buddhi) whose names are legion, are still formless, but more definitely "substantial." They are the first differentiation in the Secondary Evolution or "Creation" -- a misleading word. As the name shows, they are the prototypes of the incarnating Jivas or Monads, and are composed of the Fiery Spirit of Life. It is through these that passes, like a pure solar beam, the ray which is furnished by them with its future vehicle, the Divine Soul, Buddhi. These are directly concerned with the Hosts of the higher world of *our* system. From these twofold *Units* emanate the *threefold*.

In the cosmogony of Japan, when, out of the chaotic mass, an egglike nucleus appears, having within itself the germ and potency of all the universal as well as of all terrestrial life, it is the "three-fold" just named, which differentiates. "The male aethereal" (*Yo*) principle ascends and the female grosser or more material principle (*In*) is precipitated into the Universe of substance, when a separation occurs between the celestial and the terrestrial. From this the female, the mother, the first rudimentary objective being is born. It is ethereal, without form or sex, and yet it is from this and the mother that the Seven Divine Spirits are born, from whom will emanate *the seven creations*, just as in the Codex Nazaraeus from Karabtanos and the Mother *Spiritus* the seven *evilly disposed* (material) spirits are born. It would be too long to give here the Japanese names, but once translated they stand in this order: --

(1.) The "Invisible Celibate," which is the creative logos of the noncreating "father," or the creative potentiality of the latter made manifest.

(2.) "The Spirit (or the God) of the rayless depths" (of Chaos); which becomes differentiated matter, or the world-stuff; also the mineral realm.

(3.) "The Spirit of the Vegetable Kingdom," of the "Abundant Vegetation."

(4.) This one is of dual nature, being at the same time "The Spirit of the Earth" and "the Spirit of the Sands," the former containing the potentiality of the male element, the latter that of the female element, the two forming a combined nature.

These two were ONE; yet unconscious of being two.

In this duality were contained (*a*) the male, dark and muscular Being, *Isu no gai no Kami;* and (*b*) *Eku gai no Kami*, the female, fair and weaker or more delicate Being. Then, the: --

(5th and 6th.) Spirits who were androgynous or dual-sexed, and, finally: --

(7.) The *Seventh* Spirit, the last emanated from the "mother," appears as the first divine human form distinctly male and female. It was the seventh creation, as in the Puranas, wherein man is the seventh creation of Brahma.

These, *Tsanagi-Tsanami*, descended into the Universe by the celestial Bridge (the milky way), and "*Tsanagi*, perceiving far below a chaotic mass of cloud and water, thrust his jewelled spear into the depths, and dry land appeared." Then the two separated to explore *Onokoro*, the newly-created island-world; etc., etc. (*Omoie*).

Such are the Japanese exoteric fables, the rind that conceals the kernel of the same one truth of the Secret Doctrine. Turning back to the esoteric explanations in every cosmogony: --

(*d*) The *Third* order corresponds to the *Atma-Buddhi-Manas:* Spirit, Soul and Intellect, and is called the "Triads."

(*e*) The *Fourth* are substantial Entities. This is the highest group among the *Rupas* (Atomic Forms). It is the nursery of the human, conscious, spiritual Souls. They are called the "Imperishable Jivas," and constitute, through the order below their own, the first group of the first septenary host -- the great mystery of human conscious and intellectual Being. For the latter are the field wherein lies concealed *in its privation* the germ *that will fall into generation.* That germ will become the spiritual potency in the physical cell that guides the development of the embryo, and which is the cause of the hereditary transmission of faculties and all the inherent qualities in man. The Darwinian theory, however, of the transmission of acquired faculties, is neither taught nor accepted in Occultism. Evolution, in it, proceeds on quite other lines; the physical, according to esoteric teaching, evolving gradually from the spiritual, mental, and psychic. This inner soul of the physical cell -- this "spiritual plasm" that dominates the germinal plasm -- is the key that must open one day the gates of the terra incognita of the Biologist, now called the dark mystery of Embryology. (*See text and note infra.*)

(*f*) The Fifth group is a very mysterious one, as it is connected with the Microcosmic Pentagon, the five-pointed star representing man. In India and Egypt these Dhyanis were connected with the Crocodile, and their abode is in Capricornus. These are convertible terms in Indian astrology, as this (tenth) sign of the Zodiac is called *Makara*, loosely translated "crocodile." The word itself is occultly interpreted in various ways, as will be shown further on. In Egypt the defunct man -- whose symbol is the pentagram or the five-pointed star, the points of which represent the limbs of a man -- was shown emblematically transformed into a crocodile: Sebakh or Sevekh "or seventh," as Mr. Gerald Massey says, showing it as having been the type of intelligence, is a dragon in reality, not a crocodile. He is the "Dragon of Wisdom" or Manas, the "Human Soul," Mind, the Intelligent principle, called in our esoteric philosophy the "Fifth" principle.

Says the defunct "Osirified" in ch. lxxxviii., "Book of the Dead," or the *Ritual*, under the glyph of a mummiform god with a crocodile's head: --

(1) "I am the god (crocodile) presiding at the fear . . . at the arrival of his Soul among men. I am the god-crocodile brought for destruction" (an allusion to the destruction of divine spiritual purity when man acquires the knowledge of good and evil; also to the "fallen" gods, or angels of every theogony).

(2) "I am the fish of the great Horus (as *Mankara* is the "crocodile," the vehicle of Varuna). I am merged in Sekten."

This last sentence gives the corroboration of, and repeats the doctrine of, esoteric Buddhism, for it alludes directly to the fifth principle (Manas), or the most spiritual part of its essence rather, which merges into, is absorbed by, and made one with Atma-Buddhi after the death of man. For Se-khen is the residence or *loka* of the god Khem (Horus-Osiris, or Father and Son), hence the "Devachan" of Atma-Buddhi. In the Ritual of the Dead the defunct is shown entering into Sekhem with Horus-Thot and "emerging from it as pure spirit" (lxiv., 29). Thus the defunct says (v. 130): "I see the forms of (myself, as various) men transforming eternally . . . I know this (chapter). He who knows it . . . takes all kinds of living forms." . . .

And in verse 35, addressing in magic formula that which is called, in Egyptian esotericism, the "ancestral heart," or the re-incarnating principle, the permanent EGO, the defunct says: --

"Oh my heart, my ancestral heart necessary for my transformations, ... do not separate thyself from me before the guardian of the Scales. Thou art my personality within my breast, divine companion *watching over my fleshes* (bodies). . . . . . ."

It is in Sekhem that lies concealed "the Mysterious Face," or the real man concealed under the false personality, the triple-crocodile of Egypt, the symbol of the higher Trinity or human Triad, *Atma*, *Buddhi* and *Manas*. In all the ancient papyri the crocodile is called *Sebek* (Seventh), while the water is the fifth principle esoterically; and, as already stated, Mr. Gerald Massey shows that the crocodile was "the Seventh Soul, the supreme one of seven -- the Seer unseen." Even exoterically *Sekhem* is the residence of the god Khem, and Khem is Horus avenging the death of his father Osiris, hence punishing the Sins of man when he becomes a disembodied Soul. Thus the defunct "Osirified" became the god Khem, who "gleans the field of *Aanroo*," *i.e.*, he gleans either his reward or punishment, as that field is the celestial locality (Devachan) where the defunct is given *wheat*, the food of divine justice. The fifth group of the celestial Beings is supposed to contain in itself the dual attributes of both the spiritual and physical aspects of the Universe; the two poles, so to say, of Mahat the Universal Intelligence, and the dual nature of man, the spiritual and the physical. Hence its number Five, multiplied and made into ten, connecting it with *Makara*, the 10th sign of Zodiac.

(*g*) The sixth and seventh groups partake of the lower qualities of the Quaternary. They are conscious, ethereal Entities, as invisible as Ether, which are shot out like the boughs of a tree from the first central group of the four, and shoot out in their turn numberless side groups, the lower of which are the Nature-Spirits, or Elementals of countless kinds and varieties; from the formless and unsubstantial -- the ideal THOUGHTS of their creators -- down to the Atomic, though, to human perception, invisible organisms. The latter are considered as the "Spirits of Atoms" for they are the first remove (backwards) from the physical Atom -- sentient, if not intelligent creatures. They are all subject to Karma, and have to work it out through every cycle. For, as the doctrine teaches, there are no such privileged beings in the universe, whether in our or in other systems, in the outer or the inner worlds, as the angels of the Western Religion and the Judean. A Dhyan Chohan has to become one; he cannot be born or appear suddenly on the plane of life as a full-blown angel. The Celestial Hierarchy of the present Manvantara will find itself transferred in the next cycle of life into higher, superior worlds, and will make room for a new hierarchy, composed of the elect ones of our mankind. Being is an endless cycle within the one absolute eternity, wherein move numberless inner cycles finite and conditioned. Gods, created as such, would evince no personal merit in being gods. Such a class of beings, perfect only by virtue of the special immaculate nature inherent in them, in the face of suffering and struggling humanity, and even of the lower creation, would be the symbol of an eternal injustice quite Satanic in character, an ever present crime. It is an anomaly and an impossibility in Nature. Therefore the "Four" and the "Three" have to incarnate as all other beings have. This sixth group, moreover, remains almost inseparable from man, who draws from it all but his highest and lowest principles, or his spirit and body, the five middle human principles being the very essence of those Dhyanis. Alone, the Divine Ray (the Atman) proceeds directly from the One. When asked how that can be? How is it possible to conceive that those "gods," or angels, can be at the same time their own emanations and their personal selves? Is it in the same sense in the material world, where the son is (in one way) his father, being his blood, the bone of his bone and the flesh of his flesh? To this the teachers answer "Verily it is so." But one has to go deep into the mystery of BEING before one can fully comprehend this truth.

2. THE ONE RAY MULTIPLIES THE SMALLER RAYS. LIFE PRECEDES FORM, AND LIFE SURVIVES THE LAST ATOM (*of Form, Sthula-sarira, external body*). THROUGH THE COUNTLESS RAYS THE LIFE-RAY, THE ONE, LIKE A THREAD THROUGH MANY BEADS (*pearls*) (*a*).

(*a*) This sloka expresses the conception -- a purely Vedantic one, as already explained elsewhere -- of a life-thread, *Sutratma*, running through successive generations. How, then, can this be explained? By resorting to a simile, to a familiar illustration, though necessarily imperfect, as all our available analogies must be. Before resorting to it, however, I would ask whether it seems *unnatural*, least of all "supernatural," to any one of us, when we consider that process known as the growth and development of a foetus into a healthy baby weighing several pounds evolves from what? From the segmentation of an infinitesimally small ovum and a spermatozoon; and afterwards we see that baby develop into a six-foot man! This refers to the atomic and physical expansion from the microscopically small into something very large, from the -- to the naked eye -- unseen, into the visible and objective. Science has provided for all this; and, I dare say, her theories, embryological, biological, and physiological, are correct enough so far as exact observation of the material goes. Nevertheless, the two chief difficulties of the science of embryology -- namely, what are the forces at work in the formation of the foetus, and the cause of "hereditary transmission" of likeness, physical, moral or mental -- have never been properly answered; nor will they ever be solved till the day when scientists condescend to accept the Occult theories. But if this physical phenomenon astonishes no one, except in so far as it puzzles the Embryologists, why should our intellectual and inner growth, the evolution of the human-spiritual to the Divine-Spiritual, be regarded as, or seem, more impossible than the other? Now to the simile.

Complete the physical plasm, mentioned in the last foot-note, the "Germinal Cell" of man with all its material potentialities, with the "spiritual plasm," so to say, or the fluid that contains the five lower principles of the six-principled Dhyan -- and you have the secret, if you are spiritual enough to understand it.

"When the seed of the animal man is cast into the soil of the animal woman, that seed cannot germinate unless it has been fructified by the five virtues (the fluid of, or the emanation from the principles) of the six-fold Heavenly man. Wherefore the Microcosm is represented as a Pentagon, within the Hexagon Star, the "Macrocosm." ("[[*Anthropos*]],") a work on Occult Embryology, Book I.). Then: "The functions of *Jiva* on this Earth are of a five-fold character. In the mineral atom it is connected with the lowest principles of the Spirits of the Earth (the six-fold Dhyanis); in the vegetable particle, with their second -- the *Prana* (life); in the animal, with all these plus the third and the fourth; in man, the germ must receive the fruition of all the five. Otherwise he will be born no higher than an animal"; namely, a congenital idiot. Thus in man alone the Jiva is complete. As to his seventh principle, it is but one of the Beams of the Universal Sun. Each rational creature receives only the temporary loan of that which has to return to its source; while his physical body is shaped by the lowest terrestrial lives, through physical, chemical, and physiological evolution. "The Blessed Ones have nought to do with the purgations of matter." (Kabala, Chaldean Book of Numbers).

It comes to this: Mankind in its first prototypal, shadowy form, is the offspring of the Elohim of Life (or Pitris); in its qualitative and physical aspect it is the direct progeny of the "Ancestors," the lowest Dhyanis, or Spirits of the Earth; for its moral, psychic, and spiritual nature, it is indebted to a group of divine Beings, the name and characteristics of which will be given in Book II. Collectively, men are the handiwork of hosts of various spirits; distributively, the tabernacles of those hosts; and occasionally and singly, the vehicles of some of them. In our present all-material Fifth Race, the earthly Spirit of theFourth is still strong in us; but we are approaching the time when the pendulum of evolution will direct its swing decidedly upwards, bringing Humanity back on a parallel line with the primitive third Root-Race in Spirituality. During its childhood, mankind was composed wholly of that Angelic Host, who were the indwelling Spirits that animated the monstrous and gigantic tabernacles of clay of the Fourth Race built by (as they are now also) and composed of countless myriads of lives. This sentence will be explained later on in the present Commentary. The "tabernacles" have improved in texture and symmetry of form, growing and developing with the globe that bore them; but the physical improvement took place at the expense of the spiritual inner man and nature. The three middle principles in earth and man became with every race more material; the Soul stepping back to make room for the physical intellect; the essence of elements becoming the material and composite elements now known.

Man is not, nor could he ever be, the complete product of the "Lord God"; but he *is* the child of the *Elohim*, so arbitrarily changed into the singular masculine gender. The first Dhyanis, commissioned to "create" man in their image, could only throw off their shadows, like a delicate model for the Nature Spirits of matter to work upon. (See Book II.) Man is, beyond any doubt, formed physically out of the dust of the Earth, but his creators and fashioners were many. Nor can it be said that the "Lord God breathed into his nostrils the breath of life," unless that God is identified with the "ONE LIFE," Omnipresent though invisible, and unless the same operation is attributed to "God" on behalf of every *living Soul* -- or *Nephesch*, which is the *vital* Soul, not the divine Spirit or *Ruach*, which ensures to man alone a divine degree of immortality, that no animal, as such, could ever attain in this cycle of incarnation. It is the inadequate distinctions made by the Jews, and now by our Western metaphysicians, who, not knowing of, and being unable to understand, hence to accept, more than a triune man -- Spirit, Soul, Body -- thus confuse the "breath of life" with immortal Spirit. This applies also directly to the Protestant theologians, who, in translating verse 8 of Ch. III. in the Fourth Gospel, have entirely perverted the meaning. Indeed the verse is made to say "The *wind* bloweth where it listeth," instead of "the *Spirit* goeth where it willeth," as in the original and also in the translation of the Greek Eastern Church.

Thus the philosophy of psychic, spiritual, and mental relations with man's physical functions is in almost inextricable confusion. Neither the old Aryan, nor the Egyptian psychology are now properly understood. Nor can they be assimilated without accepting the esoteric septenary, or, at any rate, the Vedantic quinquepartite division of the human inner principles. Failing which, it will be for ever impossible to understand the metaphysical and purely psychic and even physiological relations between the Dhyan-Chohans, or Angels, on the one plane, and humanity on the other. No Eastern (Aryan) esoteric works are so far published, but we possess the Egyptian papyri which speak clearly of the seven principles or the "Seven Souls of Man." The Book of the Dead gives a complete list of the "transformations" that every defunct undergoes, while divesting himself, one by one, of all those principles -- materialised for the sake of clearness into ethereal entities or bodies. We must, moreover, remind those who try to prove that the ancient Egyptians knew nothing of and did not teach Reincarnation, that the "Soul" (the *Ego* or *Self*) of the defunct is said to be living in Eternity: it is immortal, "co-eval with, and disappearing with the Solar boat," *i.e.*, for the cycle of necessity. This "Soul" *emerges from the Tiaou* (the realm *of the cause of life*) and joins the living on Earth *by day*, to return to *Tiaou* every night. This expresses the periodical existences of the Ego. (Book of the Dead, cvxliii.)

The *shadow*, the astral form, is annihilated, "devoured by the Uraeus" (cxlix., 51), the *Manes* will be annihilated; the two twins (the 4th and 5th principles) will be scattered; but the Soul-bird, "the divine Swallow -- and the Uraeus of Flame" (Manas and Atma-Buddhi) will live in the eternity, for they are their mother's husbands.

Like alone produces like. The Earth gives Man his body, the gods (Dhyanis) his five inner principles, the psychic Shadow, of which those gods are often the animating principle. SPIRIT (Atman) is one -- and indiscrete. It is not in the *Tiaou*.

For what is the *Tiaou?* The frequent allusion to it in the "Book of the Dead" contains a mystery. *Tiaou* is the path of the Night Sun, the inferior hemisphere, or the infernal region of the Egyptians, placed by them on the *concealed side of the moon*. The human being, in their esotericism, came out from the moon (a triple mystery -- astronomical, physiological, and psychical at once); he crossed the whole cycle of existence and then returned to his birth-place before issuing from it again. Thus the defunct is shown arriving in the West, receiving his judgment before Osiris, resurrecting as the god Horus, and circling round the sidereal heavens, which is an allegorical assimilation to Ra, the Sun; then having crossed the *Noot* (the celestial abyss), returning once more to Tiaou: an assimilation to Osiris, who, as the God of life and reproduction, inhabits the moon. Plutarch (Isis and Osiris, ch. xliii.) shows the Egyptians celebrating a festival called "The Ingress of Osiris into the moon." In chapter xli. life is promised after death; and the renovation of life is placed under the patronage of Osiris-Lunus, because the moon was the symbol of life-renewals or reincarnations, owing to its growth, waning, dying, and reappearance every month. In the *Dankmoe*, (iv. 5) it is said: -- "Oh, Osiris-Lunus! That renews to thee thy renewal." And Safckh says to Seti I. (Mariette's Abydos, plate 51), "Thou renewest thyself as the god Lunus when a babe." It is still better explained in a Louvre papyrus (P. Pierret, "Etudes Egyptologiques"): "Couplings and conceptions abound when he (Osiris-Lunus) is seen in heaven on that day." Says Osiris: "Oh, sole radiant beam of the moon! I issue from the circulating multitudes (of stars) . . . . . . Open me the Tiaou, for Osiris N. I will issue by day to do what I have to do amongst the living" ("Book of the Dead," ch. ll.), -- *i.e.*, to produce conceptions.

Osiris was "God manifest in generation," because the ancients knew, far better than the moderns, the real occult influences of the lunar body upon the mysteries of conception. Later on, when the moon became connected with female goddesses -- with Diana, Isis, Artemis, Juno, etc., that connection was due to a thorough knowledge of physiology and female nature, physical as much as psychic. But, primarily, the Sun and Moon were the only visible and, so to say, *tangible* [by their effects] psychic and physiological deities -- the Father and the Son, while Space and air in general, or that expanse of Heaven called Noot by the Egyptians, was the concealed Spirit or Breath of the two. These "Father and Son" were interchangeable in their functions and worked harmoniously together in their effects upon terrestrial nature and humanity; hence they were regarded as ONE, though TWO in personified Entities. They were both males, and both had their distinct and also collaborative work in the causative generation of Humanity. So much from the astronomical and cosmic standpoints viewed and expressed in symbolical language -- which became in our last races theological and dogmatic. But behind this veil of Cosmic and Astrological symbols, there were the Occult mysteries of Anthropography and the primeval genesis of man. And in this, no knowledge of symbols -- or even the key to the *post-diluvian* symbolical language of the Jews -- will, or can help, save only with reference to that which was laid down in national scriptures for exoteric uses; the sum of which, however cleverly veiled, was only the smallest portion of the real primitive history of each people, often relating, moreover, -- as in the Hebrew Scriptures -- merely to the terrestrial human, not divine life of that nation. That psychic and spiritual element belonged to MYSTERY and INITIATION. There were things never recorded in scrolls, but, as in Central Asia, on rocks and in subterranean crypts.

Nevertheless, there was a time when the whole world was "of one lip and of one knowledge," and Man knew more of his origin than he does now, and thus knew that the Sun and Moon, however large a part they do play in the constitution, growth and development of the human body, were not the direct causative agents of his appearance on Earth; these agents being, in truth, the living and intelligent Powers which the Occultists call Dhyan Chohans.

As to this, a very learned admirer of the Jewish Esotericism tells us that "the Kabala says expressly that Elohim is a *general abstraction*; what we call in mathematics 'a constant co-efficient' or a 'general function' entering into all construction, not particular; that is, by the general ratio 1 to 31415, (the astro-Dhyanic and) Elohistic figures." To this the Eastern Occultist replies: Quite so, it is an abstraction to our physical senses. To our spiritual perceptions, however, and to our inner spiritual eye, the Elohim or Dhyanis are no more an abstraction than our soul and spirit are to us. Reject the one and you reject the other -- since that which is the *surviving Entity in us* is partly the direct emanation from, and partly *those celestial Entities themselves.* One thing is sure; the Jews were perfectly acquainted with sorcery and various maleficent forces; but, with the exception of some of their great prophets and seers like Daniel and Ezekiel (Enoch belonging to a far distant race and not to any nation but to all, as a generic character), they knew little of, nor would they deal with, the real divine Occultism, their national character being averse to anything which had no direct bearing upon their own ethnical, tribal, and individual benefits -- witness their own prophets, and the curses thundered by them against the "stiff-necked race." But even the Kabala plainly shows the direct relation between the Sephiroth, or Elohim, and men.

Therefore, when it is proved to us that the Kabalistic identification of Jehovah with Binah, a female Sephiroth, has still another, a sub-occult meaning in it, then and then only the Occultist will be ready to pass the palm of perfection to the Kabalist. Until then, it is asserted that, as Jehovah is in the abstract sense of a "one living God," a single number, a metaphysical figment, and a reality only when put in his proper place as an emanation and a Sephiroth -- we have a right to maintain that the Zohar (as witnessed by the BOOK OF NUMBERS, at any rate), gave out originally, before the Christian Kabalists had disfigured it, and still gives out the same doctrine that we do; *i.e.,* it makes Man emanate, not from one Celestial MAN, but from a Septenary group of Celestial men or Angels, just as in "Pymander, the Thought Divine."

(3) WHEN THE ONE BECOMES TWO -- THE "THREE-FOLD" APPEARS (*a*). THE THREE ARE (*linked into*) ONE; AND IT IS OUR THREAD, O LANOO, THE HEART OF THE MAN-PLANT, CALLED SAPTAPARNA (*b*).

(*a*) "When the ONE becomes two, the three-fold appears": to wit, when the One Eternal drops its reflection into the region of Manifestation, that reflection, "the Ray," differentiates the "Water of Space"; or, in the words of the "Book of the Dead"; "Chaos ceases, through the effulgence of the Ray of Primordial light dissipating total darkness by the help of the great magic power of the WORD of the (Central) Sun." Chaos becomes male-female, and Water, incubated through Light, and the "three-fold being issues as its First-born." "Osiris-Ptah (or RA) creates his own limbs (like Brahma) by creating the gods destined to personify his phases" during the Cycle (xvii., 4). The Egyptian Ra, issuing from the DEEP, is the Divine Universal Soul in its manifested aspect, and so is Narayana, the Purusha, "*concealed in Akasa and present in Ether.*"

This is the metaphysical explanation, and refers to the very beginning of Evolution, or, as we should rather say, of Theogony. The meaning of the Stanza when explained from another standpoint in its reference to the mystery of man and his origin, is still more difficult to comprehend. In order to form a clear conception of what is meant by the One becoming two, and then being transformed into the "three-fold," the student has to make himself thoroughly acquainted with what we call "Rounds." If he refers to "Esoteric Buddhism" -- the first attempt to sketch out an approximate outline of archaic Cosmogony -- he will find that by a "Round" is meant the serial evolution of nascent material nature, of the seven globes of our chain with their mineral, vegetable, and animal kingdoms (man being there included in the latter and standing at the head of it) during the whole period of a life-cycle. The latter would be called by the Brahmins "a Day of Brahma." It is, in short, one revolution of the "Wheel" (our planetary chain), which is composed of seven globes (or seven separate "Wheels," in another sense this time). When evolution has run downward into matter, from planet A to planet G, or Z, as the Western students call it, it is one Round. In the middle of the Fourth revolution, which is our present "Round": "Evolution has reached its acme of physical development, crowned its work with the perfect physical man, and, from this point, begins its work spirit-ward." All this needs little repetition, as it is well explained in "Esoteric Buddhism." That which was hardly touched upon, and of which the little that was said has misled many, is the origin of man, and it is upon this that a little more light may now be thrown, just enough to make the Stanza more comprehensible, as the process will be fully explained only in its legitimate place, in Book II.

Now every "Round" (on the descending scale) is but a repetition in a more concrete form of the Round which preceded it, as every globe -- down to our fourth sphere (the actual earth) -- is a grosser and more material copy of the more shadowy sphere which precedes it in their successive order, on the three higher planes. (See diagram in Stanza VI. Comm. 6). On its way upwards on the ascending arc, Evolution spiritualises and etherealises, so to speak, the general nature of all, bringing it on to a level with the plane on which the twin globe on the opposite side is placed; the result being, that when the seventh globe is reached (in whatever Round) the nature of everything that is evolving returns to the condition it was in at its starting point -- plus, every time, a new and superior degree in the states of consciousness. Thus it becomes clear that the "origin of man," so-called, on this our present Round, or life-cycle on this planet, must occupy the same place in the same order -- save details based on local conditions and time -- as in the preceding Round. Again, it must be explained and remembered that, as the work of each Round is said to be apportioned to a different group of so-called "Creators" or "Architects," so is that of every globe; i.e., it is under the supervision and guidance of special "Builders" and "Watchers" -- the various Dhyan-Chohans.

The group of the hierarchy which is commissioned to "create" men is a special group, then; yet it evolved shadowy man in this cycle just as a higher and still more spiritual group evolved him in the Third Round. But as it is the Sixth -- on the downward scale of Spirituality -- the last and seventh being the terrestrial Spirits (elementals) which gradually form, build, and condense his physical body -- this Sixth group evolves no more than the future man's shadowy form, a filmy, hardly visible transparent copy of themselves. It becomes the task of the fifth Hierarchy -- the mysterious beings that preside over the constellation Capricornus, Makara, or "Crocodile" in India as in Egypt -- to inform the empty and ethereal animal form and make of it the Rational Man. This is one of those subjects upon which very little may be said to the general public. It is a MYSTERY, truly, but only to him who is prepared to reject the existence of intellectual and conscious spiritual Beings in the Universe, limiting full Consciousness to man alone, and that only as a "function of the Brain." Many are those among the Spiritual Entities, who have incarnated bodily in man, since the beginning of his appearance, and who, for all that, still exist as independently as they did before, in the infinitudes of Space. . . . or taking temporary possession of a medium. Just as certain persons -- men and women, reverting to parallel cases among living persons -- whether by virtue of a peculiar organization, or through the power of acquired mystic knowledge, can be seen in their "double" in one place, while the body is many miles away; so the same thing can occur in the case of superior Beings.

Man, philosophically considered, is, in his outward form, simply an animal, hardly more perfect than his pithecoid-like ancestor of the third round. He is a living body, not a living being, since the realisation of existence, the "Ego-Sum," necessitates self-consciousness, and an animal can only have direct consciousness, or instinct. This was so well understood by the Ancients that the Kabalist even made of soul and body two lives, independent of each other. The soul, whose body vehicle is the Astral, ethero-substantial envelope, could die and man be still living on earth -- i.e., the soul could free itself from and quit the tabernacle for various reasons   such as insanity, spiritual and physical depravity, etc.   Therefore, that which living men (Initiates) can do, the Dhyanis, who have no physical body to hamper them, can do still better. This was the belief of the Antediluvians, and it is fast becoming that of modern intellectual society, in Spiritualism, besides the Greek and Roman Churches, which teach the ubiquity of their angels. The Zoroastrians regarded their Amshaspends as dual entities (Ferouers), applying this duality

-- in esoteric philosophy, at any rate -- to all the spiritual and invisible denizens of the numberless worlds in space which are visible to our eye. In a note of Damascius (sixth century) on the Chaldean oracles, we have a triple evidence of the universality of this doctrine, for he says: "In these oracles the seven Cosmocratores of the world, ('The World-Pillars,') mentioned likewise by St. Paul, are double -- one set being commissioned to rule the superior worlds the spiritual and the sidereal, and the other to guide and watch over the worlds of matter." Such is also the opinion of Jamblichus, who makes an evident distinction between the archangels and the "Archontes." (See "De Mysteriis," sec. ii., ch. 3.) The above may be applied, of course, to the distinction made between the degrees or orders of spiritual beings, and it is in this sense that the Roman Catholic Church tries to interpret and teach the difference; for while the archangels are in her teaching divine and holy, their doubles are denounced by her as devils. But the word "ferouer" is not to be understood in this sense, for it means simply the reverse or the opposite side of some attribute or quality. Thus when the Occultist says that the "Demon is the lining of God" (evil, the reverse of the medal), he does not mean two separate actualities, but the two aspects or facets of the same Unity. Now the best man living would appear, side by side with an Archangel -- as described in Theology -- a fiend. Hence a certain reason to depreciate a lower "double," immersed far deeper in matter than its original. But there is still as little cause to regard them as devils, and this is precisely what the Roman Catholics maintain against all reason and logic.

(*b*) The concluding sentence of this sloka shows how archaic is the belief and the doctrine that man is seven-fold in his constitution. The thread of being which animates man and passes through all his personalities, or rebirths on this Earth (an allusion to Sutratma), the thread on which moreover all his "Spirits" are strung -- is spun from the essence of the "threefold," the "fourfold" and the "fivefold"; which contain all the preceding. *Panchasikha*, agreeably to Bhagavata Purana (V. XX. 25-28), is one of the seven *Kumaras* who go to Sveta-Dvipa to worship Vishnu. We shall see further on, what connection there is between the "celibate" and chaste sons of Brahma, who refuse "to multiply," and terrestrial mortals. Meanwhile it is evident that "the Man-Plant," Saptaparna, thus refers to the seven principles, and man is compared to the seven-leaved plant of this name so sacred among Buddhists.

For further details as to Saptaparna and the importance of the number seven in occultism, as well as in symbology, the reader is referred to Part II., Book II., on Symbolism: Sections on "*Saptaparna*," "The Septenary in the Vedas," etc. etc.

4. IT IS THE ROOT THAT NEVER DIES, THE THREE-TONGUED FLAME OF THE FOUR WICKS (*a*) . . . THE WICKS ARE THE SPARKS, THAT DRAW FROM THE THREE-TONGUED FLAME (*their upper triad*) SHOT OUT BY THE SEVEN, THEIR FLAME; THE BEAMS AND SPARKS OF ONE MOON REFLECTED IN THE RUNNING WAVES OF ALL THE RIVERS OF THE EARTH ("*Bhumi*," *or* "*Prithivi*") (*b*).

(*a*) The "Three-tongued flame" that never dies is the immortal spiritual triad -- the Atma-Buddhi and Manas -- the fruition of the latter assimilated by the first two after every terrestrial life. The "four wicks" that go out and are extinguished, are the four lower principles, including the body.

"I am the three-wicked Flame and my wicks are immortal," says the defunct. "I enter into the domain of Sekhem (the God whose arm sows the seed of action produced by the disembodied soul) and I enter the region of the Flames who have destroyed their adversaries," *i.e.*, got rid of the sin-creating "four wicks." (See chap. i., vii., "Book of the Dead," and the "Mysteries of Ro-stan.")

(*b*) Just as milliards of bright sparks dance on the waters of an ocean above which one and the same moon is shining, so our evanescent personalities -- the illusive envelopes of the immortal MONAD-EGO -- twinkle and dance on the waves of Maya. They last and appear, as the thousands of sparks produced by the moon-beams, only so long as the Queen of the Night radiates her lustre on the running waters of life: the period of a

Manvantara; and then they disappear, the beams -- symbols of our eternal Spiritual Egos -- alone surviving, re-merged in, and being, as they were before, one with the Mother-Source.

(5) THE SPARK HANGS FROM THE FLAME BY THE FINEST THREAD OF FOHAT. IT JOURNEYS THROUGH THE SEVEN WORLDS OF MAYA (*a*). IT STOPS IN THE FIRST (*Kingdom*), AND IS A METAL AND A STONE; IT PASSES INTO THE SECOND (*Kingdom*), AND BEHOLD -- A PLANT; THE PLANT WHIRLS THROUGH SEVEN FORMS AND BECOMES A SACRED ANIMAL; (*the first shadow of the physical man*) (*b*).
FROM THE COMBINED ATTRIBUTES OF THESE, MANU (*man*), THE THINKER, IS FORMED.
WHO FORMS HIM? THE SEVEN LIVES; AND THE ONE LIFE (*c*). WHO COMPLETES HIM? THE FIVEFOLD LHA. AND WHO PERFECTS THE LAST BODY? FISH, SIN, AND SOMA (*the moon*) (*d*).

(*a*) The phrase "through the seven Worlds of Maya" refers here to the seven globes of the planetary chain and the seven rounds, or the 49 stations of active existence that are before the "Spark" or Monad, at the beginning of every "Great Life-Cycle" or Manvantara. The "thread of Fohat" is the thread of life before referred to.

This relates to the greatest problem of philosophy -- the physical and substantial nature of life, the independent nature of which is denied by modern science because that science is unable to comprehend it. The reincarnationists and believers in Karma alone dimly perceive that the whole secret of Life is in the unbroken series of its manifestations: whether in, or apart from, the physical body. Because if --

> *"Life, like a dome of many-coloured glass,*
> *Stains the white radiance of Eternity"* --

yet it is itself part and parcel of that Eternity; for life alone can understand life.
What is that "Spark" which "hangs from the flame?" It is JIVA, the MONAD in conjunction with MANAS, or rather its aroma -- that which remains from each personality, when worthy, and hangs from Atma-Buddhi, the Flame, by the thread of life. In whatever way interpreted, and into whatever number of principles the human being is divided, it may easily be shown that this doctrine is supported by all the ancient religions, from the Vedic to the Egyptian, from the Zoroastrian to the Jewish. In the case of the last-mentioned, the Kabalistic works offer abundant proof of this statement. The entire system of the Kabalistic numerals is based on the divine septenary hanging from the Triad (thus forming the *Decade*) and its permutations 7, 5, 4, and 3, which, finally, all merge into the ONE itself: an endless and boundless Circle.
"The Deity (the ever Invisible Presence)," says the Zohar, "manifests itself through the *ten* Sephiroth which are its radiating witnesses. The Deity is like the Sea from which outflows a stream called WISDOM, the waters of which fall into a lake named Intelligence. From the basin, like seven channels, issue the Seven Sephiroth. . . . . For *ten equal seven:* the Decade contains *four* Unities and *three* Binaries." The ten Sephiroth correspond to the limbs of MAN. "When I framed Adam Kadmon," the Elohim are made to say, "the Spirit of the Eternal shot out of his Body like a sheet of lightning that radiated at once on the billows of the *Seven* millions of skies, and my *ten* splendours were his limbs." But neither the Head nor the shoulders of Adam-Kadmon can be seen; therefore we read in the *Sephra Dzenioutha* (the "Book of the Concealed Mystery"): --
"In the beginning of Time, after the Elohim (the "Sons of Light and Life," or the "Builders") had shaped out of the eternal Essence the Heavens and the Earth, they formed the worlds six by six, the seventh being *Malkuth*, which is our Earth (see *Mantuan Codex*) on its plane, and the lowest on all the other planes of conscious existence. The Chaldean *Book of Numbers* contains a detailed explanation of all this. "The first triad of the body of Adam Kadmon (the three upper planes of the seven) cannot be seen before the soul stands in the presence of the Ancient of Days." The Sephiroth of this upper triad are: -- "1, *Kether* (the Crown) represented by the brow of Macroprosopos; 2, *Chochmah* (Wisdom, a male Principle) by his right shoulder; and 3, *Binah* (Intelligence, a female Principle) by the left shoulder." Then come the *seven* limbs (or Sephiroth) on the planes of manifestation,

H.P. Blavatsky   99

the totality of these four planes being represented by *Microprosopus* (the lesser Face) or Tetragrammaton, the "four-lettered" Mystery. "The seven manifested and the *three* concealed limbs are the Body of the Deity."

Thus our Earth, *Malkuth*, is both the *Seventh* and the *Fourth* world, the former when counting from the first globe above, the latter if reckoned by the planes. It is generated by the sixth globe or Sephiroth called *Yezod*, "foundation," or as said in the Book of Numbers "by Yezod, He (Adam Kadmon) fecundates the primitive Heva" (Eve or our Earth). Rendered in mystic language this is the explanation why Malkuth, called "the inferior Mother," Matrona, Queen, and the Kingdom of the Foundation, is shown as the *Bride* of Tetragrammaton or Microprosopus (the 2nd Logos) the Heavenly Man. When free from all impurity she will become united with the Spiritual *Logos*, *i.e.*, in the 7th Race of the 7th Round -- after the regeneration, on the day of "SABBATH." For the "*seventh* day" has again an occult significance undreamt of by our theologians.

"When Matronitha, the Mother, is separated and brought face to face with the King, in the excellence of the Sabbath, all things become one body," says verse 746, in chapter xxii. of "Ha Idra Zuta Kadisha." "Becomes one body" means that all is reabsorbed once more into the one element, the spirits of men becoming *Nirvanees* and the elements of everything else becoming again what they were before -- *protyle* or undifferentiated substance. "Sabbath" means *rest* or Nirvana. It is not the *seventh* day after *six* days but a period the duration of which equals that of the seven "days" or any period made up of seven parts. Thus a *pralaya* is equal in duration to the manwantara, or a night of Brahma is equal to this "day." If the Christians will follow Jewish customs they ought to adopt the spirit and not the dead letter thereof: *i.e.*, to work one week of seven days and *rest* seven days. That the word "Sabbath" had a mystic significance is shown in the contempt shown by Jesus for the Sabbath day, and by what is said in Luke xviii. 12. Sabbath is there taken *for the whole week.* (See Greek text where the week is called *Sabbath.* "I fast twice in the Sabbath.") Paul, an Initiate, knew it well when referring to the eternal rest and felicity in heaven, as Sabbath; "and their happiness will be eternal, for they will ever be (*one*) with the Lord and will enjoy *an eternal Sabbath.*" (Hebrew iv. 2.)

The difference between the two systems, taking the Kabala as contained in the Chaldean *Book of Numbers*, not as misrepresented by its now disfigured copy, the Kabala of the Christian mystics --the Kabala and the archaic esoteric Vidya, is very small indeed, being confined to unimportant divergences of form and expression. Thus Eastern occultism refers to our earth as the fourth world, the lowest of the chain, above which run upward on both its sides the six globes, three on each side. *The Zohar*, on the other hand, calls the earth the lower, or the *Seventh*, adding that upon the six depend all things which are in it, "Microprosopus." The "smaller face," smaller because manifested and finite, "is formed of *six Sephiroth*," says the same work. "Seven kings come and *die in the thrice-destroyed world*" -- (Malkuth our earth, destroyed after each of the three rounds which it has gone through). "And their reign (of the seven kings) will be broken up." (*Book of Numbers*, I. viii., 3.) This relates to the Seven Races, five of which have already appeared, and two more have still to appear in this Round.

The Shinto allegorical accounts of Cosmogony and the origin of man in Japan hint at the same belief.

Captain C. Pfoundes studied for nearly nine years in the monasteries of Japan the religion underlying the various sects of the land. . . . . . "The Shinto idea of creation," he says, "is as follows: Out of chaos (*Konton*) the earth (*in*) was the sediment precipitated, and the Heavens (*yo*) the ethereal essences which ascended: *Maa* (*jin*) appeared between the two. The first man was called Kuni-to ko tatchi-no-mikoto, and *five other names were given to him*, and then the human race appeared, male and female. Isanagi and Isanami begat *Tenshoko doijin*, the first of the five gods of the Earth." These "gods" are simply our five races, Isanagi and Isanami being the two kinds of the "ancestors," the two preceding races which give birth to animal and to rational man.

It will be shown (Vol. II. Pt. II.) that the number seven, as well as the doctrine of the septenary constitution of man, was pre-eminent in all the secret systems. It plays as important a part in Western Kabala as in Eastern Occultism. Eliphas Levi calls the number seven "the key to the Mosaic creation and the symbols of every religion." He shows the

Kabala following faithfully even the septenary division of man, as the diagram he gives in his "*Clef des Grands Mysteres*" is septenary. This may be seen at a glance on page 389, "*Une prophetic et diverses pensees de Paracelse*," however cleverly the correct thought is veiled. One needs also only to look at the diagram (Plate VII. in Mr. Mathers' Kabala) "the formation of the Soul" from the same "Key of the Great Mysteries" by Levi to find the same, though with a different interpretation.

Thus it stands with both the Kabalistic and the Occult names attached: --

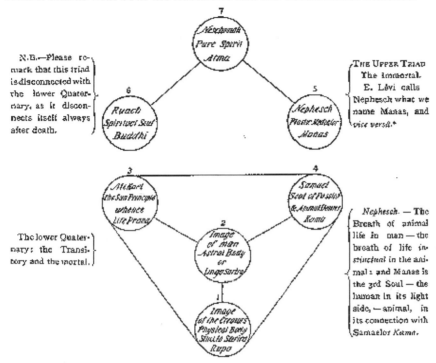

[[Footnote(s) to diagram]] --

Nephesch is the "breath of (animal) life" breathed into Adam, the man of dust; it is consequently the *Vital Spark*, the informing element. Without *Manas*, or what is miscalled in Levi's diagram Nephesch instead of Manas, "the reasoning Soul," or mind, Atma-Buddhi are irrational on this plane and cannot act. It is Buddhi which is the plastic mediator, not Manas, "the intelligent medium between the upper Triad and the lower Quaternary." But there are many such strange and curious transformations to be found in the Kabalistic works -- a convincing proof that its literature has become a sad jumble. We do not accept the classification except in this one particular, in order to show the points of agreement.

We will now give in tabular form what the very cautious Eliphas Levi says in explanation of his diagram, and what the Esoteric Doctrine teaches -- and compare the two. Levi, too, makes a distinction between Kabalistic and Occult Pneumatics. (See "*Histoire de la Magic*," pp. 388, 389.)

Says Eliphas Levi, the Kabalist: --

KABALISTIC PNEUMATICS.
1. The Soul (or EGO) is a clothed light; and this light is triple.
2. *Neschamah* -- "pure Spirit."
3. *Ruach* -- the Soul or Spirit.
4. *Nephesch* -- plastic mediator.
5. The garment of the Soul is the rind (body) of the image (astral Soul).

6. The image is double, because it reflects the good as the bad.
7. Imago, body.

OCCULT PNEUMATICS.
As given by Eliphas Levi.
1. *Nephesh* is immortal because it renews its life by the destruction of forms.
[But *Nephesh*, the "breath of
Say the Theosophists: --

ESOTERIC PNEUMATICS.
1. Ditto, for it is Atma-Buddhi-*Manas.*
2. Ditto.
3. Spiritual Soul.
4. Mediator between Spirit and its Man, the Seat of Reason, the Mind, in man.
5. Correct.
6. Too uselessly apocalyptic. Why not say that the *astral* reflects the good as well as the bad man; man, who is ever tending to the upper triangle, or else disappears with the Quaternary.
7. Ditto, the earthly image.

OCCULT PNEUMATICS.
As given by the Occultists.
1. *Manas* is immortal, because after every new incarnation it adds to Atma-Buddhi something of itself, and life," is a misnomer and a useless puzzle to the student.]
2. *Ruach* progresses by the evolution of ideas (! ?).
3. *Neschamah* is progressive without oblivion and destruction.
4. The soul has three dwellings.
5. These dwellings are: the plane of the mortals: the Superior Eden; and the Inferior Eden.
6. The image (man) is a sphinx that offers the riddle of birth.
7. The fatal image (the astral) endows Nephesch with its aptitudes; but Ruach is able to substitute for this (vitiated) Nephesch the image thus, assimilating itself to the Monad, shares its immortality.
2. *Buddhi* becomes conscious by the accretions it gets from Manas after every new incarnation and the death of man.
3. *Atma* neither progresses, forgets, nor remembers. It does not belong to this plane: it is but the ray of light eternal which shines upon and through the darkness of matter -- when the latter is willing.
4. The Soul (collectively, as the upper Triad) lives on three planes, besides its fourth, the terrestrial sphere; and it *exists* eternally on the highest of the three.
5. These dwellings are: Earth for the physical man, or the animal Soul; Kama-loka (Hades, the Limbo) for the disembodied man, or his *Shell;* Devachan for the higher Triad.
6. Correct.
7. The astral through Kama (desire) is ever drawing Manas down into the sphere of material passions and desires. But if the *better* man conquered in accordance with the inspirations of *Neschamah.*

It is very evident that the French Kabalist either did not know sufficiently the real tenet, or distorted it to suit himself and his object. Thus he says again, treating upon the same subject, and we, Occultists, answer the late Kabalist and his admirers: --
1. The body is the mould of Nephesch; Nephesch the mould of Ruach; Ruach the mould *of the garments of Neschamah.*
2. Light (the Soul) personifies in clothing itself (with a body); and personality endures only when the garment is perfect.
3. The angels aspire to become men; a perfect man, a man-god is above all the angels.
4. Every 14,000 years the soul rejuvenates and rests in the jubilean sleep of oblivion.
1. The body follows the whims, good or bad, of *Manas;* Manas tries to follow the light of Buddhi, but often fails. Buddhi is the mould of the "garments" of Atma, because Atma is

no body, or shape, or anything, and because Buddhi is its vehicle only *figuratively*.

2. The Monad becomes a personal ego when it incarnates; and something remains of that personality through Manas, when the latter is perfect enough to assimilate Buddhi.

3. Correct.

4. Within a period, "a great age" or a day of Brahrna, 14 Manus reign; after which comes Pralaya when all the Souls rest in Nirvana. (Souls = Egos).

Such are the distorted copies of the esoteric doctrine in the Kabala. But see also "The Primeval Manus of Humanity" in Book II.

To return to Stanza VII.

(*b*) The well-known Kabalistic aphorism runs: -- "A stone becomes a plant; a plant, a beast; the beast, a man; a man a spirit; and the spirit a god." The "spark" animates all the kingdoms in turn before it enters into and informs divine man, between whom and his predecessor, animal man, there is all the difference in the world. Genesis begins its anthropology at the wrong end (evidently for a blind) and lands nowhere. Had it begun as it ought, one would have found in it, first, the celestial Logos, the "Heavenly Man," which evolves as a Compound Unit of Logoi, out of whom after their pralayic sleep -- a sleep that gathers the cyphers scattered on the Mayavic plane into One, as the separate globules of quicksilver on a plate blend into one mass -- the Logoi appear in their totality as the first "male and female" or Adam Kadmon, the "Fiat Lux" of the Bible, as we have already seen. But this transformation did not take place on our Earth, nor on any material plane, but in the Spacial Depths of the first differentiation of the eternal Root-matter. On our nascent globe things proceed differently. The Monad or Jiva, as said in "Isis Unveiled," vol. i., p. 302, is, first of all, shot down by the law of Evolution into the lowest form of matter -- the mineral. After a sevenfold gyration encased in the stone (or that which will become mineral and stone in the Fourth Round), it creeps out of it, say, as a lichen. Passing thence, through all the forms of vegetable matter, into what is termed animal matter, it has now reached the point in which it has become the germ, so to speak, of the animal, that will become the physical man. All this, up to the Third Round, is formless, as matter, and senseless, as consciousness. For the Monad or Jiva *per se* cannot be even called spirit: it is a ray, a breath of the ABSOLUTE, or the Absoluteness rather, and the Absolute Homogeneity, having no relations with the conditioned and relative finiteness, is unconscious on our plane. Therefore, besides the material which will be needed for its future human form, the monad requires (*a*) a spiritual model, or prototype, for that material to shape itself into; and (*b*) an intelligent consciousness to guide its evolution and progress, neither of which is possessed by the homogeneous monad, or by senseless though living matter. The Adam of dust requires the *Soul of Life* to be breathed into him: the two middle principles, which are the *sentient* life of the irrational animal and the Human Soul, for the former is irrational without the latter. It is only when, from a potential androgyne, man has become separated into male and female, that he will be endowed with this conscious, rational, individual Soul, (*Manas*) "the principle, or the intelligence, of the Elohim," to receive which, he has to eat of the fruit of Knowledge from the Tree of Good and Evil. How is he to obtain all this? The Occult doctrine teaches that while the monad is cycling on downward into matter, these very Elohim -- or Pitris, the lower Dhyan-Chohans -- are evolving *pari passu* with it on a higher and more spiritual plane, descending also relatively into matter on their own plane of consciousness, when, after having reached a certain point, they will meet the incarnating senseless monad, encased in the lowest matter, and blending the two potencies, Spirit and Matter, the union will produce that terrestrial symbol of the "Heavenly Man" in space -- PERFECT MAN. In the Sankhya philosophy, Purusha (spirit) is spoken of as something impotent unless he mounts on the shoulders of Prakriti (matter), which, left alone, is -- senseless. But in the secret philosophy they are viewed as graduated. Though one and the same thing in their origin, Spirit and Matter, when once they are on the plane of differentiation, begin each of them their evolutionary progress in contrary directions -- Spirit falling gradually into matter, and the latter ascending to its original condition, that of a pure spiritual substance. Both are inseparable, yet ever separated. In polarity, on the physical plane, two like poles will always repel each other, while the negative and the positive are mutually attracted, so do Spirit and Matter stand to each other -- the two poles of the same homogeneous substance, the root-principle of the universe.

Therefore, when the hour strikes for Purusha to mount on Prakriti's shoulders for the formation of the Perfect Man -- rudimentary man of the first 2 1/2 Races being only the *first*, gradually evolving into *the most perfect of mammals* -- the Celestial "Ancestors" (Entities from preceding worlds, called in India the Sishta) step in on this our plane, as the Pitris had stepped in before them for the formation of the physical or animal-man, and incarnate in the latter. Thus the two processes -- for the two *creations:* the animal and the divine man -- differ greatly. The Pitris shoot out from their ethereal bodies, still more ethereal and shadowy similitudes of themselves, or what we should now call "doubles," or "astral forms," in their own likeness. This furnishes the Monad with its first dwelling, and blind matter with a model around and upon which to build henceforth. But *Man is still incomplete.* From Swayambhuva Manu (in Manu, Book I.), from whom descended the seven primitive Manus or Prajapati, each of whom gave birth to a primitive race of men, down to the Codex Nazareus, in which Karabtanos or Fetahil (blind concupiscent matter) begets on his Mother, "Spiritus," seven figures, each of which stands as the progenitor of one of the primaeval seven races -- this doctrine has left its impress on every Archaic Scripture.

"Who forms Manu (the Man) and who forms his body? The LIFE and the LIVES. Sin and the MOON." Here Manu stands for the spiritual, heavenly man, the real and non-dying EGO in us, which is the direct emanation of the "One Life" or the Absolute Deity. As to our outward physical bodies, the house of the tabernacle of the Soul, the Doctrine teaches a strange lesson; so strange that unless thoroughly explained and as rightly comprehended, it is only the exact Science of the future that is destined to vindicate the theory fully.

It has been stated before now that Occultism does not accept anything inorganic in the Kosmos. The expression employed by Science, "inorganic substance," means simply that the latent life slumbering in the molecules of so-called "inert matter" is incognizable. ALL IS LIFE, and every atom of even mineral dust is a LIFE, though beyond our comprehension and perception, because it is outside the range of the laws known to those who reject Occultism. "The very Atoms," says Tyndall, "seem instinct with a desire for life." Whence, then, we would ask, comes the tendency "to run into organic form"? Is it in any way explicable except according to the teachings of Occult Science?

"The worlds, to the profane," says a Commentary, *"are built up of the known Elements. To the conception of an Arhat, these Elements are themselves collectively a divine Life; distributively, on the plane of manifestations, the numberless and countless crores of lives. Fire alone is* **ONE**, *on the plane of the One Reality: on that of manifested, hence illusive, being, its particles are fiery lives which live and have their being at the expense of every other life that they consume. Therefore they are named the* **"DEVOURERS."** . . . *"Every visible thing in this Universe was built by such* **LIVES**, *front conscious and divine primordial man down to the unconscious agents that construct matter."* . . . *"From the* **ONE LIFE** *formless and Uncreate, proceeds the Universe of lives. First was manifested from the Deep (Chaos) cold luminous fire (gaseous light?) which formed the curds in Space."* (*Irresolvable nebulae, perhaps?*). . . . . . *"* . . . *These fought, and a great heat was developed by the encountering and collision, which produced rotation. Then came the first manifested* **MATERIAL**, *Fire, the hot flames, the wanderers in heaven (comets); heat generates moist vapour; that forms solid water (?); then dry mist, then liquid mist, watery, that puts out the luminous brightness of the pilgrims (comets?) and forms solid watery wheels (***MATTER** *globes). Bhumi (the Earth) appears with six sisters. These produce by their continuous motion the inferior fire, heat, and an aqueous mist, which yields the third World-Element --* **WATER;** *and from the breath of all (atmospheric)* **AIR** *is born. These four are the four lives of the first four periods (Rounds) of Manvantara. The three last will follow."*

This means that every new Round develops one of the Compound Elements, as now known to Science, -- which rejects the primitive nomenclature, preferring to subdivide them into constituents. If Nature is the "Ever-becoming" on the manifested plane, then those Elements are to be regarded in the same light: they have to evolve, progress, and increase to the Manvantaric end. Thus the First Round, we are taught, developed but one

Element, and a nature and humanity in what may be called one aspect of Nature -- called by some, very unscientifically, though it may be so *de facto*, "One-dimensional Space."

The Second Round brought forth and developed two Elements -- Fire and Earth -- and *its* humanity, adapted to this condition of Nature, if we can give the name Humanity to beings living under conditions unknown to men, was -- to use again a familiar phrase in a strictly figurative sense (the only way in which it can be used correctly) -- "a two-dimensional species." The processes of natural development which we are now considering will at once elucidate and discredit the fashion of speculating on the attributes of the *two*, *three*, and *four* or more "dimensional Space;" but in passing, it is worth while to point out the real significance of the sound but incomplete intuition that has prompted -- among Spiritualists and Theosophists, and several great men of Science, for the matter of that -- the use of the modern expression, "the fourth dimension of Space." To begin with, of course, the superficial absurdity of assuming that Space itself is measurable in any direction is of little consequence. The familiar phrase can only be an abbreviation of the fuller form -- the "*Fourth dimension of* MATTER *in Space.*" But it is an unhappy phrase even thus expanded, because while it is perfectly true that the progress of evolution may be destined to introduce us to new characteristics of matter, those with which we are already familiar are really more numerous than the three dimensions. The faculties, or what is perhaps the best available term, the characteristics of matter, must clearly bear a direct relation always to the senses of man. Matter has extension, colour, motion (molecular motion), taste, and smell, corresponding to the existing senses of man, and by the time that it fully develops the next characteristic -- let us call it for the moment PERMEABILITY -- this will correspond to the next sense of man -- let us call it "NORMAL CLAIRVOYANCE;" thus, when some bold thinkers have been thirsting for a fourth dimension to explain the passage of matter through matter, and the production of knots upon an endless cord, what they were really in want of, was a *sixth characteristic of matter.* The three dimensions belong really but to one attribute or characteristic of matter -- extension; and popular common sense justly rebels against the idea that under any condition of things there can be more than three of such dimensions as length, breadth, and thickness. These terms, and the term "dimension" itself, all belong to one plane of thought, to one stage of evolution, to one characteristic of matter. So long as there are foot-rules within the resources of Kosmos, to apply to matter, so long will they be able to measure it three ways and no more; and from the time the idea of measurement first occupied a place in the human understanding, it has been possible to apply measurement in three directions and no more. But these considerations do not militate in any way against the certainty that in the progress of time -- as the faculties of humanity are multiplied -- so will the characteristics of matter be multiplied also. Meanwhile, the expression is far more incorrect than even the familiar one of the "Sun rising or setting."

We now return to the consideration of material evolution through the Rounds. Matter in the *second* Round, it has been stated, may be figuratively referred to as two-dimensional. But here another *caveat* must be entered. That loose and figurative expression may be regarded -- in one plane of thought, as we have just seen -- as equivalent to the second characteristic of matter corresponding to the second perceptive faculty or sense of man. But these two linked scales of evolution are concerned with the processes going on within the limits of a single Round. The succession of primary aspects of Nature with which the succession of Rounds is concerned, has to do, as already indicated, with the development of the "Elements" (in the Occult sense) -- Fire, Air, Water, Earth. We are only in the fourth Round, and our catalogue so far stops short. The centres of consciousness (destined to develop into humanity as we know it) of the third Round arrived at a perception of the third Element Water. Those of the fourth Round have added *earth* as a state of matter to their stock as well as the three other elements in their present transformation. In short, none of the so-called elements were, in the three preceding Rounds, as they are now. For all we know, FIRE may have been *pure* AKASA, the first Matter of the *Magnum Opus of* the Creators and "Builders," that Astral Light which the paradoxical Eliphas Levi calls in one breath "the body of the Holy Ghost," and in the next "Baphomet," the "Androgyne Goat of Mendes" ; AIR, simply Nitrogen, "the breath of the Supporters of the Heavenly Dome," as the Mohammedan mystics call it; WATER, that primordial fluid which was required, according to Moses, to make *a living soul* with. And this may account for the flagrant discrepancies and unscientific statements found in Genesis. Separate the first from the second chapter; read the former as a scripture of the Elohists, and the latter as that of the far younger Jehovists; still one finds, if one reads between the lines, the same order in which things created appear -- namely, Fire (light), Air, Water, and MAN (or the Earth). For the sentence: "In the beginning God created Heaven and Earth" is a mistranslation; it is not "Heaven and Earth," but the *duplex* or dual Heaven, the *upper* and the *lower* Heavens, or the separation of primordial substance that was light in its upper and dark in its lower portions -- or the manifested Universe -- in its duality of the *invisible* (to the senses) and the *visible* to our perceptions. God divided the light from the Darkness (v. 4); and then made the firmament, air (5), "a firmament in the midst of the waters, and let it divide the waters from the waters," (6), *i.e.*, "the waters which were under the firmament (our manifested visible Universe) from the waters *above* the firmament," or the (to us) invisible planes of being. In the second chapter (the Jehovistic), plants and herbs are created before water, just as in the first, *light is produced before the Sun.* "God made the Earth and the Heavens and every plant of the field *before it was in the Earth* and every herb of the field *before it grew;* for the Elohim ('gods') had not caused it to rain upon the earth, etc." (v. 5) -- an absurdity unless the esoteric explanation is accepted. The plants *were* created before they were in the earth -- *for there was no earth then such as it is now;* and the herb of the field was in existence before it grew as it does now in the fourth Round.

Discussing and explaining the nature of the invisible Elements and the "primordial fire" mentioned above, Eliphas Levi calls it invariably the "Astral Light." It is the "grand Agent Magique" with him; undeniably it is so, but -- only so far as *Black* Magic is concerned, and on the lowest planes of what we call Ether, the noumenon of which is Akasa; and even this would be held incorrect by orthodox Occultists. The "Astral Light" is simply the older "*sidereal* Light" of Paracelsus; and to say that "everything which exists has been evolved from it, and it preserves and reproduces all forms," as he writes, is to enunciate truth only in the second proposition. The first is erroneous; for if all that exists was evolved *through* (or *via*) it, it is not the astral light. The latter is not the container of *all* things but only the reflector, at best, of this *all.* Eliphas Levi writes: --

"The great Magic agent is the fourth emanation of the life principle (we say -- it is the first in the inner, and the second in the outer (our) Universe), of which the Sun is the third form . . . for the day-star (the sun) is only the reflection and material shadow of the Central Sun of truth, which illuminates the intellectual (invisible) world of Spirit and which itself is but a gleam borrowed from the ABSOLUTE."

So far he is right enough. But when the great authority of the Western Kabalists adds that nevertheless, "it is not the immortal Spirit as the Indian Hierophants have imagined" -- we answer that he slanders the said Hierophants, as they have said nothing of the kind; while even the Puranic exoteric writings flatly contradict the assertion. No Hindu has ever mistaken *Prakriti* -- the Astral Light being only above the lowest plane of Prakriti, the material Kosmos -- for the "immortal Spirit." Prakriti is ever called *Maya*, illusion, and is doomed to disappear with the rest, the gods included, at the hour of the Pralaya; for it is shown that Akasa is not even the Ether, least of all then, we imagine, can it be the Astral Light. Those unable to penetrate beyond the dead letter of the Puranas, have occasionally confused Akasa with Prakriti, with Ether, and even with the visible Sky! It is true also that those who have invariably translated the term Akasa by "Ether" (Wilson, for instance), finding it called "the material cause of sound" possessing, moreover, this *one single property* (Vishnu Purana), have ignorantly imagined it to be "material," in the physical sense. True, again, that if the characteristics are accepted literally, then, since nothing material or physical, and therefore conditioned and temporary can be immortal -- according to metaphysics and philosophy -- it would follow that Akasa is neither infinite nor immortal. But all this is erroneous, since both the words *Pradhana* (primeval matter) and *sound*, as a property, have been misunderstood; the former term (Pradhana) being certainly synonymous with *Mulaprakriti* and Akasa, and the latter (sound) with the Verbum, the Word or the Logos. This is easy to demonstrate; for it is shown in the following sentences in Vishnu Purana: "In the beginning there was neither day nor night, nor sky, nor earth, nor darkness, nor light. . . . . Save only ONE, unapprehensible by intellect, or that which is Brahma and Pums (Spirit) and Pradhana (primordial matter)." . . . . (Book I., ch. ii.).

Now, what is Pradhana, if it is not Mulaprakriti, the root of all, in another aspect? For Pradhana, though said further on to merge into the Deity as everything else does, in order to leave the ONE absolute during the Pralaya, yet is held as infinite and immortal. The Commentator describes the Deity as: "One *Pradhanika* Brahma Spirit: THAT, was," and interprets the compound term as a substantive, not as a derivative word used attributively, *i.e.*, like something conjoined with Pradhana. Hence Pradhana even in the Puranas is an aspect of Parabrahmam, not an evolution, and must be the same as the Vedantic Mulaprakriti. "Prakriti in its *primary* state is Akasa," says a Vedantin scholar (see "Five Years of Theosophy," p. 169). It is almost abstract Nature.

Akasa, then, is Pradhana in another form, and as such cannot be Ether, the ever-invisible agent, courted even by physical Science. Nor is it Astral Light. It is, as said, the *noumenon* of the seven-fold differentiated Prakriti -- the ever immaculate "Mother" of the *fatherless* Son, who becomes "Father" on the lower manifested plane. For MAHAT is the first product of Pradhana, or Akasa, and Mahat -- Universal intelligence "whose *characteristic property* is Buddhi" -- is no other than the *Logos*, for he is called "Eswara" Brahma, Bhava, etc. (*See Linga Purana*, sec. lxx. 12 *et seq.;* and Vayu Purana, but especially the former Purana -- prior, section viii., 67-74). He is, in short, the "Creator" or the divine mind in creative operation, "the cause of all things." He is the "first-born" of whom the Puranas tell us that "Mahat and matter are the inner and outer boundaries of the Universe," or, in our language, the negative and the positive poles of dual nature (abstract and concrete), for the Purana adds: "In this manner -- as were the *seven* forms (principles) of Prakriti reckoned from Mahat to Earth -- so at the time of pralaya (pratyahara) these seven successively re-enter into each other. The egg of Brahma (Sarva-mandala) is dissolved with its seven zones (dwipa), seven oceans, seven regions, etc." (Vishnu Purana, Book vi., ch. iv.)

These are the reasons why the Occultists refuse to give the name of Astral Light to Akasa, or to call it Ether. "In my Father's house are many mansions," may be contrasted with the occult saying, "In our Mother's house there are seven mansions," or planes, the lowest of which is above and around us -- the Astral Light.

The elements, whether simple or compound, could not have remained the same since the commencement of the evolution of our chain. Everything in the Universe progresses steadily in the Great Cycle, while incessantly going up and down in the smaller cycles. Nature is never stationary during manvantara, as it is ever *becoming,* not simply *being;* and mineral, vegetable, and human life are always adapting their organisms to the then reigning Elements, and therefore *those* Elements were then fitted for them, as they are now for the life of present humanity. It will only be in the next, or fifth, Round that the fifth Element, *Ether* -- the gross body of Akasa, if it can be called even that -- will, by becoming a familiar fact of Nature to all men, as air is familiar to us now, cease to be as at present hypothetical, and also an "agent" for so many things. And only during that Round will those higher senses, the growth and development of which Akasa subserves, be susceptible of a complete expansion. As already indicated, a *partial* familiarity with the characteristic of matter -- permeability -- which should be developed concurrently with the sixth sense, may be expected to develop at the proper period in this Round. But with the next element added to our resources in the next Round, *permeability* will become so manifest a characteristic of matter, that the densest forms of this will seem to man's perceptions as obstructive to him as a thick fog, and no more.

Let us return to the life-cycle now. Without entering at length upon the description given of the *higher* LIVES, we must direct our attention at present simply to the earthly beings and the earth itself. The latter, we are told, is built up for the first Round by the "Devourers" which disintegrate and differentiate the germs of other lives in the Elements; pretty much, it must be supposed, as in the present stage of the world, the *aerobes* do, when, undermining and loosening the chemical structure in an organism, they transform animal matter and generate substances that vary in their constitutions. Thus Occultism disposes of the so-called Azoic age of Science, for it shows that there never was a time when the Earth was without life upon it. Wherever there is an atom of matter, a particle or a molecule, even in its most gaseous condition, there is life in it, however latent and unconscious. "*Whatsoever quits the Laya State, becomes active life; it is drawn into the vortex of* **MOTION** (*the alchemical solvent of Life); Spirit and Matter are the two States of the* **ONE**, *which is neither Spirit nor Matter, both being the absolute life, latent.*" (*Book of Dzyan, Comm. III., par.* **18**). . . . "*Spirit is the first differentiation of* (*and in*) **SPACE***; and Matter the first differentiation of Spirit. That, which is neither Spirit nor matter -- that is* **IT** *-- the Causeless* **CAUSE** *of Spirit and Matter, which are the Cause of Kosmos. And* **THAT** *we call the* **ONE LIFE** *or the Intra-Cosmic Breath.*"

Once more we will say -- *like must produce like.* Absolute Life cannot produce an inorganic atom whether single or complex, and there is life even in *laya* just as a man in a profound cataleptic state -- to all appearance a corpse -- is still a living being.

When the "Devourers" (in whom the men of science are invited to see, with some show of reason, atoms of the Fire-Mist, if they will, as the Occultist will offer no objection to this); when the "Devourers," we say, have differentiated "the fire-atoms" by a peculiar process of segmentation, the latter become life-germs, which aggregate according to the laws of cohesion and affinity. Then the life-germs produce lives of another kind, which work on the structure of our globes.

Thus, in the first Round, the globe, having been built by the primitive fire-lives, *i.e.*, formed into a sphere -- had no solidity, nor qualifications, save a cold brightness, nor form nor colour; it is only towards the end of the First Round that it developed one Element which from its inorganic, so to say, or simple Essence became now in our Round the fire we know throughout the system. The Earth was in her first rupa, the essence of which is the Akasic principle named   "that which is now known as, and very erroneously termed, Astral Light, which Eliphas Levi calls "the imagination of Nature,"|| probably to avoid giving it its correct name, as others do.

"*It is through and from the radiations of the seven bodies of the seven orders of Dhyanis, that the seven discrete quantities* (*Elements*), *whose motion and harmonious Union produce the manifested Universe of Matter, are born.*" (*Commentary.*)

Speaking of it in his Preface to the "History of Magic" Eliphas Levi says: "It is through this Force that all the nervous centres secretly communicate with each other; from it -- that sympathy and antipathy are born; from it -- that we have our dreams; and that the phenomena of second sight and extra-natural visions take place. . . . . Astral Light, acting under the impulsion of powerful wills, destroys, coagulates, separates, breaks, gathers in all things. . . . God created it on that day when he said: *Fiat Lux,* and it is directed by the *Egregores, i.e.,* the chiefs of the souls who are the spirits of energy and action." Eliphas Levi ought to have added that the astral light, or primordial substance, if matter at all, is that which, called *Light,* LUX, esoterically explained, *is the body of those Spirits themselves, and their very essence. Our physical light is the manifestation on our plane* and the reflected radiance of the *Divine* Light emanating from the collective body of those who are called the "LIGHTS" and the "FLAMES." But no other Kabalist has ever had the talent of heaping up one contradiction on the other, of making one paradox chase another in the same sentence and in such flowing language, as Eliphas Levi. He leads his reader through the most lovely, gorgeously blooming valleys, to strand him after all on a desert and barren rocky island.

The Second Round brings into manifestation the second element AIR, that element, the purity of which would ensure continuous life to him who would use it. There have been two occultists only in Europe who have discovered and even partially applied it in practice, though its composition has always been known among the highest Eastern Initiates. The ozone of the modern chemists is poison compared with the real universal solvent which could never be thought of unless it existed in nature. "*From the second Round, Earth -- hitherto a foetus in the matrix of Space -- began its real existence: it had developed individual sentient life, its second principle. The second corresponds to the sixth* (*principle*); *the second is life continuous, the other, temporary.*"

The *Third* Round developed the *third* Principle -- WATER; while the Fourth transformed the gaseous fluids and plastic form of our globe into the hard, crusted, grossly material sphere we are living on. "Bhumi" has reached her *fourth* principle. To this it may be objected that the law of analogy, so much insisted upon, is broken. Not at all. Earth will reach her true ultimate form -- (inversely in this to man) -- her body shell -- only toward the end of the manvantara after the Seventh Round. Eugenius Philalethes was right when he assured his readers *on his word of honour* that no one had yet seen *the Earth* (*i.e.,* MATTER in its essential form). Our globe is, so far, in its *Kamarupic* state -- the astral body of desires of *Ahamkara*, dark Egotism, the progeny of Mahat, on the lower plane. . . .

It is not molecularly constituted matter -- least of all the human body (*sthulasarira*) -- that is the grossest of all our "principles," but verily the *middle* principle, the real animal centre; whereas our body is but its shell, the irresponsible factor and medium through which the beast in us acts all its life. Every intellectual theosophist will understand my real meaning. Thus the idea that the human tabernacle is built by countless *lives*, just in the same way as the rocky crust of our Earth was, has nothing repulsive in it for the true mystic. Nor can Science oppose the occult teaching, for it is not because the microscope will ever fail to detect the ultimate living atom or life, that it can reject the doctrine.

(*c*) Science teaches us that the living as well as the dead organism of both man and animal are swarming with bacteria of a hundred various kinds; that from without we are threatened with the invasion of microbes with every breath we draw, and from within by leucomaines, aerobes, anaerobes, and what not. But Science never yet went so far as to assert with the occult doctrine that our bodies, as well as those of animals, plants, and stones, are themselves altogether built up of such beings; which, except larger species, no microscope can detect. So far, as regards the purely animal and material portion of man, Science is on its way to discoveries that will go far towards corroborating this theory. Chemistry and physiology are the two great magicians of the future, who are destined to open the eyes of mankind to the great physical truths. With every day, the identity between the animal and physical man, between the plant and man, and even between the reptile and its nest, the rock, and man -- is more and more clearly shown. The physical and chemical constituents of all being found to be identical, chemical science may well say that there is no difference between the matter which composes the ox and that which forms man. But the Occult doctrine is far more explicit. It says: --- Not only the chemical compounds are the same, but the same infinitesimal *invisible lives* compose the atoms of the bodies of the mountain and the daisy, of man and the ant, of the elephant, and of the tree which shelters him from the sun. Each particle -- whether you call it organic or inorganic -- *is a life*. Every atom and molecule in the Universe is both *life-giving* and *death-giving* to that form, inasmuch as it builds by aggregation universes and the ephemeral vehicles ready to receive the transmigrating soul, and as eternally destroys and changes the *forms* and expels those souls from their temporary abodes. It creates and kills; it is self-generating and self-destroying; it brings into being, and annihilates, that mystery of mysteries -- the *living body* of man, animal, or plant, every second in time and space; and it generates equally life and death, beauty and ugliness, good and bad, and even the agreeable and disagreeable, the beneficent and maleficent sensations. It is that mysterious LIFE, represented collectively by countless myriads of lives, that follows in its own sporadic way, the hitherto incomprehensible law of Atavism; that copies family resemblances as well as those it finds impressed in the aura of the generators of every future human being, a mystery, in short, that will receive fuller attention elsewhere. For the present, one instance may be cited in illustration. Modern science begins to find out that ptomaine (the alkaloid poison generated by decaying matter and corpses -- a *life* also) extracted with the help of volatile ether, yields a smell as strong and equal to that of the freshest orange-blossoms; but that free from oxygen, these alkaloids yield either a most sickening, disgusting smell, or the most agreeable aroma which recalls that of the most delicately scented flowers. And it is suspected that such blossoms owe their agreeable smell to the poisonous ptomaine; the venomous essence of certain mushrooms (fungi) being nearly identical with the venom of the cobra of India, the most deadly of serpents. Thus, having discovered the effects, Science has to find their PRIMARY CAUSES; and this it can never do without the help of the old sciences, of alchemy, occult botany and physics. We are taught that every physiological change, in addition to pathological phenomena; diseases -- nay, life itself -- or rather the objective phenomena of life, produced by certain conditions and changes in the tissues of the body which allow and force life to act in that body; that all this is due to those unseen CREATORS and DESTROYERS that are called in such a loose and general way, microbes. Such experimenters as Pasteur are the best friends and helpers of the Destroyers and the worst enemies of the Creators -- if the latter were not at the same time destroyers too. However it may be, one thing is sure in this: The knowledge of these primary causes and of the ultimate essence of every element, of its lives, their functions, properties, and conditions of change -- constitutes the basis of MAGIC. Paracelsus was, perhaps, the only Occultist in Europe, during the last centuries since the Christian era, who was versed in this mystery. Had not a criminal hand put an end to his life, years before the time allotted him by Nature, physiological Magic would have fewer secrets for the civilized world than it now has.

(*d*) But what has the Moon to do in all this? we may be asked. What have "Fish, Sin and Moon" in the apocalyptic saying of the Stanza to do in company with the "Life-microbes"? With the latter nothing, except availing themselves of the tabernacle of clay prepared by them; with divine perfect man everything, since "Fish, Sin and Moon" make conjointly the three symbols of the immortal Being.

This is all that can be given. Nor does the writer pretend to know more of this strange symbol than may be inferred about it from exoteric religions; from the mystery perhaps, which underlies the *Matsya* (fish) *Avatar* of Vishnu, the Chaldean Oannes -- the Man-Fish, recorded in the imperishable sign of the Zodiac, *Pisces*, and running throughout the two Testaments in the personages of Joshua "Son of the Fish (Nun)" and Jesus; the allegorical "Sin" or Fall of Spirit into matter, and the Moon -- in so far as it relates to the "Lunar" ancestors, the Pitris.

For the present it may be as well to remind the reader that while the Moon-goddesses were connected in every mythology, especially the Grecian, with child-birth, because of the lunar influence on women and conception, the occult and actual connection of our satellite with fecundation is to this day unknown to physiology, which regards every popular practice in this reference as gross superstition. As it is useless to discuss them in detail, we may only stop at present to discuss the lunar symbology casually, to show that the said superstition belongs to the most ancient beliefs, and even to Judaism -- the basis of Christianity. With the Israelites, the chief function of Jehovah was child-giving, and the esotericism of the Bible, interpreted Kabalistically, shows undeniably the Holy of Holies in the temple to be only the symbol of the womb. This is now proven beyond doubt and cavil, by the *numerical* reading of the Bible in general, and of Genesis especially. This idea must certainly have been borrowed by the Jews from the Egyptians and Indians, whose Holy of Holies was, and with the latter is to this day, symbolised by the King's chamber in the Great Pyramid (see "*Source of Measures*") and the Yoni symbols of exoteric Hinduism. To make the whole clearer and to show at the same time the enormous difference in the spirit of interpretation and the original meaning of the same symbols between the ancient Eastern Occultists and the Jewish Kabalists we refer the reader to Book II., "The Holy of Holies."

6. FROM THE FIRST-BORN (*primitive, or the first man*) THE THREAD BETWEEN THE SILENT WATCHER AND HIS SHADOW BECOMES MORE

STRONG AND RADIANT WITH EVERY CHANGE (*re-incarnation*) (*a*). THE MORNING SUN-LIGHT HAS CHANGED INTO NOON-DAY GLORY . . . .

(*a*) This sentence: "The thread between the *silent watcher* and his *shadow* (man) becomes stronger" -- with every re-incarnation -- is another psychological mystery, that will find its explanation in Book II. For the present it will suffice to say that the "Watcher" and his "Shadows" -- the latter numbering as many as there are re-incarnations for the monad -- are one. The Watcher, or the divine prototype, is at the upper rung of the ladder of being; the shadow, at the lower. Withal, the *Monad* of every living being, unless his moral turpitude breaks the connection and runs loose and "astray into the lunar path" -- to use the Occult expression -- *is an individual Dhyan Chohan, distinct from others, a kind of spiritual individuality of its own*, during one special Manvantara. Its *Primary*, the Spirit (Atman) is one, of course, with *Paramatma* (the one Universal Spirit), but the vehicle (Vahan) it is enshrined in, the *Buddhi*, is part and parcel of that Dhyan-Chohanic Essence; and it is in this that lies the mystery of that *ubiquity*, which was discussed a few pages back. "My Father, that is in Heaven, and I -- are one," -- says the Christian Scripture; in this, at any rate, it is the faithful echo of the esoteric tenet.

7. THIS IS THY PRESENT WHEEL -- SAID THE FLAME TO THE SPARK. THOU ART MYSELF, MY IMAGE AND MY SHADOW. I HAVE CLOTHED MYSELF IN THEE, AND THOU ART MY VAHAN (*vehicle*) TO THE DAY, "BE WITH US," WHEN THOU SHALT RE-BECOME MYSELF AND OTHERS, THYSELF AND ME (*a*), THEN THE BUILDERS, HAVING DONNED THEIR FIRST CLOTHING, DESCEND ON RADIANT EARTH, AND REIGN OVER MEN -- WHO ARE THEMSELVES (*b*).

(*a*) The day when "the spark will re-become the Flame (man will merge into his Dhyan Chohan) myself and others, thyself and me," as the Stanza has it -- means this: In *Paranirvana* -- when *Pralaya* will have reduced not only material and psychical bodies, but even the spiritual *Ego(s)* to their original principle -- the Past, Present, and even Future Humanities, like all things, will be one and the same. Everything will have re-entered the *Great Breath.* In other words, everything will be "merged in Brahma" or the divine unity.

Is this annihilation, as some think? Or *Atheism*, as other critics -- the worshippers of a *personal* deity and believers in an unphilosophical paradise -- are inclined to suppose? Neither. It is worse than useless to return to the question of implied atheism in that which is *spirituality* of a most refined character. To see in Nirvana annihilation amounts to saying of a man plunged in a sound *dreamless* sleep -- *one that leaves no impression on the physical memory and brain, because the sleeper's Higher Self is in its original state of absolute consciousness* during those hours -- that he, too, is annihilated. The latter simile answers only to one side of the question -- the most material; since *re-absorption* is by no means such a "dreamless sleep," but, on the contrary, *absolute* existence, an unconditioned unity, or a state, to describe which human language is absolutely and hopelessly inadequate. The only approach to anything like a comprehensive conception of it can be attempted solely in the panoramic visions of the soul, through spiritual ideations of the divine monad. Nor is the individuality -- *nor even the essence of the personality*, if any be left behind -- lost, because re-absorbed. For, however limitless -- from a human standpoint -- the paranirvanic state, it has yet a limit in Eternity. Once reached, the same monad will *re-emerge* therefrom, as a still higher being, on a far higher plane, to recommence its cycle of perfected activity. The human mind cannot in its present stage of development transcend, scarcely reach this plane of thought. It totters here, on the brink of incomprehensible Absoluteness and Eternity.

(*b*) The "Watchers" reign over man during the whole period of *Satya Yuga* and the smaller subsequent yugas, down to the beginning of the Third Root Race; after which it is the Patriarchs, Heroes, and the Manes (*see Egyptian Dynasties enumerated by the priests to Solon*), the incarnated Dhyanis of a lower order, up to King Menes and the human kings of other nations; all were recorded carefully. In the views of symbologists this *Mythopoeic Age* is of course only regarded as a fairy tale. But since traditions and even Chronicles of such dynasties of *divine* Kings -- of gods reigning over men followed by dynasties of Heroes or Giants -- exist in the annals of every nation, it is difficult to understand how all the peoples under the sun, some of whom are separated by vast oceans and belong to different hemispheres, such as the ancient Peruvians and Mexicans, as well as the Chaldeans, could have worked out the same "fairy tales" in the same order of events. However, as the Secret Doctrine teaches *history* -- which, for being esoteric and traditional, is none the less more reliable than profane history -- we are as entitled to our beliefs as anyone else, whether religionist or sceptic. And that Doctrine says that the Dhyani-Buddhas of the two higher groups, namely, the "Watchers" or the "Architects," furnished the many and various races with divine kings and leaders. It is the latter who taught humanity their arts and sciences, and the former who revealed to the incarnated Monads that had just shaken off their vehicles of the lower Kingdoms -- and who had, therefore, lost every recollection of their divine origin -- the great spiritual truths of the transcendental worlds. (See Book II., "Divine Dynasties.")

Thus, as expressed in the Stanza, the Watchers descended on Earth and reigned over men -- "*who are themselves.*" The reigning kings had finished their cycle on Earth and other worlds, in the preceding Rounds. In the future manvantaras they will have risen to higher systems than our planetary world; and it is the Elect of our Humanity, the Pioneers on the hard and difficult path of Progress, who will take the places of their predecessors. The next great Manvantara will witness the men of our own life-cycle becoming the instructors and guides of a mankind whose Monads may now yet be imprisoned -- semi-conscious -- in the most intellectual of the animal kingdom, while their lower principles will be animating, perhaps, the highest specimens of the Vegetable world.

Thus proceed the cycles of the septenary evolution, in Septennial nature; the Spiritual or divine; the psychic or semi-divine; the intellectual, the passional, the instinctual, or *cognitional;* the semi-corporeal and the purely material or physical natures. All these evolve and progress cyclically, passing from one into another, in a double, centrifugal and centripetal way, *one* in their ultimate essence, *seven* in their aspects. The lowest, of course, is the one depending upon and subservient to our five physical senses. Thus far, for individual, human, sentient, animal and vegetable life, each the microcosm of its higher macrocosm. The same for the Universe, which manifests periodically, for purposes of the collective progress of the countless *lives,* the outbreathings of the *One Life;* in order that through the *Ever-Becoming,* every cosmic atom in this infinite Universe, passing from the formless and the intangible, through the mixed natures of the semi-terrestrial, down to matter in full generation, and then back again, reascending at each new period higher and nearer the final goal; that each atom, we say, *may reach through individual merits and efforts* that plane where it re-becomes the one unconditioned ALL. But between the Alpha and the Omega there is the weary "Road" hedged in by thorns, that "goes down first, then --

Winds up hill all the way
Yes, to the very end . . . . ."

Starting upon the long journey immaculate; descending more and more into sinful matter, and having connected himself with every atom in manifested *Space* -- the *Pilgrim,* having struggled through and suffered in every form of life and being, is only at the bottom of the valley of matter, and half through his cycle, when he has identified himself with collective Humanity. This, *he has made in his own image.* In order to progress upwards and homewards, the "God" has now to ascend the weary uphill path of the Golgotha of Life. It is the martyrdom of self-conscious existence. Like Visvakarman he has to sacrifice *himself to himself* in order to redeem all creatures, to resurrect from the many into the *One Life.* Then he ascends into heaven indeed; where, plunged into the incomprehensible absolute Being and Bliss of Paranirvana, he reigns unconditionally, and whence he will re-descend again at the next "coming," which one portion of humanity expects in its dead-letter sense as the *second advent,* and the other as the last "Kalki Avatar."

SUMMING UP

"The History of Creation and of this world from its beginning up to the present time is composed of seven chapters. The seventh chapter is not yet written."
(T. Subba Row, Theosophist, 1881.)

THE first of these Seven chapters has been attempted and is now finished. However incomplete and feeble as an exposition, it is, at any rate, an approximation -- using the word in a mathematical sense -- to that which is the oldest basis for all the subsequent Cosmogonies. The attempt to render in a European tongue the grand panorama of the ever periodically recurring Law -- impressed upon the plastic minds of the first races endowed with Consciousness by those who reflected the same from the Universal Mind -- is daring, for no human language, save the Sanskrit -- which is that *of the Gods* -- can do so with any degree of adequacy. But the failures in this work must be forgiven for the sake of the motive.

As a whole, neither the foregoing nor what follows can be found in full anywhere. It is not taught in any of the six Indian schools of philosophy, for it pertains to their synthesis -- the seventh, which is the Occult doctrine. It is not traced on any crumbling papyrus of Egypt, nor is it any longer graven on Assyrian tile or granite wall. The Books of the *Vedanta* (the last word of human knowledge) give out but the metaphysical aspect of this world-Cosmogony; and their priceless thesaurus, the *Upanishads* -- *Upa-ni-shad* being a compound word meaning "the conquest of ignorance by the revelation of *secret, spiritual* knowledge" -- require now the additional possession of a Master-key to enable the student to get at their full meaning. The reason for this I venture to state here as I learned it from a Master.

The name, "*Upanishads*," is usually translated "esoteric doctrine." These treatises form part of the *Sruti* or "revealed knowledge," *Revelation*, in short, and are generally attached to the *Brahmana* portion of the Vedas, as their third division. There are over 150 *Upanishads* enumerated by, and known to, Orientalists, who credit the oldest with being written *probably* about 600 years B.C.; but of *genuine* texts there does not exist a fifth of the number. The Upanishads are to the Vedas what the Kabala is to the Jewish Bible. They treat of and expound the secret and mystic meaning of the Vedic texts. They speak of the origin of the Universe, the nature of Deity, and of Spirit and Soul, as also of the metaphysical connection of mind and matter. In a few words: They CONTAIN *the beginning and the end of all human knowledge, but they have now ceased to* REVEAL *it*, since the day of Buddha. If it were otherwise, the Upanishads could not be called *esoteric*, since they are now openly attached to the Sacred Brahmanical books, which have, in our present age, become accessible even to the *Mlechchhas* (out-*castes*) and the European Orientalists. One thing in them -- and this in all the *Upanishads* -- invariably and constantly points to their ancient origin, and proves (*a*) that they were written, in some of their portions, *before* the caste system became the tyrannical institution which it still is; and (*b*) that half of their contents have been eliminated, while some of them were rewritten and abridged. "The great Teachers of the higher Knowledge and the Brahmans are continually represented as going to Kshatriya (military caste) kings to become their pupils." As Cowell pertinently remarks, the *Upanishads* "breathe an entirely different spirit" (from other Brahmanical writings), "a freedom of thought unknown in any earlier work except in the Rig Veda hymns themselves." The second fact is explained by a tradition recorded in one of the **MSS**. on Buddha's life. It says that the Upanishads were originally attached to their Brahmanas after the beginning of a reform, which led to the exclusiveness of the present caste system among the Brahmins, a few centuries after the invasion of India by the "twice-born." They were complete in those days, and were used for the instruction of the chelas who were preparing for their initiation.

This lasted so long as the Vedas and the Brahmanas remained in the sole and exclusive keeping of the temple-Brahmins -- while no one else had the right to study or even read them outside of the *sacred* caste. Then came Gautama, the Prince of Kapilavastu. After *learning* the whole of the Brahmanical wisdom in the *Rahasya* or the *Upanishads,* and finding that the teachings differed little, if at all, from those of the "Teachers of Life" inhabiting the snowy ranges of the Himalaya, the Disciple of the Brahmins, feeling indignant because the sacred wisdom was thus withheld from all but the Brahmins, determined to save the whole world by popularizing it. Then it was that the Brahmins, seeing that their sacred knowledge and Occult wisdom was falling into the hands of the "*Mlechchhas,*" abridged the texts of the Upanishads, originally containing thrice the matter of the Vedas and the Brahmanas together, without altering, however, one word of the texts. They simply detached from the **MSS**. the most important portions containing the last word of the Mystery of Being. The key to the Brahmanical secret code remained henceforth with the initiates alone, and the Brahmins were thus in a position to publicly deny the correctness of Buddha's teaching by appealing to their *Upanishads,* silenced for ever on the chief questions. Such is the esoteric tradition beyond the Himalayas.

Sri Sankaracharya, the greatest Initiate living in the historical ages, wrote many a Bhashya on the *Upanishads.* But his original treatises, as there are reasons to suppose, have not yet fallen into the hands of the Philistines, for they are too jealously preserved in his *maths* (monasteries, *mathams*). And there are still weightier reasons to believe that the priceless Bhashyas (Commentaries) on the esoteric doctrine of the Brahmins, by their greatest expounder, will remain for ages yet a dead letter to most of the Hindus, except the *Smartava* Brahmins. This sect, founded by Sankaracharya, (which is still very powerful in Southern India) is now almost the only one to produce students who have preserved sufficient knowledge to comprehend the dead letter of the Bhashyas. The reason of this is that they alone, I am informed, have occasionally real Initiates at their head in their mathams, as for instance, in the "Sringa-giri," in the Western Ghats of Mysore. On the other hand, there is no sect in that desperately exclusive caste of the Brahmins, more exclusive than is the Smartava; and the reticence of its followers to say what they may know of the Occult sciences and the esoteric doctrine, is only equalled by their pride and learning.

Therefore the writer of the present statement must be prepared beforehand to meet with great opposition and even the denial of such statements as are brought forward in this work. Not that any claim to infallibility, or to perfect correctness in every detail of all that which is herein said, was ever put forward. Facts are there, and they can hardly be denied. But, owing to the intrinsic difficulties of the subjects treated, and the almost insurmountable limitations of the English tongue (as of all other European languages) to express certain ideas, it is more than probable that the writer has failed to present the explanations in the best and in the clearest form; yet all that could be done was done under every adverse circumstance, and this is the utmost that can be expected of any writer.

Let us recapitulate and show, by the vastness of the subjects expounded, how difficult, if not impossible, it is to do them full justice.

(1.) The Secret Doctrine is the accumulated Wisdom of the Ages, and its cosmogony alone is the most stupendous and elaborate system: *e.g.,* even in the exotericism of the Puranas. But such is the mysterious power of Occult symbolism, that the facts which have actually occupied countless generations of initiated seers and prophets to marshal, to set down and explain, in the bewildering series of evolutionary progress, are all recorded on a few pages of geometrical signs and glyphs. The flashing gaze of those seers has penetrated into the very kernel of matter, and recorded the soul of things there, where an ordinary profane, however learned, would have perceived but the external work of form. But modern science believes not in the "soul of things," and hence will reject the whole system of ancient cosmogony. It is useless to say that the system in question is no fancy of one or several isolated individuals. That it is the uninterrupted record covering thousands of generations of Seers whose respective experiences were made to test and to verify the traditions passed orally by one early race to another, of the teachings of higher and exalted beings, who watched over the childhood of Humanity. That for long ages, the "Wise Men" of the Fifth Race, of the stock saved and rescued from the last cataclysm and shifting of continents, had passed their lives *in learning, not teaching.* How did they do so? It is answered: by checking, testing, and verifying in every department of nature the traditions of old by the independent visions of great adepts; *i.e.,* men who have developed and perfected their physical, mental, psychic, and spiritual organisations to the utmost possible degree. No vision of one adept was accepted till it was checked and confirmed by the visions -- so obtained as to stand as independent evidence -- of other adepts, and by centuries of experiences.

(2.) The fundamental Law in that system, the central point from which all emerged, around and toward which all gravitates, and upon which is hung the philosophy of the rest, is the One homogeneous divine SUBSTANCE-PRINCIPLE, the one radical cause.

> . . . *"Some few, whose lamps shone brighter, have been led*
> *From cause to cause to nature's secret head,*
> *And found that one first Principle must be. . . ."*

It is called "Substance-Principle," for it becomes "substance" on the plane of the manifested Universe, an illusion, while it remains a "principle" in the beginningless and endless abstract, visible and invisible SPACE. It is the omnipresent Reality: impersonal, because it contains all and everything. *Its impersonality is the fundamental conception* of the System. It is latent in every atom in the Universe, and is the Universe itself. (See in chapters on Symbolism, "Primordial Substance, and Divine Thought.")

(3.) The Universe is the periodical manifestation of this unknown Absolute Essence. To call it "essence," however, is to sin against the very spirit of the philosophy. For though the noun may be derived in this case from the verb *esse,* "to be," yet IT cannot be identified with a *being* of any kind, that can be conceived by human intellect. IT is best described as neither Spirit nor matter, but both. "Parabrahmam and Mulaprakriti" are One, in reality, yet two in the Universal conception of the manifested, even in the conception of the One Logos, its first manifestation, to which, as the able lecturer in the "Notes on the Bhagavadgita" shows, IT appears from the objective standpoint of the One Logos as Mulaprakriti and not as Parabrahmam; as its *veil* and not the one REALITY hidden behind, which is unconditioned and absolute.

(4.) The Universe is called, with everything in it, MAYA, because all is temporary therein, from the ephemeral life of a fire-fly to that of the Sun. Compared to the eternal immutability of the ONE, and the changelessness of that Principle, the Universe, with its evanescent ever-changing forms, must be necessarily, in the mind of a philosopher, no better than a will-o'-the-wisp. Yet, the Universe is real enough to the conscious beings in it, which are as unreal as it is itself.

(5.) Everything in the Universe, throughout all its kingdoms, is CONSCIOUS: *i.e.,* endowed with a consciousness of its own kind and on its own plane of perception. We men must remember that because *we* do not perceive any signs -- which we can recognise -- of consciousness, say, in stones, we have no right to say that *no consciousness exists there.* There is no such thing as either "dead" or "blind" matter, as there is no "Blind" or "Unconscious" Law. These find no place among the conceptions of Occult philosophy. The latter never stops at surface appearances, and for it the *noumenal* essences have more reality than their objective counterparts; it resembles therein the mediaeval *Nominalists,* for whom it was the Universals that were the realities and the particulars which existed only in name and human fancy.

(6.) The Universe is worked and *guided* from *within outwards.* As above so it is below, as in heaven so on earth; and man -- the microcosm and miniature copy of the macrocosm -- is the living witness to this Universal Law, and to the mode of its action. We see that every *external* motion, act, gesture, whether voluntary or mechanical, organic or mental, is produced and preceded by *internal* feeling or emotion, will or volition, and thought or mind. As no outward motion or change, when normal, in man's external body can take place unless provoked by an inward impulse, given through one of the three functions named, so with the external or manifested Universe. The whole Kosmos is guided, controlled, and animated by almost endless series of Hierarchies of sentient Beings, each having a mission to perform, and who -- whether we give to them one name or another, and call them Dhyan-Chohans or Angels -- are "messengers" in the sense only that they are the agents of Karmic and Cosmic Laws. They vary infinitely in their respective degrees of consciousness and intelligence; and to call them all pure Spirits without any of the earthly alloy "which time is wont to prey upon" is only to indulge in poetical fancy. For each of these Beings either *was,* or prepares to become, a man, if not in the present, then in a past or a coming cycle (Manvantara). They are *perfected,* when not *incipient,* men; and differ morally from the terrestrial human beings on their higher (less material) spheres, only in that they are devoid of the feeling of personality and of the *human* emotional nature -- two purely earthly characteristics. The former, or the "perfected," have become free from those feelings, because (*a*) they have no longer fleshly bodies -- an ever-numbing weight on the Soul; and (*b*) the pure spiritual element being left untrammelled and more free, they are less influenced by *maya* than man can ever be, unless he is an adept who keeps his two personalities -- the spiritual and the physical -- entirely separated. The incipient monads, having never had terrestrial bodies yet, can have no sense of personality or EGO-ism. That which is meant by "personality," being a limitation and a relation, or, as defined by Coleridge, "individuality existing in itself but with a nature as a ground," the term cannot of course be applied to non-human entities; but, as a fact insisted upon by generations of Seers, none of these Beings, high or low, have either individuality or personality as separate Entities, *i.e.,* they have no individuality in the sense in which a man says, "*I am myself and* no one else;" in other words, they are conscious of no such distinct separateness as men and things have on earth. Individuality is the characteristic of their respective hierarchies, not of their units; and these characteristics vary only with the degree of the plane to which those hierarchies belong: the nearer to the region of Homogeneity and the One Divine, the purer and the less accentuated that individuality in the Hierarchy. They are finite, in all respects, with the exception of their higher principles -- the immortal sparks reflecting the universal divine flame -- individualized and separated only on the spheres of Illusion by a differentiation as illusive as the rest. They are "Living Ones," because they are the streams projected on the Kosmic screen of illusion from the ABSOLUTE LIFE; beings in whom life cannot become extinct, before the fire of ignorance is extinct in those who sense these "Lives." Having sprung into being under the quickening influence of the uncreated beam, the reflection of the great Central Sun that radiates on the shores of the river of Life, it is the inner principle in them which belongs to the waters of immortality, while its differentiated clothing is as perishable as man's body. Therefore Young was right in saying that

"*Angels are men of a superior kind*"

and no more. They are neither "ministering" nor "protecting" angels; nor are they "Harbingers of the Most High" still less the "Messengers of wrath" of any God such as man's fancy has created. To appeal to their protection is as foolish as to believe that their sympathy may be secured by any kind of propitiation; for they are, as much as man himself is, the slaves and creatures of immutable Karmic and Kosmic law. The reason for it is evident. Having no elements of personality in their essence they can have no personal qualities, such as attributed by men, in their exoteric religions, to their anthropomorphic God -- a jealous and exclusive God who rejoices and feels wrathful, is pleased with sacrifice, and is more despotic in his vanity than any finite foolish man. Man, as shown in Book II., being a compound of the essences of all those celestial Hierarchies may succeed in making himself, as such, superior, in one sense, to any hierarchy or class, or even combination of them. "Man can neither propitiate nor command the *Devas*," it is said. But, by paralyzing his lower personality, and arriving thereby at the full knowledge of the *non-separateness* of his higher SELF from the One absolute SELF, man can, even during his terrestrial life, become as "One of Us." Thus it is, by eating of the fruit of knowledge which dispels ignorance, that man becomes like one of the Elohim or the Dhyanis; and once on *their* plane the Spirit of Solidarity and perfect Harmony, which reigns in every Hierarchy, must extend over him and protect him in every particular.

The chief difficulty which prevents men of science from believing in divine as well as in nature Spirits is their materialism. The main impediment before the Spiritualist which hinders him from believing in the same, while preserving a blind belief in the "Spirits" of the Departed, is the general ignorance of all, except some Occultists and Kabalists, about the true essence and nature of matter. It is on the acceptance or rejection of the theory of the *Unity of all in Nature, in its ultimate Essence,* that mainly rests the belief or unbelief in the existence around us of other conscious beings besides the Spirits of the Dead.

It is on the right comprehension of the primeval Evolution of Spirit-Matter and its real essence that the student has to depend for the further elucidation in his mind of the Occult Cosmogony, and for the only sure clue which can guide his subsequent studies.

In sober truth, as just shown, every "Spirit" so-called is either a *disembodied or a future man.* As from the highest Archangel (Dhyan Chohan) down to the last conscious "Builder" (the inferior class of Spiritual Entities), all such are *men*, having lived aeons ago, in other Manvantaras, on this or other Spheres; so the inferior, semi-intelligent and non-intelligent Elementals -- are all *future* men. That fact alone -- that a Spirit is endowed with intelligence -- is a proof to the Occultist that that Being must have been a *man,* and acquired his knowledge and intelligence throughout the human cycle. There is but one indivisible and absolute Omniscience and Intelligence in the Universe, and this thrills throughout every atom and infinitesimal point of the whole finite Kosmos which hath no bounds, and which people call SPACE, considered independently of anything contained in it. But the first differentiation of its *reflection* in the manifested World is purely Spiritual, and the Beings generated in it are not endowed with a consciousness that has any relation to the one we conceive of. They can have no human consciousness or Intelligence before they have acquired such, personally and individually. This may be a mystery, yet it is a fact, in Esoteric philosophy, and a very apparent one too.

The whole order of nature evinces a progressive march towards *a higher life.* There is design in the action of the seemingly blindest forces. The whole process of evolution with its endless adaptations is a proof of this. The immutable laws that weed out the weak and feeble species, to make room for the strong, and which ensure the "survival of the fittest," though so cruel in their immediate action -- all are working toward the grand end. The very *fact* that adaptations *do* occur, that the fittest *do* survive in the struggle for existence, shows that what is called "unconscious Nature" is in reality an aggregate of forces manipulated by semi-intelligent beings (Elementals) guided by High Planetary Spirits, (Dhyan Chohans), whose collective aggregate forms the manifested *verbum* of the unmanifested LOGOS, and constitutes at one and the same time the MIND of the Universe and its immutable LAW.

Three distinct representations of the Universe in its three distinct aspects are impressed upon our thought by the esoteric philosophy: the PRE-EXISTING (evolved from) the EVER-EXISTING; and the PHENOMENAL -- the world of illusion, the reflection, and shadow thereof. During the great mystery and drama of life known as the Manvantara, real Kosmos is like the object placed behind the white screen upon which are thrown the Chinese shadows, called forth by the magic lantern. The actual figures and things remain invisible, while the wires of evolution are pulled by the unseen hands; and men and things are thus but the reflections, *on* the white field, of the realities *behind* the snares of *Mahamaya,* or the great Illusion. This was taught in every philosophy, in every religion, *ante* as well as *post* diluvian, in India and Chaldea, by the Chinese as by the Grecian Sages. In the former countries these three Universes were allegorized, in exoteric teachings, by the three trinities emanating from the Central eternal germ and forming with it a Supreme Unity: the *initial,* the *manifested,* and the *Creative* Triad, or the three in One. The last is but the symbol, in its concrete expression, of the first *ideal* two. Hence Esoteric philosophy passes over the necessarianism of this purely metaphysical conception, and calls the first one, only, the Ever Existing. This is the view of every one of the six great schools of Indian philosophy -- the *six principles of that unit body of* WISDOM *of which the "gnosis,"* the *hidden* knowledge, is the seventh.

The writer hopes that, superficially handled as may be the comments on the Seven Stanzas, enough has been given in this cosmogonic portion of the work to show Archaic teachings to be more *scientific* (in the modern sense of the word) on their very face, than any other ancient Scriptures left to be regarded and judged on their exoteric aspect. Since, however, as confessed before, this work *withholds far more than it gives out,* the student is invited to use his own intuitions. Our chief care is to elucidate that which has already been given out, and, to our regret, very incorrectly at times; to supplement the knowledge hinted at -- whenever and wherever possible -- by additional matter; and to bulwark our doctrines against the too strong attacks of modern Sectarianism, and more especially against those of our latter-day Materialism, very often miscalled Science, whereas, in reality, the words "Scientists" and "Sciolists" ought alone to bear the responsibility for the many illogical theories offered to the world. In its great ignorance, the public, while blindly accepting everything that emanates from "authorities," and feeling it to be its duty to regard every *dictum* coming from a man of Science as a proven fact -- the public, we say, is taught to scoff at anything brought forward from "heathen" sources. Therefore, as materialistic Scientists can be fought solely with their own weapons -- those of controversy and argument -- an *Addendum* is added to every Book contrasting our respective views and showing how even great authorities may often err. We believe that this can be done effectually by showing the weak points of our opponents, and by proving their too frequent sophisms -- made to pass for scientific *dicta* -- to be incorrect. We hold to Hermes and his "Wisdom" -- in its universal character; they -- to Aristotle as against intuition and the experience of the ages, fancying that Truth is the exclusive property of the Western world. Hence the disagreement. As Hermes says, "Knowledge differs much from sense; for sense is of things that surmount it, but Knowledge (gyi) is the end of sense" -- *i.e.,* of the illusion of our physical brain and its intellect; thus emphasizing the contrast between the laboriously acquired knowledge of the senses and mind (manas), and the intuitive omniscience of the Spiritual divine Soul -- Buddhi.

Whatever may be the destiny of these actual writings in a remote future, we hope to have proven so far the following facts:

(1) The Secret Doctrine teaches no *Atheism,* except in the Hindu sense of the word *nastika,* or the rejection of *idols,* including every anthropomorphic god. In this sense every Occultist is a *Nastika.*

(2) It admits a Logos or a collective "Creator" of the Universe; a *Demi-urgos* -- in the sense implied when one speaks of an "Architect" as the "Creator" of an edifice, whereas that Architect has never touched one stone of it, but, while furnishing the plan, left all the manual labour to the masons; in our case the plan was furnished by the Ideation of the Universe, and the constructive labour was left to the Hosts of intelligent Powers and Forces. But that *Demiurgos* is no *personal* deity, -- *i.e.,* an imperfect *extra-cosmic god,* -- but only the aggregate of the Dhyan-Chohans and the other forces.

As to the latter --

(3) They are dual in their character; being composed of (*a*) the irrational *brute energy,* inherent in matter, and (*b*) the intelligent soul or cosmic consciousness which directs and guides that energy, and which is the *Dhyan-Chohanic thought reflecting the Ideation of the Universal mind.* This results in a perpetual series of physical manifestations and *moral effects* on Earth, during manvantaric periods, the whole being subservient to Karma. As that process is not always perfect; and since, however many proofs it may exhibit of a guiding intelligence behind the veil, it still shows gaps and flaws, and even results very often in evident failures -- therefore, neither the collective Host (Demiurgos), nor any of the working powers individually, are proper subjects for divine honours or worship. All

are entitled to the grateful reverence of Humanity, however, and man ought to be ever striving to help the divine evolution of *Ideas,* by becoming to the best of his ability a *co-worker with nature* in the cyclic task. The ever unknowable and incognizable *Karana* alone, the *Causeless* Cause of all causes, should have its shrine and altar on the holy and ever untrodden ground of our heart -- invisible, intangible, unmentioned, save through "the still small voice" of our spiritual consciousness. Those who worship before it, ought to do so in the silence and the sanctified solitude of their Souls ; making their spirit the sole mediator between them and the *Universal Spirit,* their good actions the only priests, and their sinful intentions the only visible and objective sacrificial victims to the *Presence.*

(4) Matter is *Eternal.* It is the *Upadhi* (the physical basis) for the One infinite Universal Mind to build thereon its ideations. Therefore, the Esotericists maintain that there is no inorganic or *dead* matter in nature, the distinction between the two made by Science being as unfounded as it is arbitrary and devoid of reason.

Whatever Science may think, however -- and *exact* Science is a fickle dame, as we all know by experience -- Occultism knows and teaches differently, from time immemorial -- from *Manu* and *Hermes* down to Paracelsus and his successors.

Thus Hermes, the thrice great Trismegistus, says: "Oh, my son, matter *becomes;* formerly it *was;* for matter is the vehicle of becoming." Becoming is the mode of activity of the uncreate deity. Having been endowed with the germs of becoming, matter (objective) is brought into birth, for the creative force fashions it *according to the ideal forms.* Matter not yet engendered had no form; it becomes when it is put into operation." (*The Definitions of Asclepios,* p. 134, "Virgin of the World.")

"Everything is the product of one universal creative effort. . . . There is nothing *dead,* in Nature. *Everything is organic and living,* and therefore the whole world appears to be a living organism." (Paracelsus, "*Philosophia ad Athenienes,*" F. Hartmann's translations, p. 44.)

(5.) The Universe was evolved out of its ideal plan, upheld through Eternity in the unconsciousness of that which the Vedantins call Parabrahm. This is practically identical with the conclusions of the highest Western Philosophy -- "the innate, eternal, and self-existing Ideas" of Plato, now reflected by Von Hartmann. The "unknowable" of Herbert Spencer bears only a faint resemblance to that transcendental *Reality* believed in by Occultists, often appearing merely a personification of a "*force behind phenomena*" -- an infinite and eternal *Energy* from which all things proceed, while the author of the "Philosophy of the Unconscious" has come (in this respect only) as near to a solution of the great *Mystery* as mortal man can. Few were those, whether in ancient or mediaeval philosophy, who have dared to approach the subject or even hint at it. Paracelsus mentions it inferentially. His ideas are admirably synthesized by Dr. F. Hartmann, F.T.S., in his "Life of Paracelsus."

All the *Christian* Kabalists understood well the Eastern root idea: The active Power, the "Perpetual motion of the great Breath" only awakens Kosmos at the dawn of every new Period, setting it into motion by means of the two contrary Forces, and thus causing it to become objective on the plane of Illusion. In other words, that dual motion transfers Kosmos from the plane of the Eternal Ideal into that of finite manifestation, or from the *Noumenal* to the *Phenomenal* plane. Everything that *is, was,* and *will be,* eternally IS, even the countless forms, which are finite and perishable only in their objective, not in their *ideal* Form. They existed as Ideas, in the Eternity,   and, when they pass away, will exist as reflections. Neither the form of man, nor that of any animal, plant or stone has ever been *created,* and it is only on this plane of ours that it commenced "becoming," *i.e.,* objectivising into its present materiality, or expanding *from within outwards,* from the most sublimated and supersensuous essence into its grossest appearance. Therefore *our* human forms have existed in the Eternity as astral or ethereal prototypes; according to which models, the Spiritual Beings (or Gods) whose duty it was to bring them into objective being and terrestrial Life, evolved the protoplasmic forms of the future *Egos* from *their own essence.* After which, when this human *Upadhi,* or basic mould was ready, the natural terrestrial Forces began to work on those supersensuous moulds *which contained, besides their own, the elements of all the past vegetable and future animal forms of this globe in them.* Therefore, man's *outward* shell passed through every vegetable and animal body before it assumed the human shape. As this will be fully described in Book II., with the Commentaries thereupon, there is no need to say more of it here.

According to the Hermetico-Kabalistic philosophy of Paracelsus, it is Yliaster -- the ancestor of the just-born *Protyle,* introduced by Mr. Crookes in chemistry -- or primordial *Protomateria* that evolved out of itself the Kosmos.

"When Evolution took place the Yliaster divided itself. . . . melted and dissolved, developing from within itself the *Ideos* or Chaos, called re*spectively Mysterium magnum, Iliados, Limbus Major,* or Primordial Matter. This Primordial essence is of a monistic nature, and manifests itself not only as vital activity, a spiritual force, an invisible, incomprehensible, and indescribable power, but also as vital matter of which the substance of living beings consists." In this *Ideos* of primordial matter, or the *proto-ilos* -- which is the matrix of all created things -- is contained the substance from which everything is formed. It is the Chaos . . . out of which the Macrocosm, and, later on, by evolution and division in *Mysteria Specialia,* each separate being, came into existence. "All things and all elementary substances were contained in it *in potentia* but not in *actu*" -- which makes the translator, Dr. F. Hartmann, justly observe that "it seems that Paracelsus anticipated the modern discovery of the 'potency of matter' three hundred years ago" (P. 42).

This Magnus Limbus, then, or Yliaster of Paracelsus, is simply our old friend "Father-Mother," *within,* before it appeared in Space, of the second and other Stanzas. It is the universal matrix of Kosmos, personified in the dual character of Macro- and Microcosm (or the Universe and our Globe)　by Aditi-Prakriti, the Spiritual and the physical nature. For we find it explained in Paracelsus that "the Magnus Limbus is the nursery out of which all creatures have grown, in the same sense as a tree grows out of a small seed; with the difference, however, that the great Limbus takes its origin from the Word, while the Limbus minor (the terrestrial seed or sperm) takes it from the earth.

The great Limbus is the seed out of which all beings have come, and the little Limbus is each ultimate being that reproduces its form, and that has itself been produced by the 'great.' The latter possesses all the qualifications of the great one, in the same sense as a son has an organization similar to that of his father." (*See Comment. Book II. para. iii.*) . . . "As Yliaster dissolved, *Ares,* the dividing, differentiating, and individualising power (*Fohat,* another old friend,) . . . began to act. All production took place in consequence of separation. There were produced out of the Ideos, the elements of Fire, Water, Air and Earth, whose birth, however, did not take place in a material mode, or by simple separation," but by spiritual and dynamical, not even complex, combinations -- e.g., mechanical *mixture* as opposed to *chemical* combination -- just as fire may come out of a pebble, or a tree out of a seed, although there is originally no fire in the pebble, nor a tree in the seed. Spirit is living, and Life is Spirit, and Life and Spirit (*Prakriti Purusha*) (?) produce all things, but they are essentially one and not two. . . . The elements too, have each one its own Yliaster, because all the activity of matter in every form is only an effluvium of the same fount. But as from the seed grow the roots with their fibres, and after that the stalk with its branches and leaves, and lastly the flowers and seeds; likewise all beings were born from the elements, and consist of elementary substances out of which other forms may come into existence, bearing the characteristics of their parents." ("This doctrine, preached 300 years ago," remarks the translator, "is identical with the one that has revolutionized modern thought, after having been put into new shape and elaborated by Darwin. It was still more elaborated by Kapila in the Sankhya philosophy") . . . . The elements as the mothers of all creatures *are of an invisible, spiritual nature, and have souls.* They all spring from the "*Mysterium Magnum.*" (*Philosophia ad Athenienses.*)

Compare this with Vishnu Purana.

"From *Pradhana* (primordial substance) presided over by *Kshetrajna* (embodied Spirit?) proceeds the evolution of those qualities....... From the great Principle *Mahat* (Universal Intellect, or mind)..... proceeds the origin of the subtle elements and from these the organs of sense (*Book I., ii.*).

Thus it may be shown that all the fundamental truths of nature were universal in antiquity, and that the basic ideas upon spirit, matter, and the universe, or upon God, Substance, and man, were identical. Taking the two most ancient religious philosophies on the globe, Hinduism and Hermetism, from the scriptures of India and Egypt, the identity of the two is easily recognisable.

This becomes apparent to one who reads the latest translation and rendering of the "Hermetic Fragments" just mentioned, by our late lamented friend, Dr. Anna Kingsford. Disfigured and tortured as these have been in their passage through Sectarian Greek and Christian hands, the translator has most ably and intuitionally seized the weak points and tried to remedy them by means of explanations and foot-notes. And she says:.......... The creation of the visible world by the 'working gods' or Titans, as agents of the Supreme God, is a thoroughly Hermetic idea, *recognisable in all religious systems,* and in accordance with modern scientific research (?), which shows us everywhere the Divine power operating through natural Forces."

"That Universal Being, that contains all, and which is all, put into motion the Soul and the World, all that nature comprises, says Hermes. In the manifold unity of universal life, the innumerable individualities distinguished by their variations, are, nevertheless, united in such a manner that the whole is one, and that everything proceeds from Unity." (*Asclepios, Part I.*)

"God is not a mind, but the cause that the mind is; *not a spirit,* but the cause that the Spirit is; not light, but the cause that the Light is." (*Divine Pymander, Book IX.,* v. 64.)

The above shows plainly that "Divine Pymander," however much distorted in some passages by Christian "smoothing," was nevertheless written by a philosopher, while most of the so-called "hermetic Fragments" are the production of sectarian pagans with a tendency towards an anthropomorphic Supreme Being. Yet both are the echo of the Esoteric philosophy and the Hindu Puranas.

Compare two invocations, one to the Hermetic "Supreme All," the other to the "Supreme All" of the later Aryans. Says a Hermetic Fragment cited by Suidas (see Mrs. Kingsford's "*The Virgin of the World*"): -

"I adjure thee, Heaven, holy work of the great God; I adjure thee, Voice of the Father, uttered in the beginning when the universal world was framed; I adjure thee by the word, only Son of the Father who upholds all things; be favourable, be favourable."

This just preceded by the following: "Thus the Ideal Light was before the Ideal Light, and the luminous Intelligence of Intelligence was always, *and its unity was nothing else than the Spirit enveloping the Universe. Out of whom is neither God nor Angels, nor any other essentials, for* He (It?) is the Lord of all things and the power and the Light; and all depends on Him (It) and is in Him (It), etc." (*Fragments of the writings of Hermes to Ammon.*)

This is contradicted by the very same *Trismegistos,* who is made to say: "To speak of God is impossible. For corporeal cannot express the incorporeal. . . . . That which has not any body nor appearance, nor form, nor matter, cannot be apprehended by sense. I understand, Tatios, I understand, that which it is impossible to define -- that is God." (*Physical Eclogues, Florilegium of Stobaeus.*)

The contradiction between the two passages is evident; and this shows (*a*) that Hermes was a generic *nom-de-plume* used by a series of generations of mystics of every shade, and (*b*) that a great discernment has to be used before accepting a Fragment as esoteric teaching only because it is undeniably ancient. Let us now compare the above with a like invocation in the Hindu Scriptures -- undoubtedly as old, if not far older. Here it is *Parasara,* the Aryan "Hermes" who instructs *Maitreya,* the Indian Asclepios, and calls upon Vishnu in his triple hypostasis.

"Glory to the unchangeable, holy, eternal Supreme Vishnu, of one universal nature, the mighty over all; to him who is Hiranyagarbha, Hari, and Sankara (Brahma, Vishnu, and Siva), the creator, the preserver, and the destroyer of the world; to Vasudeva, the liberator (of his worshippers); to him whose essence is both single and manifold; who is both subtle and corporeal, indiscreet and discreet; to Vishnu the cause of final emancipation, the cause of the creation, existence, the end of the world; *who is the root of the world,* and who *consists of the world.*" (*Vish. Purana, Book L.*)

This is a grand invocation, full of philosophical meaning underlying it; but, for the profane masses, as suggestive as is the first of an anthropomorphic Being. We must respect the feeling that dictated both; but we cannot help finding it in full disharmony with its inner meaning, even with that which is found in the same Hermetic treatise where it is said:

"Reality is not upon the earth, my son, and it cannot be thereon. . . . Nothing on earth is real, there are only appearances. . . He (man) is not real, my son, as man. The real consists solely in itself and remains what it is. . . Man is transient, therefore he is not real, he is but appearance, and appearance is the supreme illusion.

Tatios: Then the *celestial bodies themselves are not real, my father, since they also vary?*

Trismegistos: That which is subject to birth and to change is not real. . . . . There is in them a certain falsity, seeing that they too are variable.......

Tatios: And what then is the primordial Reality?

Trismeg.: That which is one and alone, O Tatios; That which is not made of matter, nor in any body. Which has neither colour nor form, which changes not nor is transmitted but which always is."

This is quite consistent with the Vedantic teaching. The leading thought is Occult; and many are the passages in the Hermetic Fragments that belong bodily to the Secret Doctrine.

The latter teaches that the whole universe is ruled by intelligent and semi-intelligent Forces and Powers, as stated from the very beginning. Christian Theology admits and even *enforces* belief in such, but makes an arbitrary division and refers to them as "Angels" and "Devils." Science denies the existence of such, and ridicules the very idea. Spiritualists believe in the Spirits of the Dead, and, outside these, deny entirely any other kind or class of invisible beings. The Occultists and Kabalists are thus the only rational expounders of the ancient traditions, which have now culminated in dogmatic faith on the one hand, and dogmatic denials on the other. For, both belief and unbelief embrace but one small corner each of the infinite horizons of spiritual and physical manifestations; and thus both are right from their respective standpoints, and both are wrong in believing that they can circumscribe the whole within their own special and narrow barriers; for -- they can never do so. In this respect Science, Theology, and even Spiritualism show little more wisdom than the ostrich does, when it hides its head in the sand at its feet, feeling sure that there can be thus nothing beyond its own point of observation and the limited area occupied by its foolish head.

As the only works now extant upon the subject under consideration within reach of the profane of the Western "civilized" races are the above-mentioned Hermetic Books, or rather Hermetic Fragments, we may contrast them in the present case with the teachings of Esoteric philosophy. To quote for this purpose from any other would be useless, since the public knows nothing of the Chaldean works which are translated into Arabic and preserved by some Sufi initiates. Therefore the "Definitions of Asclepios," as lately compiled and glossed by Mrs. A. Kingsford, F.T.S., some of which sayings are in remarkable agreement with the Esoteric Eastern doctrine, have to be resorted to for comparison. Though not a few passages show a strong impression of some later Christian hand, yet on the whole the characteristics of the genii and gods are those of eastern teachings, while concerning other things there are passages which differ widely in our doctrines. The following are a few:--

EXTRACTS FROM A PRIVATE COMMENTARY, *hitherto secret:*--

(xvii.) "*The Initial Existence in the first twilight of the Maha-Manwantara (after the* MAHA-PRALAYA *that follows every age of Brahma) is a* CONSCIOUS SPIRITUAL QUALITY. *In the manifested* WORLDS (*solar systems*) *it is, in its* OBJECTIVE SUBJECTIVITY, *like the film from a Divine Breath to the gaze of the entranced seer. It spreads as it issues from* LAYA *throughout infinity as a colourless spiritual fluid. It is on the* SEVENTH PLANE, *and in its* SEVENTH STATE *in our planetary world.*

(xviii.) "*It is Substance to* OUR *spiritual sight. It cannot be called so by men in their* WAKING STATE; *therefore they have named it in their ignorance* 'God-Spirit.'

(xix.) "*It exists everywhere and forms the first UPADHI (foundation) on which our World (solar system) is built. Outside the latter it is to be found in its pristine purity only between (the solar systems or) the Stars of the Universe, the worlds already formed or forming; those in LAYA resting meanwhile in its bosom. As its substance is of a different kind from that known on earth, the inhabitants of the latter, seeing THROUGH IT, believe in their illusion and ignorance that it is empty space. There is not one finger's breath (ANGULA) of void Space in the whole Boundless (Universe)*.........*

(xx.) "*Matter or Substance is septenary within our World, as it is so beyond it. Moreover, each of its states or principles is graduated into seven degrees of density.* SURYA (*the Sun*), *in its visible reflection, exhibits the first, or lowest state of the seventh, the highest state of the Universal PRESENCE, the pure of the pure, the first manifested Breath of the ever Unmanifested SAT (Be-ness). All the Central physical or objective Suns are in their substance the lowest state of the first Principle of the BREATH. Nor are any of these any more than the REFLECTIONS of their PRIMARIES which are concealed from the gaze of all but the Dhyan Chohans, whose Corporeal substance belongs to the fifth division of the seventh Principle of the Mother substance, and is, therefore, four degrees higher than the solar reflected substance. As there are seven Dhatu (principal substances in the human body) so there are seven Forces in Man and in all Nature.*

(xxi.) "*The real substance of the concealed (Sun) is a nucleus of Mother substance. It is the heart and the matrix of all the living and existing Forces in our solar universe. It is the Kernel from which proceed to spread on their cyclic journeys all the Powers that set in action the atoms in their functional duties, and the focus within which they again meet in their SEVENTH ESSENCE every eleventh year. He who tells thee he has seen the sun, laugh at him as if he had said that the sun moves really onward on his diurnal path . . . .*

(xxiii). "*It is on account of his septenary nature that the Sun is spoken of by the ancients as one who is driven by seven horses equal to the metres of the Vedas; or, again, that, though he is identified with the SEVEN "Gaina" (classes of being) in his orb, he is distinct from them, as he is, indeed; as also that he has SEVEN RAYS, as indeed he has . . . .*

(xxv.) "*The Seven Beings in the Sun are the Seven Holy Ones, Self-born from the inherent power in the matrix of Mother substance. It is they who send the Seven Principal Forces, called rays, which at the beginning of Pralaya will centre into seven new Suns for the next Manvantara. The energy from which they spring into conscious existence in every Sun, is what some people call Vishnu (see foot-note below), which is the Breath of the ABSOLUTENESS.*

We call it the One manifested life -- itself a reflection of the Absolute.........

(xxvi.) "*The latter must never be mentioned in words or speech LEST IT SHOULD TAKE AWAY SOME OF OUR SPIRITUAL ENERGIES THAT ASPIRE towards ITS state, gravitating ever onward unto IT spiritually, as the whole physical universe gravitates towards ITS manifested centre -- cosmically.*

(xxvii.) "*The former -- the Initial existence -- which may be called while in this state of being the ONE LIFE, is, as explained, a FILM for creative or formative Purposes. It manifests in seven states, which, with their septenary sub-divisions, are the FORTY-NINE Fires mentioned in sacred books* . . . . . .

(xxix.) "*The first is the . . . . 'Mother' (prima MATERIA). Separating itself into its primary seven states, it proceeds down cyclically; when having consolidated itself in its LAST principle as GROSS MATTER, it revolves around itself and informs, with the seventh emanation of the last, the first and the lowest element (the Serpent biting its own tail). In a hierarchy, or order of being, the seventh emanation of her last principle is:* --

(*a*) *In the mineral, the spark that lies latent in it, and is called to its evanescent being by the POSITIVE awakening the NEGATIVE (and so forth)* . . . .

(*b*) *In the plant it is that vital and intelligent Force which informs the seed and develops it into the blade of grass, or the root and sapling. It is the germ which becomes the UPADHI of the seven principles of the thing it resides in, shooting them out as the latter grows and develops.*

(*c*) *In every animal it does the same. It is its life principle and vital power; its instinct and qualities; its characteristics and special idiosyncrasies* . . . .

(d) To man, it gives all that it bestows on all the rest of the manifested units in nature; but develops, furthermore, the reflection of all its FORTY-NINE FIRES in him. Each of his seven principles is an heir in full to, and a partaker of, the seven principles of the "great Mother." The breath of her first principle is his spirit (Atma). Her second principle is BUDDHI (soul). We call it, erroneously, the seventh. The third furnishes him with (a) the brain stuff on the physical plane, and (b) with the MIND that moves it [which is the human soul. -- H. P. B.] -- according to his organic capacities.

(e) It is the guiding Force in the Cosmic and terrestrial elements. It resides in the Fire provoked out of its latent into active being; for the whole of the seven subdivisions of the principle reside in the terrestrial Fire. It whirls in the breeze, blows with the hurricane, and sets the air in motion, which element participates in one of its principles also. Proceeding cyclically, it regulates the motion of the water, attracts and repels the waves according to fixed laws of which its seventh principle is the informing soul.

(f) Its four higher principles contain the germ that develops into the Cosmic Gods; its three lower ones breed the lives of the Elements (Elementals).

(g) In our Solar world, the One Existence is Heaven and the Earth, the Root and the flower, the Action and the Thought. It is in the Sun, and is as present in the glow-worm. Not an atom can escape it. Therefore, the ancient Sages have wisely called it the manifested God in Nature. . . ."

It may be interesting, in this connection, to remind the reader of what Mr. Subba Row said of the Forces -- mystically defined. See "Five Years of Theosophy" and "The Twelve Signs of the Zodiac." Thus he says:

"Kanya (the sixth sign of the Zodiac, or Virgo) means a Virgin, and represents Sakti or Mahamaya. The sign . . . is the 6th Rasi or division, and indicates that there are six primary forces in Nature (synthesized by the Seventh)" . . . These Sakti stand as follows: -

(1.) PARASAKTI. Literally the great or Supreme Force or power. It means and includes the powers of light and heat.

(2.) JNANASAKTI. . . . The power of intellect, of real Wisdom or Knowledge. It has two aspects:
The following are some of its manifestations when placed under the influence or control of material conditions. (a) The power of the mind in interpreting our sensations. (b) Its power in recalling past ideas (memory) and raising future expectation. (c) Its power as exhibited in what are called by modern psychologists "the laws of association," which enables it to form persisting connections between various groups of sensations and possibilities of sensations, and thus generate the notion or idea of an external object. (d) Its power in connecting our ideas together by the mysterious link of memory, and thus generating the notion of self or individuality; some of its manifestations when liberated from the bonds of matter are -- (a) Clairvoyance, (b) Psychometry.

(3.) ITCHASAKTI -- the power of the Will. Its most ordinary manifestation is the generation of certain nerve currents which set in motion such muscles as are required for the accomplishment of the desired object.

(4.) KRIYASAKTI. The mysterious power of thought which enables it to produce external, perceptible, phenomenal results by its own inherent energy. The ancients held that any idea will manifest itself externally if one's attention is deeply concentrated upon it. Similarly an intense volition will be followed by the desired result.
A Yogi generally performs his wonders by means of Itchasakti and Kriyasakti.

(5.) KUNDALINI SAKTI. The power or Force which moves in a curved path. It is the Universal life-Principle manifesting everywhere in nature. This force includes the two great forces of attraction and repulsion. Electricity and magnetism are but manifestations of it. This is the power which brings about that "continuous adjustment of internal relations to external relations" which is the essence of life according to Herbert Spencer, and that "continuous adjustment of external relations to internal relations" which is the basis of transmigration of souls, *punar janman* (re-birth) in the doctrines of the ancient Hindu philosophers. A Yogi must thoroughly subjugate this power before he can attain Moksham. . . .

(6.) **M**ANTRIKA-SAKTI. The force or power of letters, speech or music. The *Mantra Shastra* has for its subject-matter this force in all its manifestations......... The influence of melody is one of its ordinary manifestations. The power of the ineffable name is the crown of this Sakti.

Modern Science has but partly investigated the first, second and fifth of the forces above named, but is altogether in the dark as regards the remaining powers. The six forces are in their unity represented by the "*Daiviprakriti*" (the Seventh, the light of the LOGOS).

The above is quoted to show the real Hindu ideas on the same. It is all esoteric, though not covering the tenth part of *what might be said.* For one, the six names of the Six Forces mentioned are those of *the six Hierarchies* of Dhyan Chohans synthesized by their *Primary,* the seventh, who personify the Fifth Principle of Cosmic Nature, or of the "Mother" in its Mystical Sense. The enumeration alone of the *yogi* Powers would require ten volumes. Each of these Forces has a *living Conscious Entity* at its head, of which entity it is an emanation.

But let us compare with the commentary just cited the words of Hermes, the "thrice great":--

"The creation of Life *by the Sun* is as continuous as his light; nothing arrests or limits it. Around him, like an army of Satellites, *are innumerable choirs of genii.* These dwell in the neighbourhood of the Immortals, and thence watch over human things. They fulfil the will of the gods (Karma) *by means of storms, tempests, transitions of fire and earthquakes;* likewise by famines and wars, for the punishment of impiety. . . . It is the sun who preserves and nourishes all creatures; and even as the Ideal World which environs the sensible world fills this last with the plenitude and universal variety of forms, so also the Sun, enfolding all in his light, accomplishes everywhere the birth and development of creatures." . . . "*Under his orders is the choir of Genii,* or rather the choirs, *for there are many and diverse, and their number corresponds to that of the stars. Every star has its genii, good and evil by nature,* or rather by their *operation, for operation is the essence of the genii. . . .* All these Genii *preside over mundane affairs,* they shake and overthrow the constitution of States and of individuals; they *imprint their likeness on our Souls,* they are present in our nerves, our marrow, our veins, our arteries, and *our very brain-substance . . . .* at the moment when each of us receives life and being, he is taken in charge by the genii (Elementals) who preside over births, and who are classed beneath the astral powers (Superhuman astral Spirits.) They change perpetually, not always identically, but revolving in circles. They permeate by the body two parts of the Soul, that it may receive from each the impress of his own energy. But the reasonable part of the Soul is not subject to the genii; it is designed for the reception of (the) God, who enlightens it with a sunny ray. Those who are thus illumined are few in number, and from them the genii abstain: for neither genii nor Gods have any power in the presence of a single ray of God. But all other men, both soul and body, are directed by genii, to whom they cleave, and whose operations they affect.......... The genii have then the control of mundane things and our bodies serve them as instruments.........

The above, save a few sectarian points, represents that which was a universal belief common to all nations till about a century or so back. It is still as orthodox in its broad outlines and features among pagans and Christians alike, if one excepts a handful of materialists and men of Science.

For whether one calls the genii of Hermes and his "Gods," "Powers of Darkness" and "Angels," as in the Greek and Latin Churches; or "Spirits of the Dead," as in Spiritualism or, again, *Bhoots* and *Devas, Shaitan* or *Djin,* as they are still called in India and Mussulman countries -- *they are all one and the same thing* -- ILLUSION. Let not this, however, be misunderstood in the sense into which the great philosophical doctrine of the Vedantists has been lately perverted by Western schools.

All that which *is*, emanates from the ABSOLUTE, which, from this qualification alone, stands as the one and only reality -- hence, everything extraneous to this Absolute, the generative and causative Element, *must* be an illusion, most undeniably. But this is only so from the purely metaphysical view. A man who regards himself as mentally sane, and is so regarded by his neighbours, calls the visions of an *insane* brother -- whose hallucinations make *the victim either happy or supremely wretched,* as the case may be -- illusions and fancies likewise. But, where is that madman for whom the hideous shadows in his deranged mind, his *illusions,* are not, for the time being, as actual and as real as the things which his physician or keeper may see? Everything is relative in this Universe, everything is an illusion. But the experience of any plane is an actuality for the percipient being, whose consciousness is on that plane; though the said experience, regarded from the purely metaphysical standpoint, may be conceived to have no objective reality. But it is not against metaphysicians, but against physicists and materialists that Esoteric teachings have to fight, and for these Vital Force, Light, Sound, Electricity, even to the objectively pulling force of magnetism, have no objective being, and are said to exist merely as "modes of motion," "sensations and *affections* of matter."

Neither the Occultists generally, nor the Theosophists, reject, as erroneously believed by some, the views and theories of the modern scientists, only because these views are opposed to Theosophy. The first rule of our Society is to render unto Caesar what is Caesar's. The Theosophists, therefore, are the first to recognize the intrinsic value of science. But when its high priests resolve consciousness into a secretion from the grey matter of the brain, and everything else in nature into a mode of motion, we protest against the doctrine as being unphilosophical, self-contradictory, and simply absurd, from a *scientific* point of view, as much and even more than from the occult aspect of the esoteric knowledge.

For truly the astral light of the derided Kabalists has strange and weird secrets for him who can see in it; and the mysteries concealed within its incessantly disturbed waves *are there,* the whole body of Materialists and scoffers notwithstanding. These secrets, along with many other mysteries, will remain non-existent to the materialists of our age, in the same way as America was a non-existent myth for Europeans during the early part of the mediaeval ages, whereas Scandinavians and Norwegians had actually reached and settled in that very old "New World" several centuries before. But, as a Columbus was born to re-discover, and to force the Old World to believe in Antipodal countries, so will there be born scientists who will discover the marvels now claimed by Occultists to exist in the regions of Ether, with their varied and multiform denizens and conscious Entities. Then, *nolens volens,* Science will have to accept the old "Superstition," as it has several others. And having been once forced to accept it -- judging from past experience -- its learned professors will, in all probability, as in the case of MESMERISM and Magnetism, now re-baptised Hypnotism, father the thing and reject its name. The choice of the new appellation will depend, in its turn, on the "modes of motion," the new name for the older "automatic physical processes among the nerve fibrils of the (Scientific) brain" of Moleschott; as also, very likely, upon the last meal of the namer; since, according to the Founder of the new Hylo-Idealistic Scheme, "Cerebration is generically the same as chylification." Thus, were one to believe this preposterous proposition, the new name of the archaic thing would have to take its chance, on the inspiration of the namer's liver, and then only would these truths have a chance of becoming scientific!

But TRUTH, however distasteful to the generally blind majorities, has always had her champions, ready to die for her, and it is not the Occultists who will protest against its adoption by Science under whatever new name. But, until absolutely forced on the notice and acceptance of Scientists, many an Occult truth will be tabooed, as the phenomena of the Spiritualists and other psychic manifestations were, to be finally appropriated by its ex-traducers without the least acknowledgment or thanks. Nitrogen has added considerably to chemical knowledge, but its discoverer, Paracelsus, is to this day called a "quack."

How profoundly true are the words of H. T. Buckle, in his admirable "*History of Civilization*" (Vol. I., p. 256), when he says:

"Owing to circumstances still unknown (Karmic provision, H.P.B.) there appear from time to time great thinkers, who, devoting their lives to a single purpose, are able to anticipate the progress of mankind, and to produce a religion or a philosophy by which important effects are eventually brought about. But if we look into history we shall clearly see that, although the origin of a new opinion may be thus due to a single man, the result which the new opinion produces will depend on the condition of the people among whom it is propagated. If either a religion or a philosophy is too much in advance of a nation it can do no present service but must bide its time until the minds of men are ripe for its reception. . . . Every science, every creed has had its martyrs. *According to the ordinary course of affairs, a few generations pass away, and then there comes a period when these very truths are looked upon as commonplace facts, and a little later there comes another period in which they are declared to be necessary, and even the dullest intellect wonders how they could ever have been denied.*"

It is barely possible that the minds of the present generations are not quite ripe for the reception of Occult truths. Such will be the retrospect furnished to the advanced thinkers of the Sixth Root Race of the history of the acceptance of Esoteric Philosophy -- fully and unconditionally. Meanwhile the generations of our Fifth Race will continue to be led away by prejudice and preconceptions. Occult Sciences will have the finger of scorn pointed at them from every street corner, and everyone will seek to ridicule and crush them in the name, and for the greater glory, of Materialism and its so-called Science. The Addendum which completes the present Book shows, however, in an anticipatory answer to several of the forthcoming Scientific objections, the true and mutual positions of the defendant and plaintiff. The Theosophists and Occultists stand arraigned by public opinion, which still holds high the banner of the inductive Sciences. The latter have, then, to be examined; and it must be shown how far their achievements and discoveries in the realm of natural laws are opposed, not so much to our claims, as to the facts in nature. The hour has now struck to ascertain whether the walls of the modern Jericho are so impregnable that no blast of the Occult trumpet is ever likely to make them crumble.

The so-called *Forces,* with Light and Electricity heading them, and the constitution of the Solar orb must be carefully examined; as also Gravitation and the Nebular theories. The Natures of Ether and of other Elements must be discussed: thus contrasting scientific with other Occult teachings, while revealing some of the hitherto secret tenets of the latter. (*Vide Addendum.*)

Some fifteen years ago, the writer was the first to repeat, after the Kabalists, the wise Commandments in the Esoteric Catechism "Close thy mouth, lest thou shouldst speak of *this* (the mystery), and thy heart, lest thou shouldst think aloud; and if thy heart has escaped thee, bring it back to its place, for such is the object of our alliance." (*Sepher Jezireh, Book of Creation.*) And again: -- "This is a secret which gives death: close thy mouth lest thou shouldst reveal it to the vulgar; compress thy brain lest something should escape from it and fall outside." (Rules of Initiation.)

A few years later, a corner of the Veil of Isis had to be lifted; and now another and a larger rent is made. . . .

But old and time-honoured errors -- such as become with every day more glaring and self-evident -- stand arrayed in battle-order now, as they did then. Marshalled by blind conservatism, conceit and prejudice, they are constantly on the watch, ready to strangle every truth, which, awakening from its age-long sleep, happens to knock for admission. Such has been the case ever since man became an animal. That this proves in every case *moral death* to the revealers, who bring to light any of these old, old truths, is as certain as that it gives LIFE and REGENERATION to those who are fit to profit even by the little that is now revealed to them.

Made in United States
Orlando, FL
15 February 2023

29990926R00074